What readers are saying about this book:

"In Death We Do [...] the bereaved but it is mu[...] eat story, it contains trutl [...] in this book are some im[...] ho we are and what life [...] .nd ponder the true meanin[...] existence.

—Richard Zoll (spiritual teacher)

"I would wait until bed-time to read *In Death We Do Not Part*, as that's my favorite time to read before drifting off to sleep. One big difference I noticed was that I was having more deep, restful sleep than usual...Then my late husband, Richard, came to me in a dream. It was the first time in my dreams I was aware that he had died. Before this, I always dreamed of us when we were younger and when he was still alive. In this dream, he suddenly appeared at the top of some stairs, looked at me and smiled, came down the stairs and put his arms around me and then he kissed me. He was so warm I knew he was alive again and when I woke up I thought he really had appeared to me, as if some miracle had occurred. It's one of the nicest things that ever happened to me. I really don't totally disbelieve or believe in these things but I think reading the book allowed me to have this dream."

—Naomi Burney (widow)

"It is very exciting to think of all the people *In Death We Do Not Part* will help. All that I read felt so true and comforting. I found it very helpful in understanding better many challenges in life, including my own divorce. Also, the September 11th tragedy had disturbed me greatly but on reading what Gail Kent said about it, my peace returned. It is like the writing is from God, it is so pure and loving. This book is a very precious gift from the authors. I plan to buy several books to give to friends!"

—Nancy Christenson (divorcee)

I rate *In Death We Do Not Part* a 10 out of 10. It's a new and very helpful approach for anyone feeling the loss of a loved one. There are also great ideas for everyone to use in creating a more fulfilling life, even if afterlife communication is a questionable concept for them. The exercises in this book can be very helpful in clarifying our thoughts about various events in life."

—Betty Heyman (widow)

"What a great book! *In Death We Do Not Part* is sorely needed. It is so wonderful that the authors are putting this out there! The exercises in this book invite the reader to digest the ideas—and to use the contents for self-inquiry—they should be meditated upon. If people knew what is contained in this book, they would not fear death, nor would they react with such devastation to death. They would take comfort in knowing that they can still resolve unfinished business, express their love, and continue to gain wisdom while here on earth."

—Beth Anderson (widow)

"I wish *In Death We Do Not Part* had been written years ago as it would have been so valuable in my Beyond Loss support groups. For years I have had grievers doing certain exercises that have been very effective. After reading the explanations in this book, it is more clear to me why they work. I think that the exercises that are suggested are great for individuals and sharing them with others or in a group would make them even more powerful. This book is a beacon of hope and an excellent resource for anyone mourning the loss of a loved one as well as anyone who just wants a better understanding of life, death and grief. I find the book so full of wisdom for everyday living that I often share excerpts from it with friends, family and clients and they find them extremely insightful and helpful as do I."

—Paula Shaw , Grief Counselor,
Beyond Loss Counseling

"This book is full of wisdom, even for someone who is not grieving. It comes from a remarkable person—my mother. My mother was entirely human but so full of love that, as a child, I regarded her love as a mighty force of nature, like the winds or the tides. And while she was on this earth she showed me many profound truths. Only as an adult did I realize that not everyone attunes their heart this way, nor are all children as lucky as I and my siblings were. Her death was a shock and a huge loss, but soon I realized that her love was still with us. As this book reveals, her wisdom is still available to us too. Thank you, Mom—and Dad— for the blessing that is this book.

—Gordon Kent (Gail and Marshall's son)

IN DEATH WE DO NOT PART

An Alternative Guide to Grieving

An Uncommon Communication
Between a Husband
and his Deceased Wife.

Marshall and Gail Kent

WITH A FOREWORD BY
SIDNEY D. KIRKPATRICK and
NANCY WEBSTER-THURLBECK,
Authors, *Edgar Cayce, An American Prophet*

Alleusha Publishing

Published by:
ALLEUSHA PUBLISHING
P.O. Box 5212
Richmond, California 94805-5212
orders@alleusha-publishing.com
http://alleusha-publishing.com

First Printing, December, 2002
10 9 8 7 6 5 4 3 2 1

 Registered Trademark

Quality Books CATALOGING-IN-PUBLICATION DATA

Kent, Marshall.
  In death we do not part : an alternative guide to grieving : an uncommon communication between a husband and his deceased wife / Marshall and Gail Kent ; with a foreword by Sidney D. Kirkpatrick and Nancy Webster-Thurlbeck.
  p. cm.
  Includes index.
  LCCN 2002108393
  ISBN 0-9721761-3-6

  1. Grief. 2.Bereavement—Psychological aspects. 3. Consolation. 4. Spiritualism. 5. Kent, Marshall. 6. Kent, Gail. I. Kent, Gail. II. Title.

BF575.G7K46 2002   155.9'37'092
                                    QB102-701794

Editing, design, and production coordination by Nancy Webster-Thurlbeck
Cover by Sandra McHenry Design
Cover Art by Marshall Kent (with inspiration from Michelangelo)
Printed in the United States of America

Dedicated with love to our children.

Contents

Contents
Part Three—My Journal Entries (cont'd)

Contents
Part Three—My Journal Entries (cont'd)

Part Four—Sharing the Wisdom

Contents
Part Four—Sharing the Wisdom (cont'd)

Part Five—September 11th, 2001

Part Six—More Wisdom to Share

About the Authors

Co-author Marshall Kent is a successful retired Napa Valley contractor, architect, and real estate investor who writes for the first time about the unusual approach he took to the death, in 1996, of his beloved wife Gail. Gail Kent, using Marshall's hands, has co-authored this book from "the other side."

Gail and Marshall first met in college. It was love at first sight—on their first date they both knew they were destined for marriage. Three months later, despite the reservations of family members, they tied the knot. Little did they know when they both repeated the wedding vow, "'Til death do us part," that in fact, in death they would not part.

Gail and Marshall went on to raise a family of four children. They had a traditional marriage. Gail wanted more than anything to be a stay-at-home Mom and to be there for her children, and Marshall wanted nothing more than to succeed in the contracting/real estate business so that she could do so. They both got what they wanted.

Once the youngest child was off to college, Marshall's success in business enabled him to retire very early and the two of them traveled the world. They set constant and continuous learning as their mutual goal and saw life as one big adventure. It was Gail who would state that "death is life's greatest adventure."

When Gail died suddenly on one cold March morning, Marshall wasn't sure he could go on without her. As it turned out, he didn't have to. He took steps to remain open and to hold true to the belief that they both held—that the spirit lives on—and Gail did not disappoint him.

Marshall has had to overcome an introverted nature to share with you the very personal thoughts, feelings and experiences he had after Gail's death and to reveal to the world the mystical side that he and Gail had kept hidden from both friends and extended family. And given that in the beginning Marshall had real doubts and reservations that the communications from Gail were anything more than wishful thinking and an overactive imagination, it has taken much strength on his part to share with you his private communication with his deceased wife. Together, they offer you ways in which grievers can heal their loss and learn to continue a productive and healthy relationship with their loved ones who have passed on. They also share wisdom from the other side that is especially relevant in these difficult times and particularly in the wake of September 11th, 2001.

Foreword

Dear Reader,

When Marshall Kent first approached us to help him turn his journals into the book that would become, *In Death We Do Not Part*, we didn't know what form the final manuscript would take. We knew that the basic idea was a good one, that the story was inspiring and that the message that Marshall sought to bring forth could become a potent force in the lives of all who read it, whether or not they are grieving the loss of a loved one. What we didn't know was the remarkable wisdom that would come through Marshall from his wife, Gail, who now resides on the other side. Nor did we foresee how Gail's presence in this book would become so all pervading—saturating its pages.

Although Marshall and Gail had lived their lives with a strong spiritual foundation—and a deep interest in the mystical and esoteric—they did so privately. It was not typical of their generation to stray outside the conventional boundaries of religion. We know that to "come out of the closet" with not only an exposé of his personal trials and tribulations after the loss of his wife, but also with something so unusual as a dialogue with her on the other side, has taken a great amount of courage—courage that Marshall was not even sure he had. However, through his and Gail's writing, it becomes apparent to us that their unusual communication since her death and the publication of this book, are major portions of Marshall and Gail's life work.

When Gail was alive, there was a balanced equality in their relationship. But when it came to such endeavors as writing, or the study of the mystical side of life, it was Marshall who more often played the role of advisor and encourager. Now that Gail has the benefit of the wider view from the other side, the roles are reversed and it is remarkable that Marshall has had the daring not to control or limit Gail's marvelous influence. It is also a testament to his own humility and his deep and gracious love for her. He did not get stuck in the memories of their shared past, but is allowing the past, present and future to seamlessly take shape in his heart, his mind and his journals. That Marshall and Gail invited us to have a hand in its creation has been both a privilege and an honor, and this book has changed our lives, as it will yours.

Sidney D. Kirkpatrick and Nancy Webster-Thurlbeck
Authors, *Edgar Cayce, An American Prophet*

Marshall and Gail Kent cross-country skiing in Yellowstone, 1980.

Marshall and Gail Kent trying out Gail's 50th birthday present, 1978.

Part One

Introduction

Dear Reader,

I invite you to join me on a journey that I and my deceased wife have been taking. It is a journey of healing, full of the wonders of learning about life and death, about ourselves, and about the universe of which we are a part. All journeys have a beginning but I shall begin this one with what seems to be an ending.

Sincerely yours

Marshall Kent

Chapter 1

A Letter from Marshall Kent

Dear Reader,

As unbelievable as it may sound, my wife Gail who passed away in March of 1996, wrote parts of this book about her death. Following this letter from me, you will read a letter she wrote to you from the other side.

I feel blessed to have had Gail as my wife for 47 years. She was everything I ever wanted or needed in a woman and companion. She wasn't just my partner, but a soul-mate. Her gentle and feminine touch was everywhere present in the fabric of my life and the lives of our four children. The years we spent in our hilltop home in Northern California were not always easy or harmonious, but we viewed ourselves as travelers who had embarked upon a long journey, and were ever grateful, as parents and then grandparents, to have each other to share it with. Gail was my life and I was hers. Our children knew it, our family and neighbors knew it and even strangers noticed the connection that seemed to exist between us.

To say that I found Gail beautiful is an understatement: she had a radiance that was altogether intelligent, feminine, and open. In her youth she wasn't nearly as judgmental as I was and it showed in her face. There was a natural wave to her light brown hair which framed her smooth clear complexion. But what I found irresistible were her blue eyes. To me, they were almost magical— a mirror into her soul. I could see deep into them and I loved what I saw. I could never imagine that the day would come when I could not look into those blue eyes and see her gentle and loving soul looking back at me. Thus, I was not prepared for the sudden chain of events that took place on a chilly morning, the twenty-second of March, forty-seven-years after I had asked Gail to marry me.

That morning, at 7:15, Gail and I were laying in bed talking about a ski trip we were planning to Lake Tahoe. It would be one of those fast trips: two days together on the beginner and intermediate slopes, and one evening curled up in front of a fire at a friend's chalet. Although we often had our grown children join us, this time it would be just the two us.

I don't remember what else we talked about. I do, however, recall wrapping my arms around Gail while we lay together in bed, looking out the floor-to-ceiling windows in our bedroom. Just beyond those windows was a small lily pond and garden we had built and which was the favorite watering hole for our local deer population. Like so many other mornings, the deer that day had come up within twenty-five feet of the house.

Gail got out of bed first, and began filling the tub with water for her morning bath. For her, hot baths were a form of therapy—not only to freshen up at the start of each day, but because the heat of the water relaxed the muscles in her back which had troubled her over the years. I went into the living room and began my daily stretching exercises: a combination of head and neck rolls, deep knee bends, leg lifts and push ups. From our large picture windows in the living room I could still see the deer, only now a bank of low clouds had moved in from the north, casting a light fog that hung over the redwood trees in our yard.

I finished my ten minute routine, went back into the bedroom, and then into the bathroom to shave and shower. As I stepped into the steam-filled room, I found Gail with one hand gripping the safety bar, the other arm flailing about and her otherwise unseeing eyes looking up to the left. In that one instant I realized that something terrible had happened.

I grabbed her by the shoulders and pleaded, "Gail—talk to me." There was no answer or recognition, just a bewildered and fearful confusion, as if she had suddenly found herself plunged into darkness. I knew it was a stroke. I gently pried her hand loose from the safety bar, took her into my arms and carried her into the bedroom, where I laid her down on the bed. Then I dialed 911. I couldn't think of what else do to except to dress her, hold her hand, and remind her, over and over again, that I loved her, would not let her go and that everything would be okay.

The paramedics were quick, efficient, and kind. They put her into the ambulance and took off at high speed for the hospital, siren wailing. I raced behind them in our pick-up truck, praying that this would not be the last time Gail would see our beloved hill-top home.

In the hospital emergency room, after they had her hooked up to various monitors, I was again by Gail's side, holding her hand. The bewilderment and confusion had left her face, and even though her eyes were closed she had a look of peace and contentment. It seemed as if she needed rest, but something prompted me to gently shake her awake. When Gail opened her eyes, a streak of hope shot through me. Still holding her hand, I moved my face into her line of vision. Her blue eyes softened beautifully in recognition. Gail was back. The right side of Gail's face was paralyzed, but she nonetheless gave me a lovely half smile.

It seemed to me that her beautiful blue eyes projected a love such as I had never seen. With that look Gail seemed to be saying: "Thank you. I appreciate you, and the love we share will be ever ours." I realized at that moment that Gail knew she was dying.

The physician came in to tell us that she had suffered a stroke and that they would give her a number of tests including a CAT scan to determine its severity. He assured me that it might not be as bad as it looked. I wanted desperately to believe him but I knew in my heart of hearts that she was leaving me and had just said goodbye.

I left Gail's side briefly to call our son, Rick, who lived a short drive away. He came right away and then came again later with his wife Mercedes and daughter, Maria. Gail recognized them and smiled.

The cat-scan results showed that Gail had suffered a massive blood clot that blocked off large parts of her brain, including the speech section. The doctor said Gail had only a fifty-fifty chance of surviving, and if she did survive there would be no way of knowing the full extent of the brain damage. At best, she could probably understand very little, which would make any kind of muscular rehabilitation difficult. He said that a crisis would likely occur in two days on Sunday morning. The doctor asked me what life support systems he should use, if any. I knew that Gail would want none and told him that. He agreed with this decision

I then also called Christopher, our middle son, who lived further away. He came that evening and Gail recognized him and smiled at him too. Around 11 p.m. she seemed to fall asleep.

That evening I had asked the nurse if it would be okay if I brought my camper to the parking lot so that I could sleep there and come to see Gail throughout the night. The nurse said there was no need. I could sleep in the empty bed next to Gail—which ironically—had just been vacated that day by a friend of ours.

I spent a long sleepless night listening to Gail's labored breathing. The nurses were coming and going, periodically checking the monitors. Rick came very early the next morning.

This time he brought his guitar and softly strummed the gentle chords she loved to hear him play. She loved music especially when played by one of her children. Around eight a.m. Rick and I noticed that the monitors were showing a decided slowing of Gail's vital signs. We watched and waited, wanting badly to be with our beloved Gail when she passed on. When a new shift of nurses came onto the floor, one stepped into the room to check on Gail's status. When she saw the monitors she leaped into a great flurry of activity calling to the other nurses. As they hustled us out of the room we could see them trying to revive Gail. In our hearts, Rick and I knew that she was already gone, despite the fact that her heart and lungs were still functioning.

After a few minutes of standing nervously out in the hall, Rick went back into the room and told the nurses that we didn't want any further resuscitation. We just wanted to be alone with Gail. The nurses reluctantly retreated and we returned to her side. When Gail finally stopped breathing, approximately 24 hours after she had had her stroke, we were there with her. I was holding her hand when she took her last breath.

Rick and I stayed by her for awhile. We knew she was gone but it felt like we were abandoning her. Rick helped take off her wedding ring—I had made that ring for her and she had made mine so many years ago.

Now I had the other family members to contact. I felt badly for Gordon, our eldest son. He was in Poland beyond the reach of a telephone just finishing his two years in the Peace Corps. How terrible it would be for him to receive news—out of the blue—that his mother was dead. And there was our daughter, Laurie, to call. She had not made it to see her mother before she passed. Like her brother in Poland, she would have to find her own way of saying goodbye.

Gail—my precious wife of 47 years—was gone. And my life was suddenly taking a drastic change in direction. What would surprise me the most as the weeks, months and then years passed, was that I was able not only to come to peace with my huge loss, but to transform it into a blessing—and an experience of a lifetime. I would find myself communicating with Gail: first through feelings and intuition, later through thoughts that would enter my mind, next through mediums who would offer a "voice" for Gail to use, and then, finally, through what I like to call "inspired writing"—through a written dialogue that Gail and I could carry on between us—both of us using my hands to write or type back and forth to each other. In the beginning I thought that the messages coming through me from Gail must have been wishful thinking—my imagination working over-time. But as the communications increased in volume and intensity, and as I began to review them in their entirety and recognize the enormous wisdom and organization that was coming through, I knew it was definitely not my imagination at work.

In the early stages it was as if I both believed and didn't believe it at the same time. I think my subconscious believed it because it was a primary active participant in its happening. But my intellectual mind wasn't so sure. In fact, it doubted it and yearned for a good hard provable event that the communication was really coming from Gail. While I was determined to be open my skepticism kept intruding. I finally concluded that I should adopt the original Greek meaning of a skeptic—as one who will delay coming to a conclusion in order to entertain all possibilities. In doing this I allowed not a single validation but an accumulation of validations that it was indeed Gail communicating with me. Now my intellectual mind and subconscious are in agreement.

As time passed, communication with Gail would become more frequent—and once I learned to trust the material she would become many different things to me—a teacher, a confidante, a traveling companion, a lecturer and, as always, my friend.

I would learn from Gail about the awesome experience of death, and the purpose it serves, not only for the deceased but those left behind. I would learn that life does not cease when the human body stops breathing, that those who have passed on can still carry on a relationship with us whether we know it or not, that the living can both help and be helped, teach and learn from their loved ones on the other side. We can continue to love, heal wounds, forgive each other and grow both emotionally and intellectually through our relationship with our deceased loved ones.

I also discovered that to maintain open lines of communication with Gail required that I feel joy, rather than grief, and that I live in the "here and now." If I were to withdraw from life to focus solely on my past lovely relationship with Gail, our communications would end. Instead of shutting down, I have to live my life fully and in the present.

We were still preparing this book when September 11[th,] 2001 came and went. Like so many others, I was devastated and I badly needed answers. Gail was there for me and came through with remarkable words of wisdom that helped me enormously during that difficult time. I have incorporated those words here, throughout the book. It is our hope that they will also offer you some answers and guidance on this painful subject.

Gail and I, who loved all things mystical for most of our adult lives, nevertheless kept that part of ourselves hidden from the world. We were not ready to expose ourselves to the possible judgement and criticism of our peers. Our generation did not as readily embrace the more esoteric concepts as later generations have done. Now, it is only me—not Gail who has to worry about our friends thinking I am really weird. I'm probably going to find out that our friends always thought I was weird. Gail and I did always march to our own drummer. And writing a book with my dead wife can certainly be described as marching to my own drummer!

We are therefore, acutely aware that the path this book describes is not for everyone. And it is true that the conventional way of mourning a loved one is of very great help to many people. We don't discount the value of the hundred or more guide books and the many counselors who encourage deep grieving. If it fits, you should wear it. It just didn't fit me.

Our purpose is to provide a wider menu of choices for those who are grieving, and for those in the midst of preparing for the next stage of their spiritual journey together. To me, hopeless deep grieving is that total feeling of loss without any glimmer of light or feeling that it will ever be different: the bottomless abyss and depression that is the result of spiritual amnesia. Choosing, instead, a path of learning and development has been a wondrous help to me, as I believe it can be for you.

In the pages that follow, you will find a dialogue between me and my departed wife, Gail. The chapters in Part Two describe the events of Gail's passing. In the chapters following that, I share with you the thoughts that I wrote in my journal over the days that followed her death and then the responses that Gail gave to those thoughts—much later on. Although you will read my journal entries, each accompanied by Gail's relevant thoughts and observations, please bear in mind that I did not learn Gail's side of it until several years after my own journal entries were written.

As we proceed, Gail and I also offer suggestions on ways you can work to heal from your loss, resolve unfinished business between you and your deceased loved ones, allow them to help you, and even help your loved ones on the other side as they move forward on their journeys.

That I must share our unusual dialogue as well as what we have learned is not only Gail's wish, but may well be the primary reason that she remains "at my side." And, I believe that despite my own personal fears and trepidation, the writing and publication of this book is a task with which Gail and I have been entrusted. I believe that if I allow my own fears and self-consciousness to interfere with its dissemination, I will have failed to accomplish an important portion of my, and Gail's, life purpose.

Fifty-two years ago Gail and I exchanged wedding vows and each of us repeated the words, "'Til death do us part." Little did we know at the time, that, "In death we do not part!"

Now, Gail too has something to say. To avoid confusion Gail's words will be highlighted in bold type throughout the book. May what we share with you here transform your lives.

My best wishes to you,

Marshall Kent

Chapter 2

A Letter from Gail Kent

Dear Reader,

This is a pleasure I never thought I would have—to greet you from this side and to communicate with you through my husband. Having recently passed through death's door, I have an awareness of the process and a remembrance of the emotions that I went through. It is very different than the world anticipates. It is our chosen work to tell you about the difference so that each of you can diminish your fears and dread of death. If we succeed in this, your life will be much richer and you will have reason to love God more fully.

Unfortunately, death is much misunderstood by the majority on earth. It is regarded as the ultimate separation, the ultimate sorrow. As such, it generates much fear and grief in contemplating our own death or the death of someone near to us. Fear and thoughts of separation go hand in hand. Therefore, anything that would reduce the fear and sense of separation would bring about a better, happier, more holy world. It would be an act of healing.

These times are bringing about many changes. Some such changes are those coming about as a result of events such as the tragedy of September 11th, 2001. These kinds of events and concerns like the anthrax scare are difficult to digest. And people are going through a major priority shift. What seemed so important beforehand seemed less important afterward. And as they perceived work, suffering and difficulties ahead of them, they felt threatened and were not sure of how it would all turn out.

However, as many are observing, some good can emerge out of tragedies such as these. For instance, some of the surviving families of those who died on September 11th are beginning to realize that there *is* some kind of communication with their departed ones occurring. Others are feeling the strange "presence" of the deceased. I use the word strange only to describe a feeling of presence they never had felt before. Unfortunately, there are also many here on this side who are still trying to contact their loved ones on earth but they are not open, or don't know how to listen, or, they don't even know that communication is possible. They view their life on earth as separate.

Therefore, we are trying to help bring about a significant decrease in all forms of thoughts of separation with the corresponding increase in the awareness that *we are all one.* When we recognize that we are all *one,* then we recognize the possibility of communication with the deceased. If all those grieving ones left behind felt that it was possible to communicate with their loved one on this side they would feel uplifted. We *are* all *one.* We are all *forever.* Getting just a glimmer of these two truths can dissolve much grief.

Separation is only an illusion. On earth we tend to believe that when our loved one dies, we are separated from them. And, if our mind conceives it as so, then it is so. Since this illusion is the cause of much grief, loneliness, and unhappiness in this world, it is time to change that. To knowingly communicate with those who have passed over heals this sense of separation and diminishes the grief.

Each of us have three parts to us—our physical body, our mind and our feelings. While it is true that with death we are separated physically, this separation is not as important when we know that our minds and hearts can still be in communication.

Fortunately, the earth has also finally arrived at the stage where greater communication and less separation between realms is more widely possible. The earth at this time is experiencing vast changes in both attitude and reverence. For short we can call these times "the new millennium." Marshall and I are playing a part, as are you, in the work of this new millennium.

There is another separation that is frequently associated with death. When our loved ones were alive we felt we still had time to solve any difficulties we were having by continuing to work together. When our loved ones pass over, we assume this is no longer possible. In the instance of sudden and unexpected deaths such as those deaths that occurred on September 11th, there is no anticipation and therefore no opportunity to say goodbye or to have any closure. We may feel guilty for all sorts of things and at the same time we may harbor resentment. Now that our loved ones are gone, we believe the lack of resolution is permanent. After all, we no longer believe that we can work it out with them. We cannot talk with, fight with, apologize to, hug, kiss, forgive or ask forgiveness from them to make it better. We feel that our capacity to redo, remedy, and repair the relationship was taken away from us—permanently. We feel separated from what we need for our own growth and healing and it seems too late to recapture the lost opportunities of the past.

This feeling of separation from the capacity to heal wounds and resolve issues is also an illusion. Resolution and peace are alive and well—fully available to us—even though the physical interaction is not. Again, it is communication that unites us with our ability to reconcile.

So, can you see why communication between those on earth and us, here, is so important? The world will progress much faster, more surely and more lovingly when our sense of separation and its accompanying sorrow is reduced. The obvious result is that love and the concept of union will predominate more on earth. This is spiritual growth that will contribute to the new millennium. It is holy work.

It is our deepest desire that you will, upon reading this book and listening to your inner self, discover the splendor of who you are and of this most wonderful universe in which we all exist, know the true beneficence of God, and achieve greater awareness that we, indeed, are all *one*. From my perspective over here I can reveal to you much that you will find fascinating and also most helpful in living your life and coping with death—even untimely deaths. I feel blessed to be able to offer you this healing and information with and through my husband who is still with you on earth.

It is our goal to demonstrate that while death may separate the body, the mind and the heart can remain open to communication. This communication can ease your fears and bring enlightenment to your understanding of the magnificence of God's world.

Please know that if you think it possible to communicate with us on this side, then it becomes possible. In death *we do not part*. We *can* communicate through death. And, if you seek communication with us in the proper way, then you will certainly feel us. And later, some may even hear and see us. You will be guided by your inner self and by this book. This is a task that you, dear reader, who has suffered a loss by death, may accept.

Actually there are quite a number of people who communicate with their departed. The public is unaware of this because many of these people feel intimidated by the thought of revealing it. They don't wish to be regarded as a bit crazy—to say nothing of writing a book about it as is Marshall. It is such an intimate experience that it seems inappropriate to reveal their communication to their doubting contemporaries. Older widows and widowers are concerned that their children may take the wrong view of them if they reveal they are talking to the deceased.

Marshall has also felt this reluctance to say much about it. There is even a large part of him that is uneasy with the publishing of this book. Fortunately he is convinced the book could be very helpful to others and has taken courage in the fact that early drafts have already significantly helped some of those who read it.

I encourage you to read this book with an open mind. When you have finished it, then it is the time to look at it critically and decide for yourself the validity of what has been said. As you will read, it is most important to develop your own sense of truth and this book's purpose is to help you to do that. My husband and I always looked critically at any information presented to us and tested it to discover what validity it held for us. We invite you to do the same.

Marshall and I both enter into this work with the hope that, in these very challenging times, we may help relieve the pain and sorrow that you feel due to the loss of a loved one. And we hope to bring joy and understanding to you of your own greatness and of that of God . May we, like St. Francis, be an instrument of your peace—and an instrument of your knowing.

We are all on a spiritual path. As a friend of ours likes to say, "There is no place else for us to be." It can be a path of joy, excitement, and love.

Our blessings to you,

Gail Kent

The Prayer of St. Francis:

Lord,
Make me an instrument of Your peace;
Where there is hatred let me sow love;
Where there is injury, pardon;
Where there is doubt, faith;
Where there is despair, hope;
Where there is darkness, light;
And where there is sadness, joy.

A Note from Marshall:

Gail wrote a poem about her spiritual purpose about a year before she passed over. It came to her as a complete poem while she was meditating. It seems appropriate to include it here.

I have a function God would have me fill
From time immemorial yet with me still
To think God's thoughts, to love God's love,
To sing God's song of holy joy
One with my brother, each with the other.
Thee with me and me with thee.
I have a function God would have me fill
From time immemorial yet with me still.

Chapter 3

An Invitation

Leaving the hospital on the day that Gail died, I naturally began to think about what life was going to be like without my beloved friend and companion. Though Gail and I had previously talked about this eventuality, it was not until then, when I was actually faced with the dreaded hard reality of her death, that I would really begin to know how it feels to be without her. Now I was faced with that very cold fact: Gail was gone.

That day, as I walked out into the sunshine, it hit me that immeasurable tragedy had struck us but the world just went on anyway—with the sun shining down on us. These two distinct worlds, the tragedy and the sweet flow of life, seemed to have nothing to do with each other. But I became conscious of a third world—independent—even contrary to the other two. At some inner level, I felt that Gail and I were still together, still joined in some wonderful way.

I returned to the home that we had built with our four hands and much love over 40 years ago, fully expecting that the first night after her death would be a pure hell of longing, anguish, and grief. For she and I experienced such pleasure and intimacy in sharing the same bed. In all our years of marriage, Gail and I had only been separated for ten days, and despite the many challenges that come along with holding a marriage together, other than those 10 days, we had never slept apart.

Perhaps it was that comforting feeling that Gail was still with me—or perhaps it was from pure exhaustion, but that night I went to sleep the moment my head hit the pillow despite the empty space in the bed next to me. I woke up feeling anxious about this. I wondered how it can be that a man who has slept and made love with the same woman for forty-seven years should be able to sleep so soundly with her no longer at his side. But just as that concern crossed my mind, a thought popped into my head: "How you are feeling is a direct result of your convictions. Trust those convictions and they will serve you well."

My immediate response was to jot these words down on paper, for they made perfect sense—and I realized that the concept would be helpful later on, when I would, no doubt, be feeling even more the impact of Gail's passing. I was mindful of the fact that what had popped into my head was something that Gail would have said. She was always cautioning me to stop and examine my feelings before reacting to them.

Although it seemed difficult, I decided that I should write down all of the thoughts and experiences that had started to come to me. It would probably be therapeutic. When I went looking for something to write in I found just what I was looking for—a spiral notebook. This one had all blank pages except for the first one, which had, in Gail's hand-writing, the following words: *Meditations, Thoughts and Images, November 1991*. She had made no entries. I like to think she left it blank for me. On page two, I added: *Insights and Inspirations Since Gail's Transition, March 23, 1996. I love her so.*

In the introduction I invited you, dear reader, to join me on a journey. I am so glad that you have. We are now asking you to join in a learning process that can bring you the results that we have found so beneficial and wondrous. Throughout this book, at the end of most chapters, you will find exercises that you may do.

Our goal is to open communications as much as possible. But, some of you may not wish to do every exercise that we suggest. Although all of the exercises will be of benefit, we have identified with an asterisk (*) those exercises we feel are essential.

Join us on the path that leads to the realization that we are not separate from those who have passed on. We are all *one*—those who have passed on and we who have remained behind.

A Note from Gail:

To those of you who are grieving, do not worry about your present state. Instead be concerned with the direction you are headed. No matter what state you are now in you have the power to change the direction in which you face. If you would dearly love to communicate with your deceased one as Buck (Marshall's family nickname) **and I are now doing, realize this is something you can look forward to and something to anticipate with a happy heart. All it requires, at this point, is that you remain open, as did Buck when I passed over.**

This book gives you a case history of how it is done. It gives you exercises to do. Of course, Buck and I were and are in different circumstances than you and your departed one. We are all so individual that we are all in different circumstances. But this makes no difference. God has given us

all the same tools and powers with which to accomplish what we desire. You and your departed one can indeed do what Buck and I are doing. It is there. You can do it. God does not play favorites. Take heart, as you are the beloved child of God and He has given you what you need. You need simply open your heart to Him and turn in His direction.

> *The great thing in this world is not so much where*
> *you stand, as in what direction you are moving.*
> **—Oliver Wendell Holmes, American**
> **Author and Physician, 1809-1894**

* Exercise 1: We encourage you to find a notebook and to start writing too. Writing helps open the doors to our hearts. It has a great deal more power than thinking does just by itself. Somehow, someway, when we are writing, we are able to access our deepest feelings. Things get written that we had not previously even thought of. For instance, this book is full of concepts and ideas that are way beyond my own thinking. They came through the portal of writing.

You could start your journal with a dedication to your loved one or to an important hope or feeling that you have. You can write about your feelings and your reflections. You can write to your beloved on the other side or someone else. Write whenever and whatever comes into your mind. Begin each entry with the date.

Meditations

Thoughts and Images

November 1991

**Gail on Mount Kenya, 1972, and below,
one year before her passing, 1995.**

Part Two

About Gail's Passing

With learning being so central to who Gail and I were, I guess it should be no surprise that I should go right on trying to learn. It put me in a good frame of mind to start receiving the inspirations, the insights, and whatever else might come by way of my heightened emotional state. Right after Gail died, I began to write down my thoughts and ideas as they came along and now I wish to share them with you.

In the pages that follow I also share my story, my feelings, my reflections and even poems as they came to me over the months and years to follow. Although it would be some years before Gail would begin writing through me, I also include here those comments she wrote later which are relevant to my process and to my thoughts and words even in the early stages.

It would be some weeks before I was ready to write specifically about Gail's passing, but I will share that writing with you first.

Journal writing is a voyage to the interior.

—Christina Baldwin, *One to One:*
Self-Understanding through
Journal Writing

Exercise 2: While this may be too early in your process, at some point you might find it therapeutic to tell your story of your loved one's death. When you do this, try to take time to really reflect on the nuances and details that stood out to you—even of those events before his or her death when no one had foreseen it. These will be very helpful to your own understanding.

Chapter 4

Our Last Exchange

As I described earlier, when Gail opened her eyes and gave me that lovely half smile, it seemed to me that her beautiful blue eyes projected a love such as I had never seen. It was not the kind of love that comes between two people who share those special moments that make marriage worthwhile, but a deeper kind of love that wells from some deeper place inside that is beyond normal human reach. The only word that comes to mind is "beatific," a word which poets have used to suggest supreme happiness and a heavenly presence. I can't think of another single word to use. The look on Gail's face was almost holy, a vision that went well beyond the concerns of this earth.

With that look Gail not only seemed to be saying: "Thank you and I appreciate you, and the love we share will be ever ours," but the look in her eyes was also one of encouragement. She was telling me that she was confident that I would have the strength to carry on in her absence. And it seemed that she wanted to share this experience of dying with me. All this came to me clearly without words.

Gail and I had had some discussions about what we should do in the event that either of us would ever be unable to communicate verbally with the other. We had agreed that the survivor should both ask and answer any questions so that a squeeze of the hand could communicate.

So when I sat down next to her in the emergency room, I began to ask her questions out loud.

"Can you hear me? Squeeze my hand if you can."
She responded—her hand tightened around mine.

"You look like you are at peace. Are you?"
Again she squeezed my hand and gave me that lovely half smile.

I had heard about "near death" experiences and I felt that Gail was going through the tunnel to the light to be greeted by a spiritual being. Unfortunately, this time, "near" meant death was just hours away.

I asked, "Do you feel surrounded by the light of love?"
Gail squeezed my hand once more.

Then I found myself asking, "Is Jesus holding you by the hand?" A very hard squeeze. Although I was beside myself with worry, this exchange was beautiful and it felt holy. Gail (and I, to a lesser extent) had always felt a strong connection with Jesus.

I still wonder how I had the presence of mind to ask her the questions that I did in the emergency room. I am impressed that I had somehow sensed what was going on so that each answer could be a positive one. While part of me was rattled, another part of me was taking charge, almost without my will.

The whole thing actually amazed me. Here Gail was dying and she knew she was and what did she do? She wanted to share her passing with me. Here was the most momentous event of her life, her life's ending, and she was thinking of me, and sharing. It was also the most momentous day in my life. Writing about Gail's dying sure brings tears to my eyes but also awe that I could share such an experience. I wish I could adequately convey the immense beauty of watching my beloved friend and companion of 47 years, with whom I had experienced so many adventures, so many joys and so many difficulties, and witness her finding and feeling the true peace of God. It was the most tender experience of my life.

Here is what Gail wrote about this later:

Dearest Buck,

I was wanting to convey to you a lifetime of thanks for your companionship. When I saw that you felt this, I smiled. I so wanted you to know how I felt. I didn't know my face was half paralyzed. I felt like I was smiling at you as I always had. It was always such a good feeling to smile at you. Do you ever feel that I am smiling at you now that I am out of my body? I do and it still feels good. (Marshall: Yes, it feels like invisible sunshine.)

You were wonderful the way you asked those questions so I could squeeze your hand. Those lovely hands that I loved to hold so very much. Do you appreciate what lovely hands you have? You have never taken proper care of those beautiful hands.

You did have help in asking those questions—from your higher self—but I know it would not have happened if you had not been listening, truly open to the spiritual wonders that we were both experiencing.

Now it takes great courage to be open. And, it is particularly hard to be courageous when you are losing or have just lost your loved one. As you experienced, Buck, when you were losing me you felt as if all your courage was used up, and you needed a good deal more to get through. But you did it—and you kept yourself open.

As in the case of the September 11th deaths and many others, not everyone has the opportunity to be at their loved one's side at the time of their death or to even know that their loved one is passing over. And, not everyone wants that opportunity. Each of us are so different and have different experiences necessary to our own personal growth. But all ways of experiencing a loved one's death are valid. Each is singularly appropriate to the individuals experiencing it.

* Exercise 3: Write about your communication with your beloved when he or she died. If you weren't present at the time of death, write about the last time you saw your loved one. Looking back, do you feel there was anything special about it? Write about that. Or, if that meeting was not what you would have wanted it to be, sit back and imagine how you would have preferred it to be. Write down what you would have wanted to tell them. If you didn't say goodbye, this is a good opportunity to do so. You can write them a goodbye letter too. Many people are afraid to say goodbye thinking that this would make the separation final. We cannot deny our deceased loved ones have left the physical world, so saying goodbye is not any more inappropriate or permanent than it would be when we say goodbye to someone who is going off to college or is moving to another city. You are saying goodbye to the physical part of them—which does not end the mental or emotional connection to them.

Note from Gail: I can tell you from this side that your loved ones on this side *will* receive your message. And in receiving it, know that they will not be critical or judgmental. Instead they will be accepting of the "you that you are." It is far, far easier for us on this side to receive communication from you on earth than it is the reverse. One main reason is that here we know that such communication exists. We receive it all the time. So do not doubt that your prayers, conversations, appeals, forgiveness, and love will be received here.

Chapter 5

Gail's Last Night

I will never forget the last night I spent sleeping on the hospital bed next to Gail's. I think that all things must magnify at night. I laid awake listening to Gail breath. She would take five breaths and then there would be a long time before she would take another five. Actually she had had this pattern for a long time. That night, however, it seemed altogether different. It concerned me greatly that she might live and there would be this living remnant. That prospect seemed awful. And yet I didn't want to influence her in what to do even if I could. If she was to live, then I would accept it and love and care for her tenderly. It was a long night but I realize that I was going through a process of adjustment that was helpful.

The previous day, part of me knew that Gail was going to die and another part of me wished she would live. When the doctor had told me that Gail had had a massive stroke and her life, if it continued, would be as a vegetable, I stopped wishing she would live. I knew for a fact she wouldn't want to live that way but I also realized I didn't want to live with her that way from my own selfish point of view. That takes a bit of getting used to, selfishly hoping my dear wife would pass on. I'm glad both Gail and I agreed long ago that feeling guilty was counter productive.

My Dearest,

On arriving here on the other side I asked to see your guide. I asked him to comfort you and to ease your emotions about wanting me to die so that you would not have to incessantly care for my remnant, vegetable self. That was no more selfish on your part than my higher self wanting to die and leave you bereaved. It was only later that I found out that there was no karma*—either yours or mine—that would have brought forth such a lingering vestige of me for you to care for.

*Karma is thought of as similar to the Christian idea, "we reap what we sow." The concept of karma comes from eastern religions and suggests that there are consequences for our deeds and actions. Gail likes to view it, not as punishment nor reward—but as the lessons we still have to learn. But we can decide to learn our lessons the easy way and then we don't have to learn them the hard and painful way. More on karma later.

Exercise 4: Write about the circumstances around your beloved's death. Did you have to care for him or her? If so, what did you both gain from that? The father of a friend was nursed by his family for cancer for many months. Despite the pain, it was a wonderful experience for him as this was the first time in his life that his family was caring for him instead of vice versa. You can also write about any guilt you felt surrounding the events of his or her death. This is an almost universal feeling in the bereaved. Guilt raised its ugly head in me when I wanted Gail to die. But I also couldn't conceive of that lovely lady being a remnant. Many who have had to care for a loved one for a seeming eternity and with little hope, have gotten very tired of their situation. Guilt is hard to avoid in such circumstances. It is good to realize that if the roles were reversed your loved one would likely have felt the same as you did. Allow this realization to help you feel at one with your deceased beloved.

Note from Gail: It is also important to understand that the same circumstances do not teach the same lesson to different participants. The same situation can reveal one truth to you and another truth to another. I say this to bring out the fact that there are no correct or incorrect circumstances around a death. Do not be concerned with what others may feel about the particulars of a passing. Whatever happened will, believe it or not, contain beautiful guidance for the individual enlightenment of all concerned.

Chapter 6

Feeling Strange

As I mentioned before, on that tragic day of Gail's stroke, our son Rick came to the hospital, bringing his wife and our eight-year-old granddaughter Maria. When I got home from the hospital I found this letter from Maria:

> March 22, 1996
> Dear Grandpy, Gail is going to be all right. She ternd oround when you were not at the Hospitel.
> P.S. love and Joy!
> Love Rick, Maria, Mercedes

I am keeping that sweet letter. When Gail was being driven to the hospital with sirens going we had gone right by the elementary school where Rick was dropping Maria off for the day. Afterward Rick told me he had heard the sirens and they upset him, although he didn't know why. I vividly recall turning into the emergency entrance to the hospital, following the paramedics. I began to feel a strange almost surreal awareness. It is hard to describe. When Gail fell asleep at 11:00 that night after seeing the two of our four children we did not know she would never open her eyes again.

Dearest Husband,

Actually, I mostly left my body after you asked me those questions. I did come back when you were not there to see Rick and his family. And you know I came back to see Christopher. After that my body went into its final coma and I was gone.

Exercise 5: Did anyone have dreams, visions or feelings they couldn't explain even before they knew their departed was dying or had died? Was there evidence of any sort that your loved one stopped to visit with various family members—either by coming conscious as Gail did—or sensed in spirit by their surviving loved ones? I heard of one man who just hours before his death, kept making comments about his perceived environment which suggested that he was visiting each of his seven children in spirit. Write down the unusual feelings and happenings you or others experienced.

Chapter 7

Gail's Last Minutes

As Gail was dying and her body signs were fading fast I kept looking around the room hoping to see something like Gail out of body. I didn't but I was so emotionally full that disappointment wouldn't even register. Her vital signs quit and then started up again only to fade. The doctor said this was not unusual.

When she was fully gone I was informed that her body belonged to the Sheriff's department and might be autopsied. This was because she had died within 24 hours of being admitted to the hospital. The Sheriff wanted to be sure she had not died as a result of violence. It is a good law but it was very hard to take at the time. I tried to argue with the deputy but to no avail. He kept muttering about this aiding science, which I knew was false. It was nice of him to try. Later the doctor said he was quite sure he could talk them out of an autopsy since her death had nothing to do with a crime. I gave instructions that she was to be cremated.

My Dear Husband,

When I passed over I immediately had a feeling of coming home—even when I was traveling toward the light as I was dying. I think it was that feeling of coming home that made it so easy for me to give up my concerns about leaving you and the family. I knew that no matter what was in store for you after I left, you too would one day come home just as I did. I also had a heightened sense of God and this made it seem right—to hand over to God my concerns about my family.

One of the important components of coming home is the sense of peace that it gives you. I could have appeared to you as I was passing through but did not. I don't quite know why. I was so grateful to have been able to convey to you my thanks for sharing your life with me and all the other feelings we shared in the emergency room when I said goodbye that I felt complete. It seemed unnecessary to do more. It is most reassuring to know that the one you left behind knows there is an afterlife. I knew you believed that I survived and I knew it was inevitable that one day you too would experience what I was then experiencing. This somehow made the whole process complete so I felt good about moving on.

In life your higher self is with you always but some times it enters into your conscious mind more than others. One such time is while dying. There are those who are dying but do not know it consciously. Their higher self does, however, and is more active in this process than usual. The higher self acts like a giant pillow to the conscious mind which thinks it is falling into the abyss. The soft caress of the pillow surprises and puts wonderment into the mind of the dying.

After this the dying process proceeds in the more usual manner. The ones dying become aware of life after death, of being revitalized and being greeted with great love. Generally, any disbelief of the continuation of life is shattered by the reality of what they are experiencing. For many, this experience makes them badly want to communicate with the loved ones they have left behind to share with them their surprise and to reassure them. If your departed one was a great disbeliever, don't assume he or she will continue to be when faced with the reality of his or her continued existence. It is hard to deny what is staring them in the face. The survivors can help here by being open and receptive to us trying to communicate with them. And the survivors should not be surprised if the communicators seem considerably wiser than they would have been before they departed.

Those who are aware that they are passing and have some knowledge of the dying process have an easier transition and also know various things they may do. For this reason, the descriptions written by people who have had a near death experience are most helpful. While there is diversity, it is quite common to experience the tunnel with the light at the end of it. Most meet a loving spiritual being who revitalizes them as they welcome their return to this dimension.

Exercise 6: Given what you know of your departed, how would they have felt upon passing over? Who would they have seen? Who would have greeted them? Here is a place where you can really reach. Try asking the departed to tell you what they experienced and let them write that for you. Relax and let it flow. A few of you will be able to achieve this. But don't be discouraged if it doesn't work. It is a big stretch. You can also take this opportunity to say a prayer or send a message—written or mental—that could be of help to them if you think they would benefit from it.

Chapter 8

Our Last Hug

I remember when Gail and I were first married it felt so good to lie in bed hugging and cuddling. It seemed that any way we lay down with each other we seemed to fit so very well. I would hug Gail's back, she would hug mine, she on her side hugging me, me on my back with my arm around her. It seemed as if just every which way felt like we were designed to hug that way. I remember telling her that if I *had* to choose between making love or being able to hug her, I would chose the hugging. That's just how good it felt. Luckily we could have both. We hugged like that right up until the day of her stroke. Most people, I suspect, would find it creepy, but after Gail died, I laid down with her to hug her for one last time. I never found anything about Gail creepy. It helped me to say goodbye.

Darling,

Do you know that I was aware of you when you lay on the hospital bed with me right after I died? You hugged me as you always did. Everybody had left you alone with me in the hospital room. You climbed right into the bed with me and hugged my body for the last time. The priest was very surprised to see you there when he opened the door. I know it is not the same as when I was physically there but don't you sometimes get kind of the same feeling—like I am hugging you as you are falling asleep?

(I am pretty sure I do. But I fall asleep so quickly after I get that feeling that I can't exactly remember it.)

Exercise 7: Did you have some special physical connection with your loved one? Did you like to sit together in a favorite chair, for instance? Next time you are there or doing that, relax and see if you can't feel your loved one still there with you. Invite them to join you. It is important, both to invite them and to be open to the possibility of actually feeling them. I frequently feel a soft pressure on my upper arm where Gail used to press against me.

Chapter 9

Making Sense of Things

I had mentioned before that when I found Gail in the bathtub with her stroke she was looking up to the left apparently seeing things I could not see. This looking up to the left had a significance I cannot yet grasp. When I am quiet and think of Gail I find myself looking up to the left. Someday it will come to me what this means.

Buck,

In the bathtub when I was looking off to the upper left, I was looking at my guide who conveyed that I was dying and returning home. Coming home felt so good. I was torn because I was leaving you, causing you sorrow. This is what caused the confused look on my face. When my guide said that I would have a chance to share my death experience with you, I felt much better.

Exercise 8: Were there any unusual behaviors on the part of your loved one when he or she was getting ready to leave? Ponder what they might mean. Was there evidence that he or she was seeing or hearing things that you could not? If the passing wasn't peaceful can you discern the significance in how they went?. No matter how difficult the death, imagine how lovely it was for them to find out that they had returned home and become more fully healed, whole, and free of pain and other hardships.

INSIGHTS AND
    INSPIRATIONS
        SINCE
            GAIL'S
                TRANSITION
MARCH 23, 1996

I LOVE HER SO.

I DO NOT KNOW FROM
WHERE THIS ALL COMES
BUT I DO KNOW
THAT I AM NOT ITS
ONLY AUTHOR.

Part Three

My Journal Entries

Dear Reader,

The following are many of the entries that I made in that spiral bound notebook I found, as the days, months and years passed after Gail's death. For each entry, I have added relevant comments that Gail made in later communications. We hope that you are keeping your own journal too.

Chapter 10

Our First Communication

March 24th, 1996 (the day after Gail's death)

Since waking this morning I have been trying my best to maintain my regular routine. I did my ten minutes of stretching exercises and then took a hot shower. I haven't really been able to eat much. Later on I went to the small woods where Gail and I used to just sit and watch the birds and deer. It was far enough away from the house that I could cry and talk out loud without fear of being overheard. I went there and just sobbed. And in the midst of my sobbing I heard in my mind, "You are surrounded by God's love and my own. When you are *aware* of being surrounded by our love there is no room for fear to enter. You need not fear being alone, or being without me or anything else." It was an amazing experience. At that moment I could actually *feel* Gail's love surrounding me and my crying just stopped. It was as though love occupied a physical space around me and fear of the future just couldn't force its way in. I am doing my best to understand this intellectually but—best of all—I could really feel it. Gail, I sense, is actively communicating with me. She is trying to console me. I feel as if her spirit really has survived death—as we had always believed it would—and she is still there for me!

I know that the mind is the builder. My mind could make or allow the feeling that Gail's love surrounds me. I think it and it is. Or is it true and then I think (perceive) it? Does it matter? I know without doubt that I could *feel* its healing affection.

I feel grateful for this revelation. Even if Gail's presence in our backyard was only for a fleeting moment, a single stop on the journey to where ever it is she is going, it doesn't make the experience any less important. My emotions are running high and have swung from the depths of despair to the phenomenal feeling of joy when I think that maybe Gail will remain at my side, at least in spirit.

I believe that I have just learned, first hand, that communication between the living and the departed is not only possible, but it has happened to me. Not only did I hear Gail in my mind, but I actually felt surrounded by her love.

I feel like I have taken my first faltering and nervous steps down the path that will, I hope, ultimately bring Gail back into fuller communication with me.

Marshall's note: Emotional energy, Gail used to say, is the fuel that drives the spirit. In stressful situations, such as the loss of a job, a family crisis, or the death of a loved one, that energy becomes a powerful and sometimes frightening force. It can and frequently does overwhelm. Subsequently some shut themselves down in an effort to turn off the kinetic charges passing through them. Gail and I believed that shutting down is not the best, nor is "emotional overload" the inevitable outcome. Rather, a person could and should direct that energy in a positive and uplifting way to tap inner resources that are not otherwise available to them. I tried to do that at the hospital by holding in my heart a mental snap-shot of Gail's peaceful face whenever I felt panicky about her impending death, and I did it again when I stayed open to her communication with me back in the woods. It is somewhat similar to the adrenaline that in times of fright allows you to do physical things you could not do otherwise. This deep emotional energy allowed me to reach within my inner self and find strength I didn't know I had in a manner I could not ordinarily do.

Dearest,

It was just like you say. In your higher emotional state you could indeed cross more easily into your subconscious self. I was so happy to be able to comfort you and tell you how my love would make you invulnerable. Reciprocal love always makes you invulnerable. And, as you know, it was not just my love but God's too. And yes the love of Jesus as well.

Exercise 9: Are you open to receiving communication from your loved one? When you hear a voice, or a thought comes to you that seems like something they would say, try to pay attention. Then, try to respond—begin a conversation. Ask a question or send a message that you have been wanting to send to them. Then write it all down with gratitude.

Chapter 11

No Regrets

March 27th, 1996

Gail's sister, Violet, has chided me, "Buck, you've got to eat more." She of course means well but, as I told her, if I eat any more I will throw up. It's hard to even write. Everything I try to do seems to ache. Although, that is not completely true. There is part of me that feels enlightened and in respectful wonder. A thought enters my mind: "For giving love is to be forgiving. All you have to do is leave out the separation in between." That sounds like it is coming from Gail. Oh sweetheart, I forgive you for everything, everything, including you leaving me. And I know you forgive me for everything too." Gail and I gave each other that gift in our conversations when she was still here. We both said that we forgave each other for all the fights, the misunderstandings, and yes, all the *ineptitude*.

With Gail now gone I realize how very sincerely I meant what I had told her if I were to have died first. I told her that she should have no regrets for any part of our lives together whether it be fights or fun. And somehow my realization of the depth of my desire to be sure she would regret nothing makes me believe that she feels exactly the same way about me. And I too do not need to feel any regrets in spite of knowing there were many things I could have done much better.

Dear Buck,

In talks with those who have lost a close family member they frequently lament that now it is too late. Their loved one is gone. They no longer can correct or redo the errors between them. Their past relationship is now cast in concrete, unchangeable, permanent. And if it wasn't a very good relationship, they feel badly about it. This causes them great stress. To feel that something is irreconcilable is a most unhappy burden. Think about this a moment. What they are really saying is that the irreconcilable remains irreconcilable because it is beyond the reach of change. This is the same as saying it is beyond the reach of love. This is not true. Love always has the power to change. It happens all the time. And,

in forgiveness we experience giving up burdens we realize we don't want.

Let us take someone who had a marriage that was really more of an armed truce. They had a few good moments. There were also times when skirmishes broke out and blood was drawn. However, they limped back together for another armed truce. It seemed that there really wasn't anything that held them together. And yet they stayed together lumpy though it was. Then, let's say the husband dies just as ornery as ever.

The widow now has a hard time. Her life is drastically changed. She realizes many things about their relationship that she refused to recognize before. One realization is that even though he was a thoroughly difficult person he did have some endearing qualities that somehow got lost in the battles. She realizes now that there were many things *she* could have done but did not do that would have helped the relationship. She feels guilty—remorseful—and wishes somehow to make amends for her own peace of mind. But how can she when the relationship is now over and done with?

The truth is, the relationship is not over. Love is the tool. Love can transcend time. Love can actually go back and recreate a better feeling in the relationship. The widow can go through a healing process that will bring her enlightenment and joy.

When I left, you didn't have to go through that since we had both talked about death. We told each other that we had forgiven each other for any failures. I remember you telling me with sincerity that if you died you didn't want me to feel guilty about any tiny thing. You said we were both just learning so of course we wouldn't get every problem right. But not many couples had such discussions. It is important that they realize that what happens on this side can contribute to healing their relationships.

I can assure you that those over here are trying very hard to correct their understanding of how to transform into love the difficulties they've had with those they have left behind. Yes, and they have an easier time doing it because they now know this is a natural progression just like day follows night. When we pass over, due to a "review process" we go through, we very quickly receive a broader view of our lives and relationships.

For instance, when cranky spouses passes over they are presented with a whole new perspective of their past relationship. They get an entirely new realization of what they contributed and didn't contribute to it. They also get a better view of what it was like to be their spouse. This is quite an eye opener. As one told me, "My wife wouldn't recognize me now that I have an understanding of how we behaved to each other."

How much of a change this will bring about in each of us is up to our own free will. However, it is very, very likely that we will elevate ourselves to a higher level. This is because the lessons God gives us through transition are so very appropriate and—to use a mild term—powerful. In most instances, you would not be wrong to assume that the departed now have a much better view and you can communicate with us with the assumption that we on this side have greater understanding than we did before our death. Understanding this can, by itself, bring about a sense of healing in the bereaved.

Exercise 10: Describe how you would like your departed one to have his or her eyes opened by the review process as to how you felt about his or her relationship with you. You might also speculate what you might discover when the time comes for you to go through the review process. Understand that the departed are in the process of forgiving you—just as you can be forgiving them.

Chapter 12

Learning to Live in the *Now*

March 28, 1996

Dear God,

Thank you for your blessing of the *now*. I have but an inkling of its glory and even that overwhelms me.

Living in the *now*. This is an old mystical goal. It's not that easy to put into practice but I'm finding that it works when I can. For reasons that I don't understand today I am able to live in the *now* better than I ever have and it is very healing. The past, although it has its sweetness in all those memories is nonetheless a reminder of loss. The future can bring fear of the difficulty of living without Gail. Living in the *now* ushers in living without fear. When I live in the *now* fear or sorrow (those two have a lot in common) take a back seat. In the *now* there is the beauty that I see everywhere and the sun that I feel and the love of my family. Also in the *now,* and I don't understand this, there is a greater sense of Gail's spiritual presence. Being able to live and feel the *now* helps me greatly in dealing with Gail's loss. Another unexpected surprise.

> *Yesterday is History, Tomorrow is a Mystery.*
> *Today is a Gift, that's why we call it...The Present.*
> —**Author Unknown**

Beloved Buck,

It is a very fine *now*. Did you know it is *always* a very fine *now*? That is one of the *now's* basic characteristics. By living in the *now* do you tap into its very fine atmosphere of peace and serenity.

A deeper understanding of this reveals that the fine atmosphere is not dependent on any one or any several things. It just is. And being so, it is available to you in every circumstance. In other words, there is nothing that exists that can take away its availability to you. However, you with your free choice can deny it with closed attitudes, or more bluntly,

with your refusal to believe it exists. But it is there always and always available.

Exercise 11: Consider those moments when you feel relieved of pain and worry. You were probably present in the "now." Do not feel guilty when you experience those moments. Write down the activities, thoughts or ideas that help you to live in the "now." How does it feel when you are in the "now"? Practice bringing on these feelings consciously. In this there is a gift that God has given you and that He wants you to have. Do not deny yourself. Your beloved departed exists in the "now."

Chapter 13

Finding Significance in Small Things

March 29th, 1996

Today I went with Gordon our oldest son to pick up Gail's ashes from the funeral parlor. They came in a fancy plastic box that someone tried to make look somber. In turn, they put that into a stout plastic shopping bag and handed it to me. It was heavier than I expected. We walked down the front walk with me carrying the bag. The sun was shining and things were green and lovely. I told Gordon it seemed so strange to be walking with all that was left of my beloved Gail in a bag in my hand. All those memories, all those adventures, all that learning and loving in a plastic box that did not look a whole lot different than a box of detergent.

Poor, poor Gordon. Here he was in Poland just finishing his two years in the Peace Corps and out of the blue came the message that his mother was dead. He thought she was perfectly healthy. The Peace Corps was wonderful. They got him booked on a flight home immediately.

The previous summer he had taken his vacation in Prague in the Czech Republic and Gail and I had joined him for a visit. We three had great fun traveling together as we always had. When it came time, we took him to the train station in Prague for his return to Bialystok, Poland. We got him onto the train, said our good-byes and walked back down the platform. Just before we went down the stairs, I turned to see Gordon watching us and he had a look on his face that was full of deep meaning. It was like looking through time and space. I never forgot it. We didn't know it then but it would be the last time he would see his mother alive. I asked him today if he remembered that look and was I right that he realized that it was other-worldly. Yes, he remembered it very well indeed. He knew it was of great meaning but he didn't know of what. Strange that both he and I felt his gaze was not the ordinary goodbye. How do we perceive things like that? Science would have a hard time reducing something like that to an experiment that can be replicated.

Blessed Buck.,

Sometimes there is very great significance in seemingly small things. In small things, you can often feel more in harmony with God than you can in large. We tend to feel more gratitude for the larger things but the small things also deserve our gratitude. In small things the higher self often sees significance where the conscious mind does not. Sometimes that significance is so overpowering that it invades the conscious mind, leaving you wondering what is going on. Its meaning may puzzle you but you know it is significant, no matter what it is.

Gordon experienced such a thing in Prague when he said goodbye to me the last time. He didn't know in his conscious mind, nor did I, that that would be the last time we would see each other in this life. But his conscious mind and your conscious mind, in attunement with his, knew there was great significance in his gaze when we were leaving the train platform. We had said goodbye in foreign places before without this sense of a deeper meaning.

Gordon's higher self wanted that moment and feeling to be both felt and remembered without revealing the reason why. Your higher self wanted the same thing. After I was gone it was you that asked him about that look and now you share that common memory. You can replay it like a video in your mind allowing you to palpably feel that bond that the three of us had. What a lovely life journey we three had. And, we are still having it.

Is it not true that this one event is for both of you a key that opens to your full awareness what we three meant to each other? It includes when he was a baby and we drove home from the hospital at 20 miles an hour. We were afraid of jarring him in that old beat up pickup truck we had. It includes our trip to Africa together, our back packing together in Yosemite, and it even includes catching Gordon on the ski slopes when he was supposed to be attending university. These things and so many more are treasures that we share in the *we are all one* understanding. Did you ever think we would live to see him 50 years old? (this was written on Gordon's 50th birthday.) You can say I haven't lived that long but, in truth, I have.

We also had other life journeys with each of our other children. Each has its own special flavor, its own special dearness. They are treasures all.

Exercise 12: Write down the different ways in which you or others had somehow known that something was different about the last time you had seen your loved one. Describe the scene—just as if it was a scene in a movie. When was the last time you saw them before they died? What other special moments make up your relationship with your loved ones? Know that your higher self has arranged for that special memory.

Chapter 14

Another Communication from Gail

March 30th, 1996

After that wonderful feeling of Gail's presence in the woods behind our house, I have begun to make it a point to periodically stop and try to touch base with Gail. She might not only make her presence known, but there might be other messages to be communicated, if only I have the good sense to listen. I don't know if I will make contact but I want to try.

It has been my desire to communicate with Gail while in a restful and meditative state. Today—exactly one week after Gail's death, I had a standing appointment with my acupuncturist. It occurred to me that the conditions would be ideal. By my calculations, I would be alone and laying down in my acupuncturist's darkened room at the precise moment that Gail had died, one week earlier.

To help maintain a sense of peace, I arrived at the office early. I sat in the waiting room but as the minutes ticked by I became increasingly concerned. My acupuncturist was running late. Instead of being in a restful and meditative state, I found myself impatiently reading the minute-hand on my watch.

As the exact time came and went I was looking down at my hands in disappointment. But just then, without thinking, I suddenly had the urge to look up to my left. There, hanging on the wall was a Chinese painting of red and white mums. The flowers looked so beautiful to me—even three-dimensional—that at that moment I suddenly felt myself filled with their beauty. In my mind came the message: "When you see and feel flowers you know I am with you." As I had previously felt in the woods behind our house, I experienced an incredible sense of peace and love surrounding me. The wall-hanging itself was no different than hundreds of others I have seen in Chinese restaurants the world over but I saw it in three dimensions and in colors that only real flowers have. It riveted my attention!

Immediately afterward the doctor called me into his office, almost as if the delay had somehow been planned. It dawned on me that people can be so quick to decide what *should* be happening that they don't just relax and let things happen in their own way.

Chapter 14   Another Communication from Gail--42

I have been thinking about what Gail said to me. She had loved to garden. Getting down on her hands and knees in the dirt and planting flowers was a joy for her. Around our place she did the flower planting and I did the tree planting. The fact that flowers are everywhere—whether in arrangements, gardens or pictures on calendars—means that Gail will be with me often. Since Gail loved flowers so, they are a perfect symbol of her presence.

I feel pleased that I have taken another important and joyful step forward. Rather than dissipating my emotional energy into negative depression and grief, I am learning to deliberately redirect it into a positive creative force, into becoming open to new sensations and thoughts, however strange or foreign they are. A haiku poem is coming into my mind:

> Where do I find thee?
> With every flower I see
> That is where you'll be.

My Dear,

Yes, I wanted you to have another image of me in the now in addition to your remembrance of this past life, which is after all, now over. Your mind was still hopping, skipping and jumping all around. Then I became aware that you were expecting a message of some sort from me while lying in Dr. Ho's office with acupuncture needles in your back. But there you wouldn't be able to see any flowers. You could, however, in the waiting room. So my message came to you there. It was doubly impressive to you because you saw those flowers as live flowers which normally you can't do. Thus the message got through.

Marshall's Note: I have since learned that Gail's presence is not in the flowers but in my awareness of the beauty of flowers.

Exercise 13: Is there a symbol that would represent your loved one to you? Allow the right symbol to come into your mind. If you allow it, your departed one may help you choose the symbol. You will know it if this happens because the symbol will just pop into your head without any fanfare. You can purposefully place pictures or images of that symbol around you. Then every time you see or think of it, know that your loved one is with you.

This is a watercolor that Gail painted in 1982.

Chapter 15

Relationships Can Continue

March 31^{st,} 1996

I am realizing that some people might have difficulty with these concepts. Believing in an afterlife is hard enough without throwing in the communication with the deceased person. A valid theory (not necessarily the correct one) is that whatever is coming to me is just from my own imagination but my conscious mind likes the idea of ascribing it to Gail. The main point is, though, that somehow, some way, I am using the emotional energy generated by Gail's passing to tap inner resources and strength that were previously not easily available to me. I believe it was Gail because when she was alive we had been able to communicate mind to mind without words and we had come to recognize each other's style of thinking. The only difference now is that I can no longer confirm it with her verbally.

Darling,

Actually, there are many here who are trying to communicate with their bereaved loved ones on your plane. Many of them find it quite frustrating because the survivor is not open and will not listen. Most importantly, the survivors do not realize it is possible. On this side we want survivors to realize the great healing that can come between them. From our side I need to emphasize that the relationship that one has with their loved ones does not end when one comes to this side. It is wide, and I mean wide, open to changing for the better.

Exercise 14: When your loved one was alive, did you ever feel that you communicated with each other without speaking? Write down some examples. Now when you see, read or hear something, do you know what your deceased loved one's thoughts are on it? Do you recognize their style of thinking or speaking? Keep notes of thoughts that come into your head that sound like something they would say.

Chapter 16

Death Can Be Our Teacher

April 1, 1996

Experience, or rather experiencing, is the essence of life, its quintessential element. It keeps coming to me that I am having an *experience*—the loss of a beloved spouse—an experience that I should be aware of as an observer. What is it like? What feelings do I have? What is my natural tendency given this trauma? I am watching myself almost clinically at the very same time that I am immersed in the emotions of my beloved partner's passing.

I've talked to many people who feel that they have kind of a detached self that is above and behind their shoulder who watches everything they do. This self or awareness has no body. It is just an observation location. Although that detached self must feel encouraged or discouraged by what it sees us do, it nonetheless doesn't get involved with all the emotions we feel in the normal experience of life. I feel this detached awareness vividly, while at the very same time my heart seems totally absorbed by Gail's death.

What this detached observer sees is that I am going through a very prime and important experience which is being greatly enhanced by my *total* participation. It is a first class experience of enormous meaning and potential for understanding. And since Gail and I both loved reaching new understandings, this brings a bigger encouraging dimension to what I am going through. It doesn't diminish my loss; it adds a new opportunity that I do not want to waste. It does help put my loss into a bigger picture. Wider perspectives are always healing. I sense that if I carry it far enough I can get the full healing of knowing in my heart and mind that we are all *one*. I'm not there yet.

I intuitively feel that if I stay open and allow thoughts to come to me, then I will come to an understanding of what is taking place. I should pay attention to these thoughts and not let them slip away as dreams do when I awaken from a sleep. I already know what the understanding will be. There is an old mystical precept that applies here, difficult though it may be. Gail's death (or any other life experience) was for me, in my seeking along the spiritual path, precisely what is needed for me to gain from the lessons that are most appropriate for me to learn at this point in my life.

I realize this intellectually but I sure don't feel it emotionally. I suspect this means I have an emotional process to go through to arrive at what my intellect already knows.

I am already convinced that it was the best thing for Gail to pass on at this time even though that makes no sense from a material worldly view and would surprise our friends. We were going to go skiing. Life was great. Why end it? I will write about that another time. I'm tired

Buck,

> **God's love is the finest, most perfect love.**
> **God's creation is the finest most perfect creation.**
> **God's teaching is the finest most perfect teaching.**

God is your teacher, your personal, one-on-one, teacher. Some people think that all God has to teach us are high divine matters. They think that how to open a can of tomatoes is not a God-like subject nor one to which God has any connection. But God connects to all things because He *is* all things. There is nothing that is not God. The premise that God teaches only high divine matters creates a blinder to His wisdom. It makes us feel separated from God since most of the time we ourselves are not involved in high divine matters.

In fact, God will teach us anything and God will teach us everything. We need only to open our hearts and minds to His most perfect teaching to find enlightenment.

Ask God to be your teacher and you will let Godness become who you are. Your lessons will become holy experiences. You will see perfection where it was previously hidden from you. When you become aware that you are always both teacher and student with your brothers and sisters, who are your teachers and your students, your Oneness becomes your reality.

We feel pain, or sadness and wish we had a magic wand to take them away. If we would realize that often these negative parts of our lives are merely teaching us, or God's way of getting our attention, these parts would diminish. Volunteer to give attention to your God-given lessons and you will find the pain lessen in your life. Remember how our son, Rick, would spend vast amounts of energy and mental

ingenuity to avoid doing homework that could have been done with half the energy and thought processes? We are like that. God gives us a lesson and we squirm with how unjust the world is, how unfair it is. We would make our lives much easier if we simply said, "So this is my God-given homework. Let me start it."

Does that mean that it was God's will that terrorists attack the World Trade Center* and kill over 3,000 people? No. God gave human beings the gift of "free will" and it was the use of free will that killed all of those people. However, it is God's plan or law that with each experience we go through, we learn something that will further us on the spiritual path. There is no exception to this. Our free will granted to us by God does allow us to learn but very little, or to learn a great deal. But learn we must.

It is not only the bereaved but also those who die who learn from their death. Do you think it is possible for those 18 or 19 suicide terrorists to come over to this side, go through the review process and remain unchanged? They learned something. And so have their victims. And this is also true of you on earth who are now going through an unprecedented experience. We are all *one*.

Remember also that God in his infinite abilities can take any action done by anybody no matter how horrendous and make it a cause for spiritual advancement. So your Hitlers, your Stalins, your Bin Ladens spawn, in spite of themselves, a whole series of stimuli for spiritual advancement.

Contrary to what many might think, the unfortunate events of September 11th can provide a catalyst for the new millennium. It is as though we have been receiving our lessons for some time and have been doing our homework diligently and now comes the time for the mid-term test. Although please don't take this analogy too far and start judging whether you are passing the test or not. The results of the test will be manifest in the invisible—not the visible. Further, it isn't a test, but it does provide an acceleration of the learning opportunities.

---

*A reminder to the reader that comments from Gail that I have matched to my journal entries were given some years later—this one was obviously given after September 11th, 2001.

God is love. God is creation. God is teaching. Embrace all three. What does God want us to learn when a dear one passes away? These are common lessons aren't they? You see them everywhere. He wants us to learn many things at many different levels. None of the lessons take power away from you. Rather, they all help you to learn to love as God loves, create as God creates, and teach as God teaches. Bear in mind that we are always teacher/students. What finer thing could you be than a student of God, which is what you are? Listen to Him.

All people can find out what their lessons are. I can give you hints. First, there will be no punishment of any kind. Second, the learning of the lesson will bring you joy. Third, in learning the lesson you will not be giving up anything that is a true source of happiness. In other words, there is nothing to lose and everything to gain even if you perceive it otherwise. Too good to be true? No. Open your heart and mind and see.

* Exercise 15: Think of what lessons you might be learning on a personal level from the death of your loved one. Be open to these ideas and write them down. Also, write down what you think others have learned from the death of their loved ones. Your openness to what others have learned means that you are ready to receive the same thing. Being open is such a magical tool.

Chapter 17

Staying Open

April 2, 1996

Yesterday I wrote about staying open and letting thoughts come to me. Here are three thoughts that came to me this morning:

- To get to know the inner, let the outer give up expectations, grievances, and worries. Your inner mind uses a different language than these, and you will then be able to hear it.
- Our inner self, which we most often neglect, forgives us all the time.
- What sound does love make? It sounds exactly the same as the sun shining. And love is like the sun. It fulfills itself by shining—without concern about upon whom it shines.

Grief narrows down, closes in. And then in closing in does grief intensify. To de-intensify grief, I need to open up. Open up to what? My inner self, my inner strength and to the God within me. Be open to hearing thoughts like the three above. Have courage. Where are these thoughts coming from?

My Dear Husband,

When wisdom comes through, you are receiving something that is unknown to you. Openness then, requires courage to receive the unknown. This strikes fear in many people's hearts. They feel threatened and shut down which denies them not only new wisdom but knowing reality. It is reality that after death we exist in the spiritual world—that I can communicate with you—that we are all *one*. Closing ourselves down denies knowledge of these realities.

So the choices we make have huge consequences. Be open and become attuned to God's glorious loving reality or be closed and remain ignorant and unhappy. This is where some grief counseling falls short—it emphasizes the stages of grief. Stripped down, this is counsel of pre-determination. "You *will* go through these stages." This is not being open but closed to all but the accepted stages. Grief counselors would serve you better if they emphasized openness.

*Exercise 16: Some stages of grief that have been frequently given include: denial, isolation, shock, anxiety, depression, despair, anger, bargaining, guilt, loneliness, pain and panic. Write down all the reasons why you feel you <u>must</u> go through these stages.

Chapter 18

Ask (and Listen) and You Will Receive

April 3rd, 1996

My granddaughter made a sweet grass prayer wheel. I don't know where she got the idea. It is lovely, simple, natural and lovingly made. It is of tufts of dried grass held together with a circle of more grass bundles. What more could I want? Death seems to pull out things that are covered over within us. How long have they been waiting there? Death is a useful part of life even though most of us hesitate to view it that way.

My 47-year relationship with Gail is the platform on which I stand to view the world. Like all platforms I need not pay much attention to it in order to view the vistas it enables me to see. In other words, what I see is the result of the integration of the Gail part of me. Even though I'm outwardly not even aware of it most of the time, it adds greatly to my inner peace. We *are one*.

Yes Buck,

And as you understand deeper and deeper levels of the *we all are one* principle you will realize that sharing and communication are inevitable. But as each of us has free choice, we can *choose* not to listen. *Not listening* is the major cause of all the sadness and loneliness in your world. The Bible says, "Ask and you will receive." But it seems that there is a part left out. "Ask *and listen* and you will receive."

*Exercise 17: Write down any reasons why you or others might choose not to listen for communication from a deceased loved one. Then write down what you would gain by receiving communication—and the changes you might make to open yourself to receiving that communication.

Chapter 19

Giving Up Fear

April 4th, 1996

It is curious. I realize that my fear of the future has changed. I didn't realize how much the future concerned me. Although I thought I was generally a non-fearful person (and I guess I am compared to many of my contemporaries) I realize now that I worried about the future.

Having arrived at my late 60s I was concerned about Gail's health, and to a lesser extent, my own. Gail didn't have any real illnesses or conditions but her stamina and vitality did seem to be lessening. For instance, she could no longer go backpacking at higher altitudes. I also worried about my health—about the burden that my hereditary inclination to Alzheimer's disease could possibly place on Gail. Finances too were a concern because I wanted to be sure that if I died Gail would have enough no matter how long she lived. This was, of course, difficult because who knows when enough is enough? I was also worried about how life would be for her if I went first. I assumed I probably would, as men usually do. How would she do in taking over what I had been taking care of? She was very smart and an experienced, capable manager, but just the burden of having to take over combined with the grief could be unpleasant to overwhelming. All these worries and more.

Now, Gail is gone and the stimulus for these worries is gone too. Isn't that weird that her death could remove worries from my mind? At first blush it seems very unloving to say such a thing, but I've never doubted my total commitment to Gail. I don't worry much about my own death. Like many others I guess I do have some worries about how I might die: no protracted illnesses thank you. However, even here I feel that Gail chose her time and *way* of dying. She wanted it to be easy on all of her family. I feel that she has told me that I, too, could choose the quick and easy way of going. I don't understand why but I feel quite confident that I will die gently.

It is true that Gail's passing ushers in a whole new set of potential worries. Will I miss her so much I ache? Will I feel there is no light at the end of the tunnel? Will I even want to live since I am not that afraid of death? Will I go into long periods of depression? Will I really feel like doing anything? But all of these worries are centered on me. I find these easier to dismiss. Not dismiss exactly, but I feel they are manageable. I can handle these just as Gail wants and expects me to. She had always said she didn't want me to be defeated by her going. I won't be.

My Dear Buck,

Not being afraid is the key to life. The good things in life and fear do not go together. You cannot love, you cannot have joy and you cannot truly be grateful and be afraid at the same time. You cannot fulfill your spiritual self if you are afraid. Nor can you communicate with your higher self in meditation or through creativity. That is because fear creates separation. Separation—any separation—separates you from God. There is no true "evil" in the world—but fear comes closest to it. The more advanced you are spiritually the less fear you have.

Your reasons for fear are all self made. You can remove fear from your life by understanding God's gifts to you. There are three great gifts:

♦ **The first gift is that we are all *one*. If this is true then it is impossible for you to be separated in any way. Nothing important can happen to you that would not happen to the All. All the strife is but temporary illusion that cannot affect you unless you choose to let it.**

♦ **The second great gift is that you are immortal. You are forever. So what is there to fear.**

♦ **The third gift that you have been given by God is free choice. You therefore do not need to fear *having* to do something, for you can choose not to. There are many who think of karma as being something that you cannot escape. You will have to be paid back an eye for an eye, a tooth for a tooth. But, you can escape your "bad" karma in an instant if you choose to learn the lessons contained in that karma. If you learn those lessons, you will feel so much better, that you will understand that the karma was actually a gift just waiting for your acceptance.**

You do not need to have fears in your life. You can choose to give them all up—all at once if you want. But if this seems

too daunting, then give up your fears little by little. And avoid making more of them. To the degree that you give up fears you will increase your happiness, and more importantly, your self-fulfillment.

Fear on earth is an all-pervading power. God has given us choices and so many earth decisions are made with fear as the dominant factor. Fear is a confession of vulnerability. Yet God made you invulnerable. When I died at the hospital the staff saw me as vulnerable to the stroke I had. That is the narrow perspective. In the wider perspective I was not vulnerable. After all, I am still here enjoying life given me by God.

When you come over here you feel much less vulnerable so the influence of fear will disappear. For some whose earthly life was dominated by fear, it is hard to give up the fear. Therefore, if you can reduce the role of fear in your life now and in the future, it will be very helpful when you pass on.

Exercise 18: Take a moment to write in your notebook what you are most afraid of. Consider what underlying beliefs these fears reveal. Write: I am afraid of ....therefore I must believe.....Then write down the beliefs that would remove those fears. It can be hard to remove fears, to turn them off. But, you can turn down the volume and then you can turn down the volume yet again. Then you will be in command of your fears instead of your fears being in command of you.

Chapter 20

Acceptance and Getting Rid of Expectations

April 5th, 1996

God please help me to accept Gail's death. That is incorrect. I do accept Gail's death. God please help me to accept the wisdom and value you have made available to me in Gail's passing. I do understand that acceptance is not passive as we tend to think it is. It is actively opening our minds and hearts to the gifts that lay hidden in what we are experiencing. We will find these gifts only if we seek them. And we will seek them only if we know they are there to find. Acceptance is actively minimizing expectations and maximizing openness. Guide me to this understanding.

Later this poem came to me:

> ACCEPTANCE
>
> We're two old pines anchored to the shore.
> How long have our roots mingled
> In this ancient soil, living the repeated seasons
> Each granting us a tree ring of truth.
> Has wisdom's girth fulfilled the task
> Of life's many journeys to be our last?
> Our souls await with patience and acceptance
> The place of our being in God's plan.

Dearest Buck,

You are right. Acceptance is not passive. And it is as important a concept here on this side as it is on earth. As far as I can tell, the acceptance principle goes up through all levels to God Himself. He could only have given us free will and choice as He has done if He was ready to accept the choices we make. An all-accepting God is very hard for the earth's religions to understand. If God is all accepting what difference does it make if we are bad or good, cruel or kind? In a true sense, none. However, there is more to the universe than arbitrary behavior. More about that later.

Expectations have the effect of closing the mind. If your expectations are not fulfilled then all other outcomes are more likely to appear negative. This can literally close you off from recognizing positive aspects of alternative outcomes. In this way you refuse to see the great benefits that all of your experiences contain. This specifically applies to the death of loved ones. Their death may not have been a part of your expectations—even if you had some notice of it. When you don't expect it, your resistance to it can be even greater. Resistance just gives you that much more to overcome. There is already a great deal to overcome in a death. Beware that expectations don't just add to those burdens.

> *Acceptance is not passivity, rather it is the*
> *active opening of the mind to learning what*
> *your experiences are meant to teach you.*
> **— Marshall Kent**

*Exercise 19: Write down what your expectations are or have been in and around your life with your beloved departed. Then describe all the ways those expectations could limit you and your experiences.

Chapter 21

Help from the Other Side

April 6th, 1996

The message from Gail in the acupuncturist's office was so encouraging and so uplifting that I have been staying open for more messages from her. I did not have to wait long. My next communication, while not something I could "take to the bank," has resulted in something I could plant in the ground.

Neither Gail nor I wanted a public memorial service, a grave or the like. We both wanted to be returned to the soil where our ashes might contribute to something living and this without a plaque or such. Just a simple recycling to the living. So for our family memorial gathering on this coming Easter Sunday I have decided to plant a tree and mix Gail's ashes in the soil around the tree.

Forty years ago, when we first bought our 13 acre knoll, we planted a black oak tree right by our house and it is now a big lovely tree. We had always talked about planting another one but had never gotten around to it. Now a black oak seems to be the most appropriate. I telephoned our local nursery and they said they had no black oaks. They couldn't even order me one because it was the wrong time of year. I called other nurseries in adjacent towns and, sadly, no black oaks. I went to the library and looked in the yellow pages for all the nurseries within 100 miles and I called them all. I had luck with only one nursery. They said they had a shipment of 10 black oaks coming in Friday and to call back then.

When on Friday I called, they told me that they had rejected the shipment of the oaks. They were not of good enough quality. I was terribly disappointed and reluctantly concluded that we would have to plant my second choice, which was a redwood tree. But we already have quite a number of redwoods on our hill and one more doesn't seem quite unique or special enough to honor Gail. However, I tried my best. Today I went down to the same local nursery that I had first called to shop for a redwood.

I confess that shopping and I do not mix well. If I must shop I walk straight to what I want to buy then I pay for it and leave. Most men are like this I think and most wives shake their heads in despair for their husband's peculiar ways. Gail, of course, liked to browse around. There I was walking into the nursery to buy the redwood tree and be gone when into my mind came this thought, "Don't be so silly. What makes you think they know what they have in their own inventory? Walk around." I immediately knew that this was Gail's thinking. After living with her for 47 years I knew how Gail's mind worked and this was her style—not mine. Being committed to staying open, I immediately changed course and headed up an aisle of plants. There, at the very end of that aisle, up against the fence—lo and behold—were three black oaks! One of them had an outstanding shape and I would have picked it out of 100 trees as Gail's tree. It has the most wonderful character. I found myself laughing and, in my mind, giving thanks to Gail. Of course I bought that tree. It seems as if Gail arranged the whole thing including the frustration of finding the tree in the first place. She would know that would get my attention. What a lovely, humorous, and gentle way for her to let me know of her presence and of how she could help me. I felt so amazed and overjoyed to hear Gail's wonderful voice again. Much to the curiosity of the customers around me, I laughed out loud when I heard it. I feel certain now that Gail's presence is not a figment of my imagination. Although I couldn't see her, I am absolutely positive that Gail was standing there beside me.

Darling Buck,

Do you recall how when we worked together remodeling the house we would just know how the other person needed to be helped and we just did it even without talking? It was a good feeling to mesh together in that way. In a way this is what we were doing when we were getting the black oak tree. On the surface it might seem that I was working against you by frustrating your search for the tree. I knew that the tree was not the object of your true search. You were searching for something that would tell you I was there with you even though I am "gone".

Yes, I made suggestions to you that contributed to your frustration. I knew that you would search diligently for what you thought was right. You have always been that way. I also knew I could depend upon you to accept the inevitable and go get a redwood tree. Best of all, I knew with the buildup I had helped create that I could depend upon you to receive the gift you really wanted: knowledge that I was alive and attuned

with you and your life—after my death. It was the same pattern as our raising the 4 x 12 beams in the living room ceiling. We each played our part like the glove does to the hand.

Marshall's note: I have a widow friend who does not believe in all this afterlife stuff. One day her paper shredder jammed and she could not get it working even with a few kicks. In disgust she stepped back and said, "Okay Bill fix it." Her deceased husband had the knack for fixing anything. The shredder made a noise, spit out the jammed material and it has worked ever since!

Exercise 20: Can you think of a time when you felt the influence of your deceased loved one since his or her death? Did you remain open to it? Write down a description and how it helped you. If you cut it off or if you dismissed it as your imagination, realize you can reopen the communication. Take yourself back to that time and situation. With an open mind write and ask for the communication to be reopened. Actually this is a very good way to break through any blocks.

Chapter 22

Accepting Help from the Other Side

April 6th, 1996 Evening

I honestly believe that Gail arranged for the purchase of that tree, including my frustration in finding it, knowing that this was a lovely, humorous, and gentle way to get my attention. Again I am reminded that there is a lesson to be learned in every challenge and every apparent setback. This was another example of the value of unconditional acceptance of experiences. I will work hard to continue to be accepting.

My Dear Buck,

You have described how I frustrated you in finding a black oak tree for my memorial. It makes it sound as though I had the power to manipulate events. If that were true, then I would be interfering with your free will. Was I in fact frustrating your free will? No, I wasn't and couldn't. Your free will and the free will of every soul is inviolate.

To understand all this we should go to the basics. Free will is a gift given to us by God. Nobody has the power to take that away from us. We always have free will to decide for ourselves. Nobody can decide for us unless we first *choose* to let them do so. This applies equally to us over here. We too have free choice. We too are free of having other people choose for us *unless* we choose to let them do so.

With the black oak tree situation, I just took advantage of what was already there. The oak tree had been there for some time and, not surprisingly, it had been forgotten by the nurseryman who you talked to. I did convey to you suggestions but you had the free will to accept or reject those suggestions. Because of the harmony we have built up over the years, I was not surprised that you picked them up. I knew better than you did that what you were *really* seeking was not the oak tree but validation that I was with you and helping you. I also knew the skeptic that you are and wanted to demonstrate my presence in a way that would impress you and allow no other interpretation.

Exercise 21: Do you ever feel that your departed loved ones are somehow presenting you with thoughts and actions you could choose to take? Write down some examples of these, including what you perceive their reasons would be for doing so.

Chapter 23

A Memorial Service for Gail

April 7, 1996

Today is Easter and we had a memorial service for Gail. I wasn't sure I could handle it. Gail's twin brother is here from Ohio with his wife and children. Gail's sister and all four of our kids and their children and spouses were also here. The weather was fine.

I selected a spot that I thought would be good for the black oak tree. It is next to a small contained garden. It also has a lovely view to the southwest. Earlier I dug a big hole and put the pile of dirt by its side. This is all about 60 feet from the house.

We started the ceremony in the garden right outside of the bedroom window that we looked out of together every morning when we awoke. I had Bud, Gail's twin, hold the sturdy wood box filled with Gail's ashes that I had made with great pride. In fact, when I got back from picking up Gail's ashes, I couldn't wait to make a wooden box for them. The plastic container just wasn't Gail. So I went to my shop room and got some re-sawn redwood that our son, Rick, had gotten for me and some 2-inch pine left over from when Gail and I had remodeled our house with our own hands. I made a nice flush-sided box and fitted the top on tightly so that no hinges were needed. Instead I put a lift handle on it. As I was doing this I was overcome with the sense that this was not the first time I had built a box for my dearly departed wife. I felt as if I had done this before—in another lifetime—but it was a full sized coffin that time. Strangely enough, the feeling was comforting as it gave to me the great sense of the continuity of all things. I am a carpenter in this life and was in others before. My wife had also died before me in that lifetime, but it wouldn't be the last time I would see her.

For the ceremony I carried with me a beautiful copy of Teilhard de Chardin's* statement: "Joy is the most infallible sign

Pierre Teilhard de Chardin (1881-1955) is among the few leaders of thought in the last century to integrate pure scientific research with a religious vocation. This paleontologist and Jesuit priest made it his mission to reconstruct the most basic Christian doctrines from the perspectives of science and, at the same time, to reconstruct science from the perspectives of faith.

of the presence of God." It was a print of the statement in calligraphy, which Gail and I got in Ojai.

Gail's joy was such a wonderful thing to live with so it seemed fitting. She had hand colored it and framed it. It hung in our bathroom where she had her stroke. It will continue to hang there.

I spoke about how fortunate we all were to have had Gail in our lives. And I explained that I carried this framed statement because it was so central to her life, to our life. She knew joy and she knew it both with and without adversity. Then I suggested we plant the tree. Everyone lined up while I got on my knees to lift the tree into the hole. Bud stood beside me with the box of ashes. Each person came up, took some ashes and some dirt from the pile and sprinkled them into the hole while I tamped it down. They then would each stand back to make room for the next person.

After filling in the hole I stood beside the tree feeling reluctant to move from it. My two granddaughters came up and hugged my legs and started to cry. My grandson William came too and we all clung to each other and sobbed. It was very moving— they all loved their grandma so.

The ceremony was more or less unplanned—without much structure. Improvising was very characteristic of our family life and still is. When the ceremony was over we had an outdoor dinner. It was teary but went well. We only used part of the ashes. The rest I will take up to the Sierras to a spot that Gail and I had visited often and had selected as our personal sacred site.

Beloved Buck,

At that time of great family sorrow, my memorial service, I was appreciative of the love that was shown toward me. It is strange from this perspective to know you have just a completed a whole life devoted to family and to see them all together at your earthly completion. And there you all were— thinking of your relationship with me over our long associations together.

I was so pleased with you. You did the service impromptu. We were always at our best improvising. It seemed fitting that you were still improvising with me then. It was like when I shared my death experience with you. It is just the way we did things. I was so glad that you used Teilhard de Chardin's

statement of Joy and God. I do want to be thought of as joyful and grateful to God. The sorrow can be healed by joy. With joy you cannot dwell in mourning for the past. It was a very nice service and I thank you for it.

The most pampered tree in our county.

Exercise 22 : Write down what your beloved departed would have thought about the memorial or gathering that you had for them. What would they have appreciated about it? Know that they were there. Did you discern any evidence of that?

Chapter 24

The Invisible Acts Upon the Visible

April 8th, 1996

When Gail passed away we were studying the workbook from *A Course In Miracles* (ACIM for short). Today I have been rereading the lessons of the Workbook that we were reading at that time. They seem uncommonly appropriate. The day before Gail's stroke we were on Lesson 278 and Gail had been reading out loud:

If I am bound, my Father is not free.

If I accept that I am prisoner within a body, in a world in which all things that seem to live appear to die, then is my Father prisoner with me. And this I do believe, when I maintain the laws the world obeys must I obey; the frailties and the sins which I perceive are real, and cannot be escaped. If I am bound in any way, I do not know my Father nor my Self. And I am lost to all reality. For truth is free, and what is bound is not part of the truth.

As I read this now it seems as if Gail was ready to accept the invitation to be set free. For those not familiar with ACIM, a main tenet is that this life is but a dream. Gail is choosing to leave this dream and return to God. I find it amazing that it is so clearly appropriate.

The next morning she had her stroke before we could meditate and do the next lesson. That lesson seems to me to be about her acceptance of the invitation to leave her body. Perhaps her stroke was her acceptance. I have changed the gender in the quote.

Creation's freedom promises my own.

The end of dreams is promised me, because God's Daughter is not abandoned by His Love. Only in dreams is there a time when she appears to be in prison, and awaits a future freedom, if it be at all. Yet in reality her dreams are gone, with truth established in their place. And now is freedom hers already. Should I wait in chains which have been severed for release, when God is offering me freedom now?

To me the last sentence should read, "Should *she* wait in chains which have been severed for release, when God is offering her freedom now?" This seems to be telling me to take joy in Gail's passing. She is free now. I am trying to do this and in the trying I am succeeding somewhat. This lesson touched me deeply. It was as if I was reading this to her, to honor her and accept her decision to leave her body and to leave me.

The next lesson (280) seems custom made for me:

What limits can I place on God's child...

Whom God created limitless is free? I can invent imprisonment for her, but only in illusions, not in truth. No thought of God has left its Father's Mind. No thought of God is limited at all. No thought of God is but forever pure. Can I lay limits on the Child of God, whose Father willed that she be limitless, and like Himself in freedom and in love?

Today let me give honor to Your Daughter, for thus alone I find the way to You. Father, I lay no limits on the Daughter You love and You created limitless. The honor I give to her is Yours, and what is Yours belongs to me as well.

This says exactly what I am feeling. I do indeed *"give honor to God's daughter."* And I do so with gladness in my heart. All three lessons so accurately describe what is going on and in the right sequence. It is uncanny. Call it all coincidence if you want. I don't.

My Dearest,

For you on earth, it can be difficult to realize how basically and how often the invisible affects the visible in your world. There are signs everywhere that this is true. You won't see them unless you are looking for them. When I passed on we were reading ACIM. Because you thought to look at ACIM to see where we stopped our reading, you discovered that the last three readings were strangely appropriate. You would have never discovered this if you had not thought to look in the first place, and having looked, observed the synchronicity. Many people would not have thought to look, therefore many examples of the invisible acting on the visible go unnoticed. These rarely observed synchronicities are put in place in the

visible world by the invisible. When you start seeking them you find them everywhere.

One reason you won't notice them is that you tend to judge everything as good or bad, welcome, painful or unpleasant. Synchronicities end up just being there and tend to become simply background to our good and bad evaluations.

Exercise 23: Have you observed amazing synchronicities in your life? Evidence of the invisible acting on the visible? Describe in your journal some examples of these. If you look for it, you will even find good reasons for what appear to be bad things that happen to you. When you get stuck in traffic or a lunch date doesn't show up, instead of getting upset, try looking for some other reason for you being where you find yourself. Maybe you are being saved from a bad accident—or being guided toward a particular person you need to meet. The more you look for it, the more you will see evidence of the invisible acting in your world.

Chapter 25

A Message in My Dreams

April 9th, 1996

Each night I have been asking to communicate with Gail in my dreams. It seems to be happening. Last night I dreamt we were in an undeveloped part of the city. We were surprised to see a white raccoon. There was a large excavation in which the footings had already been poured and the reinforcing bars were protruding up 10 feet or so. There were no workmen but somehow I was involved with the construction. Gail and I were in a car and I told her that I needed to get some crushed rock fill from someplace to put in a void where we were getting ready for another pour of concrete.

She had been driving and restarted the car with great confidence. She drove straight ahead to the top edge of the excavation, and then drove right off the edge. I yelled at her to stop, that she would get us both killed. She turned and smiled at me and I realized we had not been killed but were down at a place where there was crushed rock. We both got out of the car (uninjured) and she walked me over to the gravel right in front of the car. She picked up the shovel that was there and handed it to me and said, "Here's the gravel that you needed." She then said something to the effect that she knew what she was doing and that I should trust her. She had done the whole thing with complete assurance.

It was interesting that the dream was ushered in by a white raccoon. Having had a pet raccoon, both Gail and I viewed them as very intelligent animals. The color white so often symbolizes spirituality. The white raccoon was a symbol, I think, of the spiritual wisdom that was being offered. And the spiritual wisdom was that Gail knew what she was doing when she died –that there was nothing to fear and that she was taking the lead for both of us to grow into new areas spiritually. All I had to do was to trust her. Driving off the top of the excavation represented her death which scared me but didn't scare her. The construction was the symbol of our new life that was in the early stages of development and required building upon from a new foundation. I had work to do and her death was the means of giving me the tool (shovel) and the material (gravel) I needed to build that foundation. I should trust her and remain open and I too would find it all fits together into our holy relationship.

Dearest Dreamer,

As your dream told you I was not at all afraid of death. That surprised me as I thought when death came I might be scared. I wasn't. Many things come into understanding when you pass over, particularly at the beginning.

 Sleep is a state of *being* that opens doors through dreams to a whole new vast world of thoughts, images and meanings. In the bible, Joseph's* interpretation of the pharaoh's dream changed history. Years ago, I had an important dream that changed our lives when it told me to accept your early retirement. Even more surprising was that this dream was a complete therapy that removed the emotional fears I had at the time. It was like magic. Not many psychiatrists can do such a complete and quick job as my dream had done for me.

*Joseph was a biblical character who analyzed an Egyptian Pharaoh's dream and then recommended a course of action which saved the country from starvation during a 7 year drought.

*Exercise 24: Dreams can teach us a lot. Before going to sleep at night, instruct yourself as to what wisdom you would like to gain from your dreams. Put your journal and pen by your bed and when you awaken, lay still as long as you can and focus attention on your dreams. Dream memories are fragile—the movements of your body disrupt your memory. Play your dreams in your mind over a few times. Once you have transferred the memories of your dream from your sub-conscious mind to your conscious mind, you can write them down.

Chapter 26

This Day I Choose Joy

April 10th, 1996

Lesson 284 in A Course in Miracles says that joy is God's gift and being joyous is the truth. *"The Holy Spirit converts the physical world into remembrance of God's world when we feel the joy in the world. Feeling joy is a remembrance of God. Joy is without boundaries."* In the morning, when I first get up, I find it helps me greatly just to say, "I choose Joy."

To me joy is that sense of wonderful well being that comes from inside of me and is not dependent on anything from outside of myself. In contrast, happiness is that reaction I have to favorable events that occur outside of me—for example, when the problem I am having with my car turns out to be just minor.

Using these definitions, joy is an inner resource we can choose to tap. I am choosing joy with the knowledge that each time I do so I get better and better at it. With this understanding I don't fret so much when I choose joy and it doesn't seem to work so well. After all, I am just an apprentice and I just lost my beloved wife.

My Dear Buck,

Any experience you've had in the physical with the feelings of joy is *so valuable*. You and I sensed that joy was a good and wonderful thing but I want you to know that we really had no idea of the great value of joy. You are right. Joy is even greater than happiness. Joy comes from within and does not depend upon outer circumstances, as does happiness.

Exercise 25 : Write down a list of those things that make you happy. Now, write down a list of what it is that brings you joy. What is the difference between the two lists? Write that down too.

Chapter 27

Converting Grief

April 11th, 1996

Here I am with Gail gone and I feel two very different ways. The first is what you would call traditional grief and separation. Fortunately for me it is not the principal emotion. The second is much more unconventional. I am deliberately trying to take the high emotional energy that is a result of my loss and divert it to my higher, inner self. Perhaps it would be better to call it being in touch with the spiritual side—not only the spiritual side of myself but that of the world. The professional grief counselors will probably describe this as some form of grief repression. But those considered as authorities are not always correct.

Despite my own skepticism and disbelief in my own abilities, I am astounded to find that I can indeed divert this emotional energy away from grief and into communicating with my higher self. I can't always achieve this but when I do it feels so good. When I do, I feel I understand why Gail left when she did and why I am still here. I also feel I understand why she left with only 24 hours notice. And all of that seems so naturally correct. When I sense this I feel that Gail is close and that she is encouraging me and telling me things will be good. And lo and behold they are.

My rational mind wants to know what this experience is and how it comes about. Perhaps it will become clearer if I first describe its opposite, grief. With grief I am very conscious of the boundaries that are around me. It is a very self-centered ME-consciousness that knows that I have lost my beloved wife of 47 years. There is a very big and distinct boundary that separates me and my loss from the person ahead of me in the checkout line and everyone else. Gail being physically gone is another very distinct and inviolate boundary. I will never see her again. There are so many other boundaries that I can allow to make me feel hemmed in and with no way out. That is why grief and its depression seem so hopeless. There are barriers and boundaries between me and any future happiness I can have.

I realize that all of these boundaries are created by no one other than myself, although it is with the encouragement of my culture. Therefore I have the choice to dissolve these boundaries of my own creation. This doesn't imply that it is easy, just that it is within my jurisdiction.

Just the opposite of feeling bound, is the opening of my mind to my spiritual self and its connection with the spiritual world and to Gail. The boundaries are dissolved almost by definition. The verb to open, is quite the opposite of to bind. When I am open, the first thing I notice is that the grief that is dependent upon my feelings of being bound and isolated is gone. Grief is impossible for a truly open person to feel.

The second thing I notice is that the separation that I feel from Gail (because she can no longer be physically present) is also gone. This separation too requires a boundary—between the dead and the living. Take the boundary away and the sense of separation is gone. It is so logically simple. And what takes place instead is a sense of her presence that is lovely to feel. I will let others argue over whether it is actually Gail's presence I feel or whether it is a figment of my imagination. But I do know that I like it and this is a time when I am searching diligently for things to like. I also know that I can almost feel it dissolve my grief. It is this last feeling that convinces me that I'm not repressing my trauma. I'm converting it.

Dear Buck,

Let me give you something to mull over. *All* is just acceptance without boundaries. When you feel this acceptance you have peace and communication. And you know how dear the concept of communication is to my heart. As children we find a secret place and feel immediately attuned with it. Later, as adults, we try to recapture that feeling but seldom do. This is because we have created boundaries and reinforced them to the point that we can no longer penetrate them. Children are without these boundaries and have a much easier time of it.

Keep yourself open. Do not judge. Do not judge yourself or myself as being unable to do this or that. I love you. Enjoy this day in the *now*. You actively enhance your awareness of the joy of the *now* by actively diminishing your expectations and fears. You have nothing to fear.

The world is bountiful. God's gifts are so abundant. When you are aware of them it is difficult not to feel joy. If you feel in a morass, just wait with the patience Edgar Cayce* extolled and it will all change.

However, I have to be careful here. You do not simply wait and do nothing. You must try your inspired best, but you need not be discouraged by any apparent lack of results. In a way, you are being tested but there is no time limit to the test nor is there a point when you get a grade of pass or fail. You are evolving as your inner understanding progresses. Your outer world comes and goes and changes to reflect your inner understanding. This is why that inner self that you are constantly creating and recreating is so important. Recognizing your own invulnerability, your own immortality helps greatly with your inner being and therefore with your outer circumstances.

*Edgar Cayce was the famous American psychic also known as "the sleeping prophet" who died in 1945. He called patience the fourth dimension.

*Exercise 26: Figure out what invisible boundaries you have created for yourself and write them down. Now see them dissolving.

Chapter 28

Feeling Out of Balance

April 12th, 1996

I realize that Gail and I lived a balanced life—full of good things and experiences most of the time. Now she has died, and a new element, a new condition has been introduced into my life. My task is to bring my life back into balance while incorporating this new condition.

I don't think I will achieve balance if I feel that her death was unfair or that I was a victim of some sort. I also have faith that God created us with the tools we need to meet all of our experiences. So I must ask myself, "What has God given me to handle this trauma?" I have that energy that I spoke of earlier that is difficult to turn off. It was not my usual energy of *wanting* to do something. It is the opposite. There is little I want to do. It is a ceaseless mind energy. Thoughts, episodes, memories and speculations keep boiling up in my mind.

How am I supposed to use this? I feel out of balance and I want to get back into balance. I realize that my boundaries are what keep me on just one side of the scale. The idea comes to me that this energy I have can be used to bust out of my boundaries.

For instance, before Gail died I believed I wouldn't want to go on living without her. I have to break out of this very limiting boundary. I also had doubts about the afterlife and the spiritual world as I think I understood it. It came to me that I should believe that *all* things are possible. This is not the same as saying that any crazy idea I come up with is true. It is just that it *could* be true pending the gathering of more experience or data. In other words, I shouldn't dismiss things as impossible or ridiculous unless they have been proven as such.

A simple openness is all it takes. It is good to remain skeptical *as long as it doesn't inhibit me from being open.* I can continue to be skeptical–but as an observer, *not as a participant!* A true observer watches what happens but does not try to affect it or change it. Participating skeptics, in encountering something they think is outlandish, will shut it off and thus lose the stimulus to grow. They will not allow something new to enter their thinking. I must remain open and eliminate boundaries and limitations. I am on the road to regaining my balance.

Dear Buck,

Let us talk about volcanoes. It is recognized that they bring about exquisite balance despite their tremendous explosiveness. How can all that power and chaos bring balance? Many on earth feel that the world is dominated by chaos both man-made and natural. In truth, balance is far more powerful than chaos as the chemists and the physicists have demonstrated in their formulas. So why do we think that our lives are a series of random and chaotic events and coincidences?

Our lives on earth start with the introduction of something new to be added, our birth. If properly handled, we create with our parents a new balance. To this balance is added again something new—our growth. As we grow and can do more things, again a balance is sought and achieved. This is the dance of life. Something new is added and a new balance occurs to which something new is again added which in turn demands balance. This is the proper play-out of life and results in growth and advancement. Improperly fulfilled, our lives do not find balance but become a series of seemingly imposed new events and conditions which we never digest or adapt to. We try to run away or remove them. Narrowing perspectives brings about imbalance. In contrast, widening your perspective just like a tightrope walker spreads out his arms for balance—or keeping yourself open—will help you to regain your balance. Bringing balance into your life is a difficult process but very rewarding.

Exercise 27: Write a description of the imbalances caused by the loss of your loved one. Think about ways that you can bring yourself back into balance. What boundaries can you dissolve? Think about how staying open helps you in this process.

Chapter 29

A Birthday Gift from Gail

April 18th, 1996

April 18th, 1996

My birthday. Not much to celebrate? Hardly. I have had a lovely companion and lived with her in a lovely life. How can I complain? I don't.

Dear Buck,

Happy birthday! I have a present to give you. Do you remember as a child how you looked at things and just wondered about them—like the time you really looked at that hawk's feather? It seemed so impossibly intricate. There was no end of little hairs all very neatly arranged. How did it know to grow that way? And that feather had soared in the high up sky. What did it feel like to glide way up there with the air flowing over it?

This morning you took your bath. Stop and wonder about the water molecules that surrounded you. Think of all the places they have been, all the activities they have been part of. There are some bits of that water that were in the blood that flowed through a brontosaurus. Other bits were big raindrops in a thundershower. Some have flowed past the gills of the great white shark or the gold fish. Some have meandered for centuries through dark fissures in the rocks beneath us. And there are the clouds suspended above us that give rides to the water bits. Think of the kayak-like rides over great waterfalls, joyously and harmlessly roaring about. The water that surrounds you has been in countless rainbows cambering over landscapes beautiful beyond description. All this and more the waters that you sit in each day have experienced.

You too have had so many experiences. Who you are is the result of your participation in all of these events. Although you don't remember the specifics you do remember the glory. The eye that you have for beauty, the open heart that puts forth love, the ear that sings of music, the awe you feel toward all creation, all of these are yours because of the memory within you of all that you have experienced.

On a cool day the sunshine feels so good upon your skin. There is a sunshine within you that also feels so good if you let it shine. It is there as a result of all the experiences you have had and is the treasure of your lives on earth.

Buck as a child.

Exercise 28: Take a few minutes out and ponder the miracles and beauty of life. What are the things on earth that you love? What are the things on earth that inspire wonder and awe? Consider the immortality of the bits of water and the particles of dust—consider your own immortality. Write down your thoughts.

Chapter 30

The Question of An Afterlife

April 19ᵗʰ, 1996

I find myself truly believing in the afterlife—and in communication with the departed. Many assume that unless something has been proven by science it does not exist. It is true that no kind of afterlife has been proven using the scientific methodology. However we make many decisions and many of our actions are not based on scientific methodology. Most businesses, for instance, operate by their owners making decisions on incomplete data. And their success or failure is heavily dependent on the intangible unscientific "judgments" of those running the business. In truth, much of what we enjoy and devote our time to has little scientific basis.

Also, if an afterlife has not been proved by science it is equally true that it has not been *dis*proved by science. As Kierkegaard* said, there are two ways to be fooled. One is to believe what *isn't* so and the other is to refuse to believe what *is* so. Or as Daniel Boorstin** said, "The main obstacle to progress is not ignorance, but the illusion of knowledge."

Concepts such as heaven, nirvana and reincarnation which are advanced by various religions are all theories. We can choose to believe the one of our choice and have a strong inner conviction of its essential truth for us, or we can choose not to believe there is an afterlife. Nonetheless, they are all theories—theories that have not been disproved and therefore you are not being unrealistic to believe in any of them.

We can see that in the matter of an afterlife, all we have are theories and beliefs, none of which have been proven or disproved by science and which may never be. Yet each of us, at the termination of this life, will be confronted with whatever is true.

---

*Soren D. Kierkegaard was a nineteenth century existentialist philosopher. **Daniel Boorstin is a public servant, historian, Pulitzer-prize winning author and Librarian of Congress Emeritus. Gail and I met him and his wife Ruth on a trip to Antarctica. I had mentioned to him my brother's statement, " The best and the worst is done by amateurs and the mediocre is left to the professionals." He was so delighted with it he asked permission to use it in an upcoming book.

Just as the law of gravity functions with the same perfection whether mankind believes in it or not, so too will whatever happens to us after death.

I feel that my belief system—I also like to call it my filter/grid system—is working for me. I am learning to maintain my balance and enjoyment of life after receiving a severe traumatic blow. I have adopted a process of deliberately opening my filter system to receive whatever comes without immediate judgment. I am also deliberately putting my filter/grid into an open-to-revision mode and I am open to significant change. This is bringing me results for which I am grateful. It has brought me a sense of closeness to Gail. I feel that I am learning with Gail. I feel that through me she is also getting stimulus to her learning. Grief seems to be a more distant phenomena each day.

Dear Buck:

Let us touch again on the concept of boundaries. They are, of course, a device used to separate *this* from *that*. Our minds create the idea of a boundary and then we often physically try to put it into place. Boundaries are also means of protecting ourselves against perceived threats. The latter may be physical territorial threats or they may be threats to the mind or, more particularly, the system of the mind that seeks to preserve itself.

A not very scientific (because he is closed-minded) scientist may scoff at psychic phenomena by drawing a boundary between what is scientifically proven and what is not scientifically proven. Thus will the boundary protect his system of thought and allow it to perpetuate itself. Psychic events threaten his belief system and hence the need to draw a boundary against them. Although this scientist would shudder at the thought, he is no different from the religious adherent who separates the believers from the infidels or the gentiles from the chosen ones.

The intention here is not to pick on scientists or religious adherents. Large numbers of people in all walks of life do this very same thing. But I am saying that the drawing of boundaries is a poor solution to the problem that the boundaries are supposed to remedy. The impetus to draw the

boundary comes from fear. When you make choices based on fear they are likely to have meager results.

You have the situation where you are over here and the thing you fear is over there. You draw a boundary between you to protect yourself and keep what you fear outside, on the other side of the boundary. When you undertake this separation tactic you usually don't even consider what is in the best interest of that which you have barricaded outside of yourself. This is basically why separation leads *away* from the joining and sharing that is involved in the *All that is One*.

True solutions come from the realization that we are all *one*. This realization can only occur when you dissolve the boundaries rather than create them. Creating boundaries narrows the perspective while dissolving the boundaries broadens the perspective. Boundaries and their narrow perspectives lead to short term solutions that have within them the seeds that bring long term renewed conflict. The removal of boundaries on the other hand leads to solutions that will be lasting because the thoughts and desires of all have been brought within the broadened perspective. With an attitude that we are all *one* can we create inclusive solutions.

Boundaries are also created to help organize thoughts and things. This is a different mode. Firstly it is not based on fear. Secondly it is prompted by a desire to include not exclude. In fact, one reason you feel the need to draw boundaries in organization is that you have so much within your purview that you can't keep it all straight without organizing it with boundaries or groupings. You are doing this to allow yourself to include much more in your mind. If the data were all random and disorganized you couldn't keep track of it. So you organize it, and in so doing, allow yourself to include in your thinking a broader amount of data. So organization allows a larger perspective, a greater inclusiveness of data. Thus does it also move in the direction of the *All that is One*.

So here are two ways of drawing boundaries that have opposite results. One is fear induced and the other induced by inclusiveness. This is somewhat contrary to what you previously thought, Buck, but do you see its validity?

Marshall: Yes I do. But, before this, I didn't see that grouping for organizational reasons was an inclusive device.

Exercise 29: Write a short list of boundaries that you draw for purposes of inclusion. Then, write out a list of boundaries that you draw that have the effect of separating.

Chapter 31

Imagine that We Are Immortal

April 20th, 1996

I am so, so glad that I have been guided to try transforming my emotional energy into a door opener to the spiritual side. It removes so many fears and worries about the future. I don't know what my future will be any more than anyone else but I do know I need not fear it. It will be full of good things. In fact, life is full of good things now.

I feel my love for Gail without fear. *A Course In Miracles* indicates fear is the opposite of love. Other philosophies say that feelings are the point of it all—to experience what it feels like to love, for instance.

But does Gail still exist in some way on some other side? I remember, it must have been 20 years ago she said she had a revelation. That is a big word or event but she meant it. She was in the kitchen and she suddenly *knew* from inside that she was immortal. She didn't have to wait to die first. She was immortal now, in the *now*—the eternal *now*. This seemed so sure to her, not just intellectually but emotionally, that she felt it a revelation indeed. She and I both thought this conceptually but now she *knew* this was the truth. She did her best to share it with me but I couldn't feel it internally as she did. I was so glad for her. But now I do feel it. I feel it with her and I feel my love for Gail without fear.

Beloved Buck,

Life is indeed good. And it never ends. Isn't that almost unbelievable? I remember when I had that revelation that I was immortal. As an intellectual concept, of course, we were both very familiar with it. However the revelation that I had made it so real. My whole body and soul felt at one and I *knew* I was forever. I've talked before about perspective and how a narrow perspective leaves you open to negative outlooks, judgment, and dissatisfaction. A wider perspective leads to joy, understanding, and serenity. If our brothers and sisters would truly *feel* their immortality it would make a huge difference in their ability to see the broader perspective with all its

wonderful attributes. They would find that their worries, which so debilitate their happiness, would seem even myopic to them. They would know that the deceased loved ones over whom they are now so distraught are immortal too and are therefore, in fact, invulnerable.

Your invulnerability is so little recognized in your earth trials. Yet it is a gift given to you in love by your God. In your earth life it is hard to feel this, but this does not mean that you cannot begin to sense this invulnerability. To start this process, considering two concepts will help you.

♦ First, realize that you are much, much more than the conscious awareness that you live in each day. This realization opens the door to an understanding that there is much more going on inside of you than the prattle of your conscious mind. Trust this unconscious activity as being for your own good, which it most certainly is.

♦ Second, think in terms that you are indeed immortal. Don't think of life stopping when you die. Know that it will just carry on. You have absolutely no personal experience that proves this is not true.

You cannot recall a time at which you were not conscious. People base their belief that their consciousness ends on the fact that those they know who have died no longer seem to partake in life. They assume, without justification, that this means that the consciousness is also gone. The truth is that even when the deceased were alive other people had no direct knowledge that they had a consciousness because they were not literally partaking in it, only in their own consciousness.

I agree the departed *appeared* to have consciousness, but people could not be directly aware of it as this consciousness was outside their purview. So it can be argued that people have no direct proof that others do have consciousness nor do they have any proof that such consciousness, if it exists, ceases upon death.

If people were to keep these two ideas in the forefront of their minds, they would see how their perspectives would change. The difficulties in their lives would be diminished.

While they wouldn't disappear entirely, they would be less distracting.

Exercise 30: Imagine yourself and your deceased loved ones to be immortal. How does your view of life change? How do your actions change? How do your feelings change? Write this all down.

Chapter 32

The Meaning of Joy

April 21st, 1996

It strikes me that the illusionary world is but a series of symbols chosen by the mind. They can be symbols of the ego system but I will choose to make them symbols of God by feeling joy, by seeing beauty and by giving love. What do I expect joy to be? True joy has no lack. How then can I feel joy and at the same time realistically know that Gail is gone? True joy, which I can choose and which I can feel, requires that I feel no lack of my dear Gail. And, strangely enough, somehow, someway, feeling joy brings me into Gail's unspecified presence. How illogical. And how wonderful that I can feel joy in the first place in order to discover this. And having done this once it is much easier to do again. I seem to be talking a lot about joy.

Dearest Buck,

Joy is the clothing we wear when we are close to God. And wisdom is what brings us closer to God. Therefore, with wisdom comes joy. Ultimately, it is wisdom that is our goal. And learning is the means to wisdom. Everything that happens to us is to help us learn—to develop wisdom.

Another definition of joy is: knowing that God selected the experience you are having for your benefit. This knowledge will convert what seems like bad experiences into good. Believe in the total appropriateness of what you are experiencing. It has been "hand selected" by God for you. If you truly understand this you will be absolutely thrilled with what God has chosen for you. A narrow view of our experiences will blind us to the benefits that the experiences contain. Broadening our perspective will allow us to see the benefit of every moment of our lives.

> *Know that in whatever state ye find thyself,*
> *that—at the moment—is best for thee.*
> **—Edgar Cayce**

Exercise 31: Consider what gains you have made as a result of some of the more difficult times in your life. Write those down and allow yourself to feel joy and gratitude for those experiences.

Chapter 33

Preparing for Life After Death

April 22nd, 1996

Over the years Gail and I had tried to set our affairs in good order so that when one of us died the other would be less burdened by the loss. Believing that I would probably be the first one to die, I had tried to prepare Gail emotionally for my passing. However, I had not been able to imagine my own life continuing on without Gail. Thus, I was not fully prepared for this sudden chain of events ending in her death. No matter how much one thinks about it, how one will actually react to such a crisis is beyond one's knowing. I felt certain that if she died first I would be a puddle of tears on the floor. I often wondered as I got into my 60s whether I would want to go on living if she went first. I even conjured up the idea that if she went, I would go up to our beloved Sierras and just hike until hypothermia took over. Gail and I had loved to go hiking there.

My Dear Buck,

Little did you know that I could continue to be with you when you visit our beloved Sierras. I can truly continue to enjoy them—through your feelings of joy when you are there.

It is so very interesting. Many people prepare for death by setting things up for those who will be left behind. This is a very caring and good thing to do. What most don't realize is how many things they can also do to prepare themselves for this side too. Do not misunderstand me. This side accepts everyone. But if you evolve and understand that there is much more than just the material world you can enter this side with an ease and joy. Your stumbling around is much reduced.

If you feel like doing some experimenting, try filling your life with conscious love—love for yourself, love for your fellowman, love for the people who annoy you and even love for the politicians you don't agree with. Just respond to everything with love. It will prepare you for this dimension when you come over. It will help you in your adjustment.

Love is the greatest power in life, in the universe. We think of it as a thought or a feeling only, but it is more. It is a power. It has energy. It can solve problems. It can harmonize

situations. It can create. There is just no limit to what love can do. It is almost like the basic energy—like you have electricity on the earth plane. It is not electricity here but it has the power to create, to move and so forth. It is fantastic. It is the answer, the key. It is the cause—it is what is used in the first cause. The Creative Source Himself uses love to create. These are exercises in *being* rather than *doing*. Rather than "*Do* unto others as you would have other do unto you," it should read, "*Be* unto others, as you would have God *be* unto you." I'll expand on this another time.

Exercise 32: Here is an exercise to try. When you have a situation, a question, a puzzle or you have to make a decision, first define it and make it clear in your mind what it is you need to know. And then conjure up in yourself a feeling of love and bring that question into that love energy. Let it sit there and let it cook. The answer or response that will come to you will be much more enlightened than if you just try to figure it out with your conscious mind. We can enhance our conscious mind's activities by taking it through the love energy or the love atmosphere. Think of it anyway you want.

Chapter 34

Only the Present Can Bring You Joy

April 23rd, 1996

Don't contaminate today with tomorrow's worries. I remember when Gail and I came up with this thought. We both felt we were living in halcyon days—days that we would probably longingly look back on with pleasure. Indeed we were right. I do look back on them with great enjoyment.

We were in our early sixties and it seemed like every health insurance company in the world was doing their best to remind us that the sunset years are full of hovering illnesses and we needed insurance right now. Then we thought of what it would be like later if indeed we had one of those illnesses or that one of us had passed away. Undoubtedly we would look back on these halcyon days and wish we could return to them.

If some magic would let us do so, we would also, in that future time, realize at once that we were making a huge mistake by worrying about future illness or widowhood. What a waste of golden times to contaminate them with those future worries. We resolved right then and there that we would accept the future no matter what it was, but today we owed it to ourselves to love the very wonderful times we were then living. And we did and that pleased us greatly then. I didn't realize that this was giving me practice for my widower-hood. Peculiarly, this can be just as true for me today as it was then. Every moment is to be cherished.

It is interesting too that all those fears I described are gone. This all makes it easier to live in the *now. And to choose joy.* Yet another surprise. The *now* is a much more interesting place than I thought it was. I always knew that we chose our own happiness or sorrow but also that it was difficult at times to choose happiness over sorrow. Like right now, for example, when we have lost someone we love. I am discovering that this choice is much easier to exercise when I live in the *now.* I can wake up and choose joy and it is there. I'm getting better at this. The past and the future are heavy weights that hamper one's ability to choose joy. The *now* gives me lightness in my attitude to life.

It is true that the chosen joy sometimes evaporates too quickly. But if I don't get too bogged down in something less pleasant and remember that I am still in the *now,* I can chose again and my balance returns. How empowering it is to live in my *now* and not my past, as wonderful as it was. I feel that I am faithfully doing this, that is, living in the *now* and fully engaging in what I have left to do on this earth. Thus Gail remains open to me. And what a treasure that is! And it doesn't stop there. I think that if I always live in my *now*, joy will always be mine.

Dear Buck.

I remember that poem you wrote for Claudio:

> **It is the past from which**
> **All your grievances come.**
> **It is the future that**
> **Harbors all your fears.**
> **It is only the present**
> **That can bring you joy.**

The earth perspective does give too much priority and too much attention to both the past and the future, as you envision them. It also suggests that you are limited in your understanding of the *now* or the present. There is much, much more to the present than just a fleeting moment that bridges your past to your future.

First you assume the *now* must be some kind of frozen or static instant. As such it is quite unexciting. Even though this is your common view of the present you nonetheless have had many experiences in the *now* that transcend this.

You have experienced hearing music that reaches something inside you and suddenly the past and the future are forgotten. You are transported. More accurately you are experiencing a joining. You and the music join and are one. This is a *now* experience. In fact, music truly *only* displays itself in the *now*.

Similarly, when you are playing your own music, particularly with others—when the harmony chords change and you all change together it is the lovely feeling of the *now* that you are experiencing. It is also the ecstasy experienced in making love. All these and many more are experiences that you have had in the *now* that should make you aware that there is far more to it than you recognize.

Chapter 34 Only the Present Can Bring You Joy--91

Exercise 33: Jot down those times when you have felt you were living in the "now." Then, take a moment to write down what you perceive to be the primary characteristics of these precious "now" moments. Then practice bringing them on at will.

Chapter 35

We Are Not Separate

April 24th, 1996

I realize that the fear or the experience of separation from Gail is the quintessential ego thought system based on "separateness." Right mindedness and right perception as discussed in *A Course in Miracles* reveals that I am not and *cannot* be separate from Gail.

A friend of mine says everyone is on the spiritual path: there is nowhere else to be. Rephrased, Gail is with me now, there is no place else for her to be. Mind is not limited to time and place, neither is hers nor mine.

I know as no one else does how Gail was the very center of my life and how she had become so over those many lovely years. With her gone, if she truly was gone, my life would be impossible for me to endure without the deepest of grief. But I don't have that grief and in fact I have happiness and joy. How come? I would never be able to convince anyone else but I know the answer. Gail is not only with me, she is part of me—only 11 words but what a miracle and impact on my life. I am her and she is me and if we could remember it, we would also know that we are God.

I had always read that we are all *one*. This appeals to me and I came to believe it intellectually. However, I must admit that when I looked around the world I didn't feel much like I was *one* with everyone else. Quite the contrary, I felt distinctly separate and often I was glad of it.

With Gail gone though, I want to be *one* with her. In a way I cannot understand or describe, I do feel more at *one* with her. Part of it is that I realize more fully what an influence she has been in my life. Put more strongly, much of what I am today is a result of the interplay and mutual growth Gail and I had together. So that part of Gail is me already. Her death somehow allows me to see that more clearly and dearly.

We did indeed have interplay. I am a maverick and tend to challenge rather than accept authority. Along with this I am stubborn. It seems to run in the male side of my family. The nicer way to say it is that I am persistent. Being married to a persistent maverick has its problems. Gail was soft and gentle until she thought something was important enough, and then she had a backbone of iron. After a rough introduction (read big, big fights) to this part of her I came to respect it a great deal.

I *do* feel her presence at times. It is very hard to define what I feel but it is distinct. I don't believe it is my imagination, as I cannot *mak*e it happen. I wish I could. It just suddenly is. So here I am feeling much more at *one*, not only with Gail, but also with many others. This feels right.

Dear Buck,

I have said many times that the world has many things backwards. This is really not much of a surprise for the following reason: The basic law of the universe is that we are all *one*—connected together in a giant pattern of association. Despite that, our tenure on earth has been characterized by trying to separate things, the opposite of uniting things.

We separate time into past, present, and future which is the opposite of the eternal *now*. We separate our selves, our being, over and over again. We see each individual as separate. We see each family as being separate. We see each town as separate. We see each nation as separate and so on. We separate diseases. We separate our children into grade levels. We segregate a whole group of teenagers into one school and are surprised at how difficult they can be. I don't need to go on with separation examples; distinguishing one thing from another is the basic thing this world does.

Conclusions drawn from this separation perspective will be the opposite of conclusions drawn from a union perception, because separation and union are opposite. Now this separation is not all bad. Science and engineering tools are based on separating the various factors in any phenomena, examining them in detail (again a separation) and then drawing conclusions as to how each element functions. This has brought about tremendous knowledge and understanding of how the material world works. So the separation approach has had its use. It has, by our experiencing it, given us knowledge which we need. But, we now have the task of integrating that into the whole that is God. More on that later.

Exercise 34: Experiment with thinking the opposite of what you have been taught. If you find yourself thinking, "My loved one is gone," think instead, "My loved one is here with me now." If you find yourself thinking, "We will never be together again," try thinking, "We will be together forever." Write down the thoughts about your beloved deceased that you find painful and then write their opposite. The opposite thoughts will more likely bring to you joy—and will more likely represent the truth.

Chapter 36

Training in God's Gymnasium

April 25th, 1996

Lesson 282 in A Course in Miracles speaks of being "asleep in dreams of death." In truth, Gail's death is but my dream from which I can choose to awaken.

Darling,

You look at the material world and it seems very real to you. It is your reality and you have difficulty in recognizing it as an illusion. To think you live in an illusionary world is disquieting and an idea you do not welcome. The easiest reality for you to recognize is the material world, therefore the great majority of people believe the material world is real and all else is illusionary by comparison. Again the world has it backwards.

It is important to understand that the only way you *know* the world is through your perception of it. Let me state it more clearly. If you do not perceive it you have no idea it is there. This is peculiar because that means that the only way you know what is outside of you is through your perception which is inside of you. So reality, which you always seek, comes back to what is inside of you. This is a profound understanding.

Please note, however, that the fact that the material world is illusionary does not mean that you should not live in it and in the process, learn. Being an illusion does not mean it has no meaning or use, or that it should be avoided. On the contrary, God gave the illusions to us, or rather, the power for us to create illusions for our own use. He did so with the understanding that we would always be presented with those circumstances that were most appropriate for what we currently need to learn. This brings us to the metaphor that God has given us "a gymnasium" in which to develop ourselves and to train ourselves in the skills to fulfill our goals.

In truth, whether you regard the world as illusionary or reality is not that important. What *is* important is the nature of who you are, where you are going and who you are becoming. These will be greatly enhanced if you realize that either the realities or the illusions (your choice) are simply tools for your utilization. Being a co-creator with God you create the reality of who you are. That is the only reality that counts. All other realities are simple backdrops and staging upon which you act to consummate your true self.

Exercise 35 : Think about how the "gymnasium" that God has provided you with—or you have created for yourself—has helped you become a better person. Write about who you think you are becoming.

Chapter 37

Finding Our Own Truth

April 27th, 1996

Writing about this is becoming much easier and without doubt makes me feel better. Gail and I had such a wonderful life. I am so appreciative of the vast dimensions that she added to my life.

My wife and I loved to learn not simply as scholars but as practitioners of life. We felt that God had indeed given us a book of instructions when we were delivered into this life. And the language of that book was in the experiences we were given. Through feelings, perception and intuition we could find the meaning and the love in life that is far more visible and abundant than most of us realize.

Before we met, we both intuitively felt there was a great deal more to life than was obvious. There was the invisible and we were curious about it. We didn't know what it was but we were willing to look. A number of things happened to us that led us on a seeker's path toward spiritual enlightenment.

One example involves Christopher, our middle son, when he first began to speak. He was very late in talking, and like any parents, that worried us. Gail and I tried all kinds of stratagems to induce him to talk—but with no results. Then, to our relief, one day he started talking in sentences. His first sentence was, "It's mine, I had it first."

His next sentence was, "The fire engines are coming to our house." Gail—ever alert—asked why and he responded, "Because our house is on fire." And indeed it was. I had purchased at the Goodwill Thrift Shop a used record player for the kids to play their records on. The transformer had shorted out and billows of black smoke were pouring forth. Pulling out the plug easily put out the fire.

But it is the third sentence that is the point of this story. One day, he sort of said to himself, "I used to be an old man and now I'm a baby." There was nothing in our house or our conversation that would stimulate such a comment. We had known what reincarnation was. But we hadn't talked about it nor had we really believed in it. This prodded us to think about this whole arena.

I know from a scientific viewpoint this proves nothing as it is merely anecdotal. But when your toddler says something like that and you know there was no place for him to pick it up you sit up and pay attention. Over the next forty years we studied and pondered over a lot of the mystical literature and became firm believers that our inner selves were the key to the realization of the Oneness to which we all belong. My particular interest was to see how the spiritual laws worked from a purely practical point of view. It just did not make sense to me that we would be placed on this earth only to find it an inhospitable place with no room for spiritual laws to manifest. For my practical mind the spiritual laws had to work in the real world or they were not valid.

Yes, I also saw some of the evil in the world. At the end of World War II, I saw Rotterdam, Warsaw, Gdansk, and other urban shells which were demonstrations of man's destructive power. Actually, that was one reason I was drawn to construction as a career. I had no desire to be destructive.

My Husband,

It is fun learning together! And we delighted in knowing that we would love learning together for the length of our earthly life together. Remember that? Little did we realize that it would extend beyond death. You on earth have so little realization of how continuity functions. Your addiction to separation causes your failure to see the continuity that surrounds you. You see the world continue every day of your life, but it never occurs to you that this is a lesson from God to illustrate the continuity of the mind and the spirit. These are the laws: As above so below: as within so without. To which we can add: as with the visible so with the invisible. It is the thoughts of God that show themselves as the laws of the universe. These laws include gravity and electricity, for example. They also includes the law of karma, the *we are all one* principle and other spiritual laws. All must be done within God's laws which provide gentle loving opportunities to recognize that there is wisdom, joy and serenity in choosing harmony or love over fear and anger.

It is not so much a matter of *what* is done as it is the *attitude* with which something is done. What you are *doing* is not as important as what you are *being*. Long ago we said that

you can do anything including murder and it could be a virtuous act if done with the right attitude.

In the case of the World Trade Center tragedy, when it comes to spiritual evolution, what we do is not as important as what our thoughts are when we are doing it.

Americans and others are now fighting a war against terrorism. In the actions of prosecuting this war some are intent on revenge and paying back the terrorists for the World Trade Center destruction. This is their mind set. Others involved in the fight are not thinking of retaliation but of correction, sustenance and reconstruction. Thus, while they are trying to root out the terrorists, food is also being dropped and fund raising undertaken to help the children and refugees. Although not perfect, this is their thinking and it reflects the presence in their being of spiritual principles.

Even though these latter are taking part in some of the violence, their attitude will help usher in a healing, whereas the former group who seek only revenge will continue to exacerbate the seesaw of revenge and counter revenge. This, in spite of the fact that each is participating in the same actions.

God has created natural laws that subtly but inevitably move us ever upward. There are many opportunities to bring this about. One thing we can all agree on is that there is always change. Nothing stays the same. This constant of change requires us to consistently recreate our own personal truth. We cannot settle into a fixed unchanging life even though vast numbers of souls would like to do nothing better. This is one of the purposes of getting older and dying. These are changes we have to accommodate in the truth that we create for ourselves. We are required to continually update our own truth as we go through life. God has given us choice. Choice to do what? To find our own truth. More explicitly—to create our own truth.

And in this creating, other laws and tendencies push us upward. Toward what? The goal can be expressed in quite a few different ways, all of them valid. We are to return to God. We are to learn that our will is God's will. We are to remember who we really are: spiritual beings who are integral parts of the *All that is One*. And ultimately, we are to develop a truth that is congruent—that is harmonious—with God's truth: again, that we are all *one*.

Exercise 36: Write about what truths about life and death you believe in. If you have trouble figuring that out—first think about what you feel about different aspects of life and death. Are those feelings evidence that you believe we are "one"? Or that we are separate? Then write down all the beliefs that would make you feel better—if they are different from the beliefs you now hold.

Chapter 38

There is No Finality

April 28th, 1996

I wish Gail were here to see that little fawn lying down in the baby tears. It is there right now in our back door garden two feet from the door. This is such a serene place. Recently I talked to an old college friend. Along with condolences he asked me if I felt a sense of completeness with Gail's passing. That surprised me because I do and it's a nice feeling. Here is her whole life no longer threatened by disease, her backaches, disappointments, or anything else. The complete life was good, in fact marvelous. It had in it what she wanted: children, adventure, learning, romance, travel, and lots of love. I know this because she told me so more than once when she was alive. What a gift she gave me in telling me that. I truly appreciate knowing this now.

Dear Buck,

Did you ever wonder why serenity is so lovely to feel? It is really a state of feeling *complete*—where you demand nothing and wish for nothing except what *is*. It is also complete in its closeness to the *we are all one* principle where there is no lack in serenity. You have it all. Serenity is a fulfillment of yourself. It is a fulfillment of your nature given to you by God.

Did you know that you don't have to die to feel this sense of completeness? It is attainable in the world that you are now in. You can achieve it with meditation. You can also achieve it with feeling gratitude toward God for your blessings. Serenity is what you feel in a sacred place with God's sacred creatures being at peace in our garden, curled up without fear. Fear and serenity cannot co-exist in our minds or hearts. Serenity is good for our soul. Feel blessed when you are serene for you are so.

Do you feel the sense of connection between serenity and beauty? They are not the same but beauty can be a channel to serenity. One reason people are so attracted to beauty in all its forms is the serenity-like character that comes with it. There is no sense of lack. You feel complete.

We must be careful though, not to confuse the concepts of completeness with finality. *There is no such thing as final**. Because we are immortal, because we are all *one*, there is never a final anything at which point there would be no more. We go through vast changes, transformation, and transitions but something always comes out on the other side. Even those things that come to an end such as the 1991 football season reappear as the 1992 season. The events that took place in the Roman Coliseum, which have come to an end from earth's viewpoint have not disappeared. When you have a true understanding of time this becomes clear.

It is the illusionary belief in finality that is a cause of your grief there on earth. You do not need to feel that grief. There is no finality.

*Final is from the Latin "finalis" which means "end." Complete, in contrast, is from the Latin, "complere" which means "to fill out."

M.KENT 88

Marshall's brush-painting of a deer.
This was used in Gail's death announcement.

Exercise 37: In what ways can you describe your loved ones' lives as complete? If they were young when they died, was there something especially wise or unique about them? So often, we hear people speak of children who have died as "saints." Perhaps they had reached a level of completion in their short lives.

Chapter 39

The Spiritual Power of Beauty

April 29th, 1996

An analogy has come to my masculine mind that helps me understand what is happening. Gail and I, when she was here, were playing a team sport, say doubles tennis. We enjoyed the game, how it is played, scoring points, being skillful, and having that camaraderie. Now that she is gone I have to change my game—to golf, let's say. It would just sadden me to try to keep playing doubles tennis. I must become absorbed in the new rules, new skills, and new ways to use my body. I never have to get involved with whether tennis or golf is the best game. Each has its aura and each are splendid games. I can chose to *enjoy* the game of golf and allow myself to get all wrapped up in it. I think my golf game will be artistic—painting, sculpture, composing and playing music, and this—writing.

Dearest,

What you speak of is creating beauty. Beauty goes well beyond having something pleasant to see, as nice as that is. Beauty is actually a spiritual power. It is one of the principles of the universe, and as such, has a place in the absolute.

Yes it is true that on earth beauty seems to be relative. This painter created better masterpieces than did that painter. This woman is more beautiful than that woman. Yosemite is more beautiful than Capitol Reefs. And of course others might differ from these comparisons and arrange their beauty scale in a different order. All this keeps you on the surface and obscures the true principle of beauty. This is the same pattern as love. There are all kinds of earthly love, all of which are very nice, but divine love is of a whole different principle.

As has often been written, we are love made manifest. The result of this manifestation is beauty. The principle of beauty is that God created all things to be beautiful no matter what scale you are using. The night sky with millions of stars is beautiful, as is the delicacy of the wings of a housefly. The beauty aspect is an integral part of its being and is created by the fulfillment of the God given nature in all things.

Then, when you seek *to perceive* the perfection in the world about you and *attune* yourself to the fulfillment of all things to their own nature as given to them by God, you will see the beauty principle. In turn, sensing this perfection in the world allows you peace and serenity. Peace and serenity brings you back into communication with God. Do you understand how this all fits together? It is beautiful isn't it? Notice I used the word beautiful appropriately to describe this wonder.

Although she just dabbled, Gail was a fine artist herself. This water-color painting she did has beautiful colors but looks surprisingly good in shades of gray.

Exercise 38: With your tennis partner gone, what game will you play now? Write down all of those things you would love to do by yourself or with friends. Will they bring you closer to living in the "now"? Will they bring to you more beauty, serenity and peace— more of a sense of completion? Pick one or two favorites and write a start date on your calendar. Then begin to do the homework you need to do to get started on time.

Chapter 40

Be Not Afraid to Communicate

April 30th, 1996

There is a traditional mystical concept that when a loved one dies you should not try to hang on to them by seeking communication. It is explained that they have work to do on the other side and that by your wish to communicate with them you keep them earthbound. If this is true, then obviously, as you wish the best for your departed one, you would try not to reach out to them. You should get on with your life, and abandon any attempt at communication.

However, I feel as if I have gotten strong communication from Gail that this is only partially true. The ideas coming into my mind are that on the other side they can do more than one thing at a time. To imagine that it is the same there as it is on this side is but a false transfer of our own earthly limitations. The other side does not have these limitations. I feel that Gail is perfectly capable of doing what she needs to do on the other side and concurrently communicate with me. And I sense that she likes to do this. However, and this is a very important however, I know that I need to get on with my life on this earth. I need to address what I still have to do here and not live in the past nor hunger for what can no longer be. If I can be true to that, I feel that I can have much communication with Gail to the benefit and pleasure of us both.

This is like receiving secret knowledge. However, the mystical tradition of letting the departed one get on with their life on the other side without calling them back to earth could have validity—but more for the benefit of the bereaved—those who are grieving and who otherwise might not get on with their life's work.

My Dear Husband,

Here I am by your side as always. You are right, it is easy to be here even though I am in other places as well. I'm glad you received and believed my message that we here can be in more than one place and do more than one thing at a time.

The question is, "Can the survivor on earth do something, like try to hang onto the deceased, which will have a negative influence on the departed?" You often read this in

the esoteric literature that the survivor should let the deceased go so they are not held back from what they have to do on the other side. This strongly infers that what the survivor *does* can have a direct effect on the progress of the deceased on this side. To understand all this we should again go back to the basics.

Free will is a gift given to us by God and nobody has the power to take that away from us. Others can decide for us, only if we choose to *allow* them to decide for us and this applies equally to us on this side. We too have free choice.

Why am I now communicating with you as if I were not dead—gone and silent as most people think I should be? It is because I *choose* to do so. Why is it you are receiving what I am saying? It is because *you* choose to do so. If I choose to communicate with you and you choose not to listen, what would happen? Nothing would happen. I do not have the power to suspend your free will and impose mine upon yours. Nor does anyone else.

Also, you do not have the power to do something, like try to hang onto me, that would prevent me from doing what I should be doing on this side. I have the free choice to do what I need to do on this side. You cannot be and are not responsible for what I do here. I am responsible.

The above is a clear statement of how free will functions. However, other factors must also be considered. When I died I was very concerned with leaving you and my family behind. My heart went out to you. It was not a pleasant feeling. On the contrary it was very unsettling. I wanted to reach out to all of you and in some way heal your grief. These feelings and desires are, however, all free will choices I had made over this lifetime.

With guidance and help I was soon able to give up these unhappy feelings. My broadened perspective, which I choose with my free will, let me know that you all were properly in God's hands and I knew that each of you had individually chosen to go through my leaving so as to be presented with the learning opportunity involved. With this knowledge I could relax and feel good about your futures. You could say that with my free will I liberated myself from these concerns and was free then to go on with what I needed to do on this side.

Where it may appear fuzzy but is not, is that we on this side are understandably concerned with how you on earth are handling our departure and choose, with our free will, to try to help you. We send you communications. We send you healing. But you on earth may choose to dismiss them, discount them as imagination or whatever. This is your proper jurisdiction to accept or reject what we try to send you. We, of course, want you to receive our communications but know well that we cannot force you to do so and would not *want* to force you to do so. Do you see how this is?

I'm glad that you are deliberately and conscientiously engaging yourself in your life. This is allowing me to continue my closeness to you. Not all people can do this on your side nor on my side but this doesn't mean that many more could not also do this. *It really gets down to what you think is possible.* This is a most profound statement that is not fully appreciated on your side. *It really gets down to what you think is possible!* Things become only because you *think* they can become.

If you do not feel that it is possible for you to communicate with your deceased one then I can assure you, you will not. The very first requirement in communication is to open your side of the communication. Otherwise it is impossible to hear what is coming to you whether it be God or your beloved departed wishing to communicate with you.

Know that when you place limitations on your capacity to receive information you are deliberately limiting a child of God in what he or she can do. You would not want to do this anymore than you would want to place limitations of what talents your children have. You all have many abilities that are latent within you—even if you feel them beyond you. They are not. Open yourself. Be not afraid. You are immortal.

Exercise 39: Do you believe that you can communicate with your beloved? If not, why not? Write down all the reasons why you feel you can't communicate with them. Then, if you wish to receive communication remove the barriers, one by one. Once the barriers are removed, pay close attention—to the thoughts, ideas, voices and visions that you see. The closer you pay attention, the clearer and the more frequent the communications will become. It is like exercising your muscles.

Chapter 41

Learning Together Still

May 1st, 1996

Gail and I loved to learn from our experiences in life and we shared this learning with each other with excitement. I feel that we still can do this. I feel that I am like a monitoring device on this earth, which both she and I can access to transform my current experiences into our joint stimulus for insight. And even more miraculous, her understandings from the other side can be accessible to me in the same way. As a matter of fact, I believe that I am accessing her understanding right now. I believe that this is the source of much that I write here.

Here are a few things that are coming to me.

- Be still to listen. Close your eyes to hear what only you can teach yourself.
- To see into the other world find spirituality in this world.
- While *having* something and *doing* something satisfies the appetites, *being* someone satisfies the soul.
- Do not seek or copy another's enlightenment, rather discover your inner self.

Statements like these come into my mind and I have to be sure to write them down quickly. If I don't, they disappear like dreams and I can't remember them. I've already lost a few of them for lack of something to write them on.

My Dear Buck,

It is such a privilege to be able to communicate with you, to be able to learn with you and share with each other what we know. This privilege is granted everyone but few are consciously aware of this ability. We are so blessed because we know this and practice it as we are right now.

You are thinking about what it is that I am learning from you. You are aware of how I can partake in what you feel and see as though you were my own personal wandering video camera. There is much more than this that I am learning from

you. It would be fun for you to puzzle this out. I will give you a hint. It has to do with how we are all *one*.

You on the earth see very little of the ramifications you have in people's lives in the way you live yours, or the way we lived our lives. It is probably well that you don't. On this side much of this is revealed as it is quite instructive and I must say surprising. And of course some of it was not of outward benefit to others. In our early years I would watch you and see you unintentionally hurt people's feelings. You didn't even know you were doing it. As I saw many times, the instant you realized you were hurting somebody's feelings you stopped and tried to make them feel better. But often you just didn't see it. This doesn't excuse you but often that adversity was instructive even though difficult for the ones you hurt.

The way all these things weave together is truly miraculous. It is also amazing how there always seems to be deeper and deeper meanings in all things and also higher and higher meanings. There is no part or no event in the universe that does not dovetail into all other parts. The *All that is One* is just that. It is true there is one gigantic pattern of which everyone is part. We see but pieces of this grand pattern. And even these are so awesome we find them difficult to comprehend.

Do you remember when I was so excited that we were studying mysticism together and I exclaimed, "And we will always find this study fascinating because it goes on and on without end. We will always love studying it." At that time I was only thinking of our lifetime together. Now here we are still studying it together and here I am over here. And Buck, when you get here we will still go on learning together. We've been on this joint path for many lifetimes.

Exercise 40: Try opening yourself to being a vehicle for your beloved departed to learn. Write down what you think they might be able to learn through you right now.

Chapter 42

Love, Joy and Beauty

May 3rd, 1996

I have been writing about Gail's dying. It sure brings tears to my eyes but also awe that I could share such an experience. In March of 1995, a year before she died, Gail wrote two poems. They seem to be about passing on:

THE ANGEL

The Angel of the Lord spoke to me.
The Angel of the Lord held my hands
And lifted me on high
and said, "Your heart is filled
with the Love of God
Your grievances are left below
As merely dust to scatter
With the wind, meaningless.

IN HEAVEN

There is no one to thank
No one to forgive
Nothing to endure
Naught to overcome
Only Love
And the joy of creation

Dearest Buck,

You are so dear to me. We were so fortunate to be with each other again in this last life. I was writing of love and joy. Those two principles and the beauty principle are all different aspects of one and the same. Through any one of these aspects you can reach the other two.

All three of these are *above* the principle of forgiveness. And in truth, as vital and important as forgiveness is, it does not have absolute existence as a principle. Forgiveness, which you know I treasured on earth, is a process, a journey to a destination. Once you arrive at the destination, the journey is over and it is no longer necessary. You then have arrived at the principles which just "are". You unite with these principles by just *being*, in contrast to *doing*. In *being* do you prepare yourself to become love, joy, and beauty. In becoming love, joy and beauty do you prepare yourself for this side.

Exercise 41: Consider the love, joy and beauty you have or have had in your life. Write a description in your notebook of some of those instances.

Chapter 43

Together Still

May 4th, 2001

Well intentioned friends continue to call me, offering condolences and frequently with the advice to keep busy. In other words, it is best for me to be so active that I have no time to think about Gail or the life we shared together. Time heals all wounds, and I can put Gail's death behind me if only I could occupy my time thinking about other things, such as building a new deck off of the living room, or teaching the grandchildren to ride bicycles. "Take a vacation!" one well meaning friend told me.

I appreciate my friends' concerns, but in truth, I am not feeling the slightest inclination to busy myself with anything in particular, or to surround myself constantly with family and friends. Despite the fact that I desperately miss the company of the physical Gail, I am filled with gratitude with each message from Gail and I am deriving real enjoyment from our new "relationship." The greatest challenge is communicating my feelings to people who loved Gail and me the most. After all, the assumption is that the sudden loss of a loved one is a devastating thing, and that if I am not devastated, something must be wrong. Either my love was not deep enough or I am in denial.

I am doing my best to put our friends and family at ease. I try to explain that in marriage, like in business, I have always believed that you cannot solve a problem by either pretending it isn't there or sugarcoating it. Facing the unvarnished truth, in my life experience, has always been a successful technique, and I have no wish to abandon my trusted tool now. What I don't feel comfortable communicating to many is my conviction that Gail's death is not a "problem" or a "challenge" to overcome, because I believe that death hasn't severed my *spiritual* connection with her.

Buck,

I have been with you so many times and I have watched you, and loved you. I will love you forever. And if you only KNEW how thin the veil is between us. But I suppose if we really knew we would be distracted from what it is we're supposed to be doing in the present situation that we find ourselves.

I am with you so often in thought that I cannot enumerate all the times but what I can say to you is that when you sense that I am near or that I'm thinking about you, trust those times. Don't try to talk yourself out of them. Trust them.

I am looking forward to being back together with you—perhaps a little too much—and I'm going to have to release it some. In time I am also going to have to move further away in my activities and in my consciousness. But do not think that I will ever forget you. I never will. And so if you sense I'm not around for a while, just realize that I'm doing what I am given to do and I want you to do what you are given to do.

I'm so grateful that I can reach you. It is very difficult to be loved to the extent that you have loved me and not be able to reach back in a satisfying manner, to let you know that I'm aware of you and I'm loving you as much as ever. I am so grateful .

Exercise 42: Take note of it whenever you get the sense your loved one is near. If you can, stop and write down the circumstances and what made you notice their presence. The more you pay attention, the more often it will happen.

Chapter 44

More on Regrets

May 5th, 1996

We all have feelings of regrets in our relationships with a departed one for those things which we either did or did not do that we now wish we had done differently. When I think of those things that I could have done for Gail and didn't, it seems like she substitutes in my mind those things that I actually did do.

She was always a great one for doing projects around the house. And of course these projects needed me to do some of the work. I confess that I was often not too enthusiastic for some of the jobs I was to do. I think of those now and she fills my mind with all the projects we *did* do together. We did a major remodeling of our house, just the two of us. It took us months. It included about four weeks in the summer when most of the roof was off our living room. We would sit on the couch to watch the evening news and we could look up and see the clouds reflecting the sunset. Occasionally a butterfly would come in and join us.

Dear Husband of Mine,

One thing we must always remember is that our lives together were meaningful and purposeful. They were not—and are not—just happenstance. So rather than get bogged down in regrets, joyously embrace the experience. I couldn't have had a more wonderful experience of life than this last one—especially when it comes to family being responsive and loving and having a strong desire to grow together.

*Exercise 43: Write out the regrets you feel or that you think your loved one might have about your life together. For everything you feel you didn't do—write something that you did do—together or for each other. Then write to your loved one that you forgive them any regrets they might have and ask for their forgiveness for your own. Don't forget to forgive yourself too.

Chapter 45

Feeling Joy

May 7th, 1996

My rational mind tugs at me and asks how I can feel joy sometimes but not others. When I feel bad and would like to get this good feeling why can't I just ask it to come forth? My guess is that I have to create within me receptive conditions or attitudes that will allow it to happen. Furthermore, these conditions go against standard belief systems. One would think that the deeper one's depression the greater the chance of getting relief by feeling your unbounded spiritual side. But I think it is the opposite. I think you need to create a boundless sense of joy within yourself.

And how does one create a boundless sense of joy within when a loved one has recently died? I'm not sure I can answer how, but I know I am doing it sometimes. There are a few things that help. When I look at the world and sense how beautiful it is, it is easier to feel joy. When I sense the love I see between other people or directed toward me, it is easier to feel boundless. When I live in the *now* joy seems to come with it.

Darling,

Since arriving here, I have learned even more about joy and the crucial role it plays in communication between us. There is a peculiar thing that happens that can be misunderstood. We can share your feelings with you from this side, only when your feelings are joyous and full of gratitude—like the feelings you have when you watch our grandchildren with love and wonder.

If your feelings are not positive, that sharing with us is cut off. This sounds like we are selfishly saying we only want to share your good times. This isn't true. One reason is that, on this side, only the good stuff remains in existence.

If you are always feeling sad and lonely and trying to hang on to the life that my passing brought to an end, you are closing us out of your present experiences, just as you are closing yourself out of the present experiences you should be having. We live in the *now*—not in the past. So then, you have to do your own homework. You can't pull us in to do it for you

because then you are cut off from us and you can feel that separation.

      In addition, you cannot communicate with us unless you *fully* engage in your current life on earth, in other words, in your *now*. If in your wish to communicate with me you withdrew in part from your life, or stated another way, if communicating with me were to become a substitute for fully living your life now, communication would be blocked.

      The reason for this is quite simple. You are still on earth because your current earth experiences are ideal for you to learn the lessons you need to learn. My passing over was one of those lessons for you. If you withdraw from your life in favor of trying to hang onto me, you are abdicating your responsibilities as a student of God to utilize the opportunities He has made available to you in your life. This is obviously harmful to you and your growth. This will hamper your realization of who you truly are, a child of God and part of the One. Since this withdrawal is not good for you, we on this side cannot partake in it by continuing to communicate with you. Thus will our communications dry up.

      When we were both on earth the impact of our lessons involved us both. The good and the bad intertwined us whether we choose it or not. But when one of us goes to the other side this is no longer the case. Now we can share only the love and the beauty. We here can observe the pain and have great sympathy for you, but we cannot actively share it. We do our best, however, to cheer you on even if you are not aware of it.

* Exercise 44: Write down a list of the people, thoughts or things which are joyous to you. When your heart fills with these feelings, know that your loved one is best able to commune with you. And allow yourself to feel joy without guilt. Many struggle with feeling joy when they have lost a loved one. They are afraid that they are being disloyal. But grief denies the fact that your loved one continues to live. Think of it this way—your joy can be a result of feeling the presence of your loved one. Actively look forward to the time when you <u>will</u> be in communication with your loved one. Know, that what you are doing is not only for yourself, but it is the work of God.

Chapter 46

Husband, Lover, Friend and Foe

May 8th, 1996

If you are going to live with someone 47 years, you're going to have fights, in fact lots of them. Gail and I did. Boy did we had some lulus! They came mostly when we were both overworked in our twenties. Gail was taking care of four children—all born within a six year period. And I was starting a construction business with only one employee—me.

In general, Gail was very easy to get along with. That is, until I tried to do something with which she strongly disagreed. She was not one to waste disagreement on small things, thank God. In our early marriage I would run into this with great surprise. Here was this harmonious wife suddenly changed into a brick wall. Being typically male I tried to overpower her with, again to my surprise, a total lack of any success. We would have a big argument and I would lose.

After a number of these I came to understand how it was. I would look back on what we argued about and I would have to agree that as things worked out she was right and I was wrong. I then came to respect her disagreements with me. Fortunately she tried to keep them to a minimum. When they occurred again I would know immediately that this was something that required extra scrutiny and that what she was saying needed serious consideration.

As we got older we were able to handle our disagreements much better. We would start going after each other and then one of us would start laughing because sometimes we were just acting out the typical masculine and feminine roles.

After Gail passed on I was going through some of her things and found a poem she had written and had never told me about. What a surprise!

GRATITUDE

How can I thank thee, how can I show
The love within me that I know.
Husband, lover, friend and foe,
Perfect partner made for me.

Chapter 46   Husband, Lover, Friend and Foe--118

What guiding hand, what loving care
Brought us together, our lives to share.

At first I was a bit concerned with her calling me a foe and maybe that is why she didn't show it to me. But when I thought about it, it was true. The masculine and the feminine have a lot to fight about. But equally true is that we were loving foes.

Gail and I went to a wedding of a Christian and a Jew. The Rabbi who performed the ceremony said something to the effect that some people may be disturbed by a mixed marriage but in truth any marriage between a man and a woman is a mixed marriage. Gail and I loved it. Together then, through foemanship we came to follow a path in life that was better, happier and more fulfilling. Yes, and to the point, more loving.

Dear Husband, Lover, Friend and Foe,

You recognize my greeting. It is from the poem I wrote about us that I never showed you. And you are right. I didn't show it to you because I didn't think you would like my use of the word foe. I should have known better. You do understand.

All those bereaved you talk to do not understand that the foe part of their relationship was and is not negative and certainly not something to feel guilty about. It is not something that detracts from what was good in their lives. Yet many feel exactly this way. They feel that the opposition that existed between themselves and their beloved diminished the love and the friendship they shared. It is just not true!

Part of their relationship was that of being a foe, an opposition to what the other wanted to do or think. In fact, this is a very important ingredient in a relationship. As you used to say, "failure is the greatest teacher of success," so too is "foemanship the greatest teacher of love." The growth of the relationship and each partner in it comes from experiencing foemanship.

In a couple's relationship this foemanship does not always come out to resolution as you described. In fact most of the time it does not. In our marriage it did not always resolve itself. This isn't a great problem. All those aches and remembrances of what your spouse did to you or didn't do to you as well as what you did or failed to do with your spouse are

not unchangeable burdens that you have to forget to find peace. They are now subject to change, understanding and enlightenment both for the survivor and the departed.

As we have discussed before, the departed are trying hard to correct their understanding of how to transform the foemanship into love. And they have an easier time doing it because they now know this is a natural progression.

I can also assure you that there are many here who are trying to communicate this understanding and healing of the foemanship to the bereaved on your plane. Many here find it quite frustrating because the survivor is not open and will not listen. Most importantly, they frequently do not realize it is possible. From this side we want survivors to realize the great healing that comes in forgiving each other for the stupid things that we did to each other. Actually as you know, they were not stupid at all. Rather it was ineptitude—lack of skill. It is so important to understand the degree of healing that can come to the bereaved when you realize all those negative things are but incidents of ineptitude, not uncaring.

Exercise 45: Describe the ways in which you and your departed were foes. Then describe the ineptitude that was behind it all. What did you both learn from your foemanship?

Chapter 47

Still Able to Make Amends

May 10th, 1996

One thing Gail and I never doubted was that we were committed to each other. And we really truly did try to forgive each other everything. When I think about it, it is really ignorance or inexperience behind the mistakes I made. When we are in a relationship it is easy to think that the other one is mean spirited—deliberately trying to tear us down, trying to hurt us—is uncaring, revengeful, deliberately trying to disturb our peace, incapable of being satisfied, selfish, and the list goes on and on. This judgment makes us question their basic love for us and their commitment to our relationship. Now with our loved one gone we are mad at them for what they did or didn't do and often at the same time unforgiving of ourselves for how we acted.

We need to realize that our judgment is incorrect—that neither we nor our beloved was acting in all these despicable ways. In fact what was going on was that each of us felt placed in a position where the best thing (and I emphasize the *best thing*) we could think to do in our difficult situations was to do precisely what we did, negative as it was. We made this nasty choice out of incompetence. We would have made a better choice if we had the competence to do so. How do I know this? Because the choices we made were usually not in our own self-interest. And no one makes choices contrary to their own self-interest if they can avoid doing so. And how do I know these nasty choices were against our own self interest? Because right now those choices that we made are making us unhappy! If we had had the insight to foresee the unhappy result we feel now for our previous bad choices, we would have sought another, better solution.

Those things we regret we would like to do over and in doing so would make a better choice. We are learning now. We are becoming more competent. So, there is no need to condemn ourselves or the deceased for our shared incompetence.

Dear Buck,

From my side I need to emphasize that the relationships that the bereaved have with their deceased loved ones does not end

when one comes to this side. The relationship continues to be open to changing for the better. If there is anything in a relationship with their departed that the bereaved would like to change or redo, they can do so. And they can do so now. They can tell the departed how they feel and what they would do differently. Do not doubt. The veil seems thicker from your world to ours than vice versa. This means that your departed will have a much clearer idea of what you think, feel and want to change than you will have of what is going on with them. However, realize that with practice the bereaved too will have a clearer understanding of the deceased. I am asking you to please try it. Follow your heart.

Exercise 46: If there is anything in your relationship with your departed one that you would like to change or redo, you can work on that now. Talk to them or write to them, telling them how you feel and what you would do differently.

Chapter 48

Forgiveness is an Ever-Present Choice

May 11th, 1996

In truth, is it not easier to forgive ourselves for our transgressions and to forgive our deceased beloved for his/her transgressions when we realize we and they acted out of incompetence and not meanness? This is not window dressing; this is a truer picture of what was going on. When we accept this understanding we are allowing these episodes of foemanship to transform into love as they were meant to do.

When Gail was alive I remember discussing whether it was actually possible to truly forgive someone absolutely and completely. It seemed very difficult. Now there is no doubt in my mind that I forgive Gail completely and she does me. It was all part of a lovely learning experience. Forgiving completely is such a wonderful release of burdens, it makes you want to do it with everybody.

Dearest,

One of the key things in our experience that so helped me in transition is that I knew that you forgave me for everything. When we were together we told each other often as to how much we appreciated each other. All the mistakes we made were of no consequence when placed within the great bowl of experience in which we had lived together in this last lifetime. It wasn't until I was here that I realized how much our past lives together also contributed to this. This forgiveness helps greatly to the sense of completeness to which I referred to above.

But, I do not want what I said above to discourage others who did not talk about forgiveness and haven't really forgiven yet. Forgiveness is an ever-present choice. God never withdraws this from us. It is available every second, every minute in endless opportunities. I know there are many people who would like to forgive but do not know how. In spite of this the major step in forgiving is to truly *want* to forgive.

And what does it take to want to forgive? It requires that you do not require anything from the person who you

think needs your forgiveness. They don't have to confess their sins to you. They don't even have to be aware that you feel they sinned against you. Nor is there any requirement upon them to seek your forgiveness. To truly want to forgive, you must need nothing from them. Forgiveness is within your power alone and it doesn't depend—at all—upon what the other party does.

When you understand this you will be pleased that it doesn't require anything on their part, only yours. Because this means the power is within you alone and no one can prevent you, by his or her action or inaction, from forgiving. This is quite liberating. After all, one of the reasons you feel you need to forgive somebody is because they seemed so insensitive to your feelings in the first place. If forgiveness depended upon them becoming aware of their insensitivity to you, it could postpone your forgiveness for a long, long time. Fortunately, forgiveness is within your jurisdiction and not theirs.

If they have passed on it can be easier to forgive when you realize you are in total control of your forgiveness. And as I have said before, the dying experience changes your life. It most certainly will change the life of the one you want to forgive. The whole process of death was created by God to enlighten the dying person and to make them acutely aware of how the way they behaved while alive affected others. Your departed one cannot escape this. Nor as they experience this do they want to.

You can be sure that your departed one is much more enlightened about you and life in general than when you last were aware of his or her outlook. The true question is, can you in your turn become more enlightened sufficiently to keep up with them? Forgiveness, as I have described it above, is a very effective way of doing this.

Exercise 47: Do you carry with you hurt feelings or anger over unfinished business between you and your deceased loved one? Try forgiving them and <u>know</u> that they have forgiven you. Life is but a school and most of the time our mistakes are simply ineptitude on our part. Write to them, forgiving them for every mistake you can remember they ever made. You have a gift to give them. Then, ask them to forgive you.

Chapter 49

Family is Like a Rental Agency

May 12th, 1996

Writing yesterday about our early days brought back memories. Early in our marriage, it seemed as if Gail was pregnant most of the time and taking care of these little kids all day long. It was exactly what she wanted to be doing but still she was ready for some relief and adult talk when I got home.

I of course would leave the house at 7:00 a.m. each day for my half hour drive to the job site. It would take another half hour to set things up and then at 8:00 I would be doing what needed to be done, swinging a hammer or digging a ditch. Then, at the end of the day I drove home all tired out. The kids would rush out and want to play with their daddy and that was fun and unwinding, but bore no resemblance to resting. Gail could join in this sometimes but then she had to go in and cook supper. She was busy, busy, busy. After eating there was cleaning up to do and putting the kids to bed which, they, like all kids, resisted. Their parents, of course, just wanted to sit down together and not move.

Looking back on it, I sometimes wonder how we did it. It helped that a long time ago Gail and I decided that life was like a rental agency. We rented out a tool, an experience, a companionship, and a home. In fact everything we had and every experience in life had a beginning and an end. This was our rental period. From this idea we felt that everything we had, including each other, we had only temporarily. This made it important to utilize and appreciate what we had while we had it.

When our children were small they were so dear and so much fun. Four kids in six years made an immense amount of work. But the realization that the sweet little gang were ours to enjoy only for our rental period, enhanced our enjoyment of them and increased our energy to deal with the task side of it.

But the kids were wonderful and so very responsive to life and to us. They were interested in everything. I remember telling Gail that my career's main purpose was to provide her time and money to raise the kids as we both felt they should be raised, full of fun, learning, and a vast variety of experiences. We were so fortunate we had four very bright, energetic kids.

At the end of World War II when I was in Poland I saw lethargic half starved kids there. That tore my heart out. That too really helped me appreciate our four healthy ones.

Here are some poems by Gail about children that she wrote from time to time.

JOY

To see a child unfold in love.
Lover of earth and play,
and yet aware of that
which guides the way.
The moral, true and holy union
That wraps us all in a single net.
To you ecology; to me it's God.
I care not which word you say.
You bring me joy, you child of heaven.

GLORY

A precious babe, a pure delight.
Hidden within a glorious light.
A love out flowing, clearly showing
Loves sweet power and holy might.

INNOCENT

An innocent child with eyes so pure
Looks out upon a world so sure.
Faith in father, trust for mother.
Seeing the best in one another.
Oh child of mine, hold fast that view
And let its love encircle you.

Dear, Dear, Buck,

We have so many wonderful memories of all our babies. They were such treasures. I'm proud of them because they all have contributed to making the world a better place. There is no holier role to play on this earth than as a mother. Nor is there any role in which we have greater opportunity to do as love would do. Motherhood gives us the channel for bringing love to a love-starved world. And, in spite of all the trials, disappointments, scares, and anxieties there is great self-

fulfillment to be found. Parenthood presents us with very high caliber learning possibilities.

As you know, my girlhood dreams were to marry a wonderful, loving man and raise a family of exciting children. I was totally family oriented. In my life I devoted most of my energies to you and the children and I loved it. In this last lifetime, I did not want a career. Fortunately for me this coincided with the "cultural construct" of what I should be doing. It made it much nicer for me because you told me when all those babies were coming, that the purpose of your career was to buy the time and wherewithal to allow me to mother our family. And you really meant it. Thus, at age 44, when the children were going off to college, you were able to give up your career without regret—partly because you had fulfilled that task. And partly, once the children were more independent, the two of us could do things together such as travel the world.

In family relations, particularly as a parent, there are great responsibilities to be assumed. We were constantly asking ourselves, "Are we being too protective or should we let them learn by experiencing life's harsh realities?" In some ways we never knew whether we did it right or not. One thing that I did learn was that by being *ourselves* we relay to our children the encouragement to be *themselves*.

You and I were always proud that our four children were all so very different, each following their own path. Family is a strange mix of guidance, support, discipline, and yet letting go. Fortunately, parents are aided in this by the built-in desire of children to grow up and be on their own. While this can cause some strife, if we realize that our child is in the process of just learning how to be independent, it makes it easier to understand his or her ineptitude in doing so.

We are all learning all the time. And since we are learning new things, it is understood that we don't know how to do the new things very well. Thus we need to accept not only our own ineptitude but also the ineptitude of those around us. It is so much easier to be forgiving and to be tolerant, if we understand that it is simply ineptitude. And nowhere do we need this forgiveness and tolerance more than for our *own* ineptitude.

This should be one of the basics of family life. Here is where we should be able to stumble all over ourselves and yet still feel part of the family. Family is a balancing act of the first order. Each family will seek its own fulfillment according to its own unique nature. In this process each family member is given a learning environment appropriate to him or her. Even after the death of a family member, this learning environment continues for both the bereaved and the departed.

The Kent Family on our hilltop, late 1960's.

Exercise 48: Ponder and write down how the family you were born into, or the family you created when you grew up provided a learning environment for you. Despite your beloved's death, write how your family continues to learn. And know that we here on the other side continue to learn with and through you.

Chapter 50

Having Doubts

May 13th, 1996

As I have suggested before, the fear or the experience of the separation from Gail is the result of the quintessential ego thought system based on separateness. But I believe that I am not and cannot be separate from Gail.

The first requirement or demand the ego system makes is that we give it importance. The first requirement in setting the ego system aside is to recognize the ego's great unimportance. Therefore to wrestle long and hard over the spiritually correct response to an ego system situation is to inadvertently assign the ego system too much importance. The true path lies in the recognition that it makes no difference how I respond to an ego situation because it is all a dream and an illusion and of no importance. Gail's death has triggered a mixture of ego response and spirituality. I notice that it is the ego side that seems to promote the grief and the spiritual side that brings comfort and joy.

I suppose that having doubts is an integral part of perception and the ego's view of things. Even right perception has its tinge of doubt. This is a dual world and doubt is the other duality to truth. I do not need to be overly concerned with doubt or give it importance. Doubt has no effect on truth. It only diminishes my openness.

Dearest Buck,

You know, to get encouraging results you do not have to be perfect. You *can* have doubts—even that there is an afterlife. You can have doubts that communicating with the deceased is possible. And you can doubt that you have the ability to communicate with the departed. But *if you are just open* to the possibilities of an afterlife and communications, then you are on the road to success.

God does not require perfection from you in order for you to progress toward perfection. God in His mercy embraces you as you are. And He provides you with opportunities to learn.

Exercise 49: List any doubts you may have about an afterlife existing or about the possibility of communication with someone who has passed over. Take note of how you can have doubts and still remain open to these possibilities.

Chapter 51

Life In-Between

May 14th, 1996

I've always been an avid reader. Since Gail passed on, however, I have not been able to read. After a few paragraphs my mind just drifts off and the words on the page have no meaning for me. You would think reading would be a great source of relief. So I am now pleased that I found a fascinating book—*Journey of Souls*—written by Dr. Michael Newton. He tells of his research through regression hypnosis of what the spirit world is like in between lives. Since this is where Gail is now it is of great interest to me as I want to know what "life" is like for her and what she is doing. It is written in a clear organized manner that reflects an author not given to fancy flights of credulity.

I think I am going to try to get hypnotized by Dr. Newton even though he is retired. He obviously is a very curious man and perhaps if I send him a draft of the piece I'm writing about Gail's death he may be sufficiently intrigued to take me. It is worth a try.

My Dear Buck,

You wish to know what I am doing. We always wanted to know what each other was doing. I am resting in a way. Actually it is more like digesting. I am learning. I am in a place where learning takes place quite differently from classrooms there. Although there are also similar classrooms and institutions here for the purpose of learning.

I have been learning a great deal about love—both sending and receiving love. In the spiritual plane it is quite different than where you are. Here we do less guessing as to what someone needs or wants. We can perceive more clearly what is needed. But, although we can give love, how it is received, as on earth, is up to the receiver. You don't know what choice the receiver will make in accepting our gift.

There has also been some past life evaluation and learning but now I am studying what seems like a new subject. It is like taking Physics 201 instead of Physics 101. It is not just physics but a subject beyond which I recall learning before. It is a preparation. I am being prepared for what comes next in

the life experience, which is eternal. So if you like to learn you will definitely enjoy this.

I must say to you I am learning some wonderful, wonderful things beyond anything that I have ever dreamed of. This eternal experiment is almost beyond what we can imagine or cope with, so it has to be done in little increments—just like kindergarten, first and second grade. It is thrilling! It is like—oh I wish I could transfer to you what it's like. It is beyond anything you could ever imagine. On your plane you would call it illumination—sometimes we have short periods of illumination and then there are huge bursts. It is like this intense experience of light within, which allows us to somehow see and understand the whole picture. Although there is a limit to how much we can cope with and we have to be careful when we do this. On your plane you have to be careful too. Where I am we have careful monitoring, for which we are all very grateful. It gives us a freedom from any kind of fear or anxiety about this because it can be overwhelming at times.

When we pass over, some issues and aspects of ourselves are carried over and have to be dealt with, internalized and cleared up or transformed. We have to be brought to a certain level of consciousness and understanding in order to be allowed to go up to the next level. We cannot make any steps upward or ahead without properly preparing the groundwork. Now that's the level where I'm working right now.

But, this is not what happens in everyone's interim experience between physical lives. Wherever we find ourselves is very purposeful and very appropriate. There are not any negative feelings but there is the realization of that which requires clarification, healing or cleansing as part of the preparation. It is mostly healing. It could be a healing of a misunderstanding or a misuse of information or an inappropriate response to something. It just has to be made more appropriate so that when you move along its energy is in keeping with what's ahead.

Exercise 50 : Try to imagine what your beloved might be doing. While writing, relax and see if you can't receive a description from them.

Chapter 52

Facing in the Right Direction

May 15th, 1996

In A Course in Miracles I am reading: "The past is over. It can touch me not." Today the past includes Gail's death. This means her death is over. But the joining of our inner selves is not over. It is in the *now*—the here and *now*—that her death and separation is gone. It is past. Understanding that her death is past will allow me to see the real world, which is obscured by perceiving or remembering the past.

Elsewhere ACIM repeatedly says that all our loving actions remain and are preserved by the Holy Spirit. All of the love therefore that Gail and I experienced in the past is not over but present in our *now*. It is very strange but I feel this.

My Darling Husband,

This moment of your *now* is always the most appropriate time for you to choose to be open. There is only one place to start, ever, and that is where you are. It is never too late. *The now does not allow anything to be too late.* And, it is true that nothing loving is ever irreversibly lost. God's world is so perfect that growth is always available to you. It is never shut off except by your choice. No matter what stage you may be in—with a loved one by your side or over here with me— choosing openness will reward you beyond measure. The wonders and miracles of God's world are so numerous and ever-present that to open yourself to even an inkling of them will bring you joy and purpose in living. Cherish every moment.

But, it may seem unfair to those who have lost a loved one that they need to be engaged in the *now* and to be upbeat in order to establish communication. As I have explained, we are not permitted to partake in the depression as it is not good for the grieving. Nor can we do your homework for you. This need not be discouraging.

Buck, do you remember when you started your business and you needed a loan? You couldn't get one because we didn't have enough assets. You said disgustedly that the

only people the bank wanted to lend to were those who had money and therefore really didn't need a loan.

The readers may feel this same way. Those who have survived the death of a loved one and who are living in the *now* and who feel positive about life are *not* those who are desperately in need of the reassurance of communication from the departed. It is those who feel depressed, guilty, and weighed down with grief who need help in overcoming their discouragement.

Fortunately God is ever merciful. He has set us on the path to achieving perfection of self. To make progress on this path does not require us to be perfect first. We can be quite imperfect indeed and still make holy progress in our evolvement. Common sense would tell us that if God intends us to go from here to there He must give us the means to progress forward, whatever our current level of evolvement.

No matter how depressed or how sad we may be, God gives us the means to see light ahead and to progress toward that light. In view of what I said at the beginning about having to be positive in order to communicate with us, how does this work?

This brings us to the importance of the direction in which we are faced. You on earth seem to place great emphasis on where you are. You may feel you seem to get mired down all the time. Here you are with your loved one taken away from you and you are unable to shake off the depression. You feel that where you are is a very bad place. What I want to tell you is that where you are is not nearly as important as is the direction in which you are faced. In other words, you can stay right in the same place you are. The biggest step you can take is not to move from here to there but to turn from facing in the wrong direction to the right direction. After this most important change in direction occurs then progress becomes much, much easier.

What I am saying is that those who are in grief need not worry about their present state. No matter what state they are now in they have the power to change the direction in which they are facing. And those who would dearly love to communicate with their deceased loved one, should realize that this is something they *can* look forward to, something to anticipate with a happy heart.

Exercise 51: If you are having difficulty in feeling joy or living in the "now," stop and try to determine what direction you are faced. Are you faced toward the hope of eventually feeling connected and at one with your loved one? If not, write down which direction you need to turn toward to accomplish this.

> *Those who stare at the past have*
> *their backs turned to the future.*
>   **—Unknown**

Chapter 53

A Catharsis Complete

May 16th, 1996

I have finished writing about Gail's day of dying (which is given earlier in the book). It was good for me. I have no idea whether it is well written or not but it makes no difference as it was just for me.

Dearest Buck,

You do a better job of writing when you think no one else will see it. Your desire for privacy is understood. I was the same way. The need to do service, however, is greater than the ego driven desire for privacy. It will be best to just leave it alone for a while and let its therapeutic effects soak in.

Exercise 52: When you are ready to do so, try writing about your beloved's death. You may find it to be therapeutic for you too.

Chapter 54

Embracing Life

May 18th, 1996

What is it in me that feels separated from Gail? I cannot touch her or be with her and I miss this joining. But there were other joinings we had then and I have now. Many times when I was with her I would just soften and melt with feelings of love for her. That's a wonderful feeling.

I remember times when she would be sitting on the couch reading or relaxing and I would walk by. Without saying anything she would pat the place beside her asking me in body language to join her by sitting next to her. And I would sit down and we would just feel that lovely being together. We would just *be*. I feel that now at times. It just comes sometimes all by itself. I wish I could make it happen whenever I want it to but maybe I would overuse it. I'm going to think about how this comes about.

My Dear Husband,

So you remember when I would pat the seat next to me on the couch and you would sit down? We would sit in silence but we were also sitting in *at-one-ment*. At those times we felt our holy relationship. Do you feel it now?

You have a mind, a body, and a heart—as did I. Now our bodies have truly been separated. The heart and the mind, however, have not been. Of these three the most important is the heart. The mind is the next most important. Lastly is the body. Even on earth people dread losing their minds more than losing bodily health. Upon death the body is truly gone but the heart and mind come over to this side. It is only reasonable, then, that your heart and mind can communicate with my heart and mind.

And, did you know that communications open when you think of me in a loving way? The reverse is true too. When I think of you in a loving way communication with you is opened as well. However there is a difference for you on earth versus those of us on this side. You are in a denser world, one that tends to close things off. In other words, it separates. If I think of you and open communications with you it will happen

only if you are open to receive. As you are in a world of closings, you are not always open.

We on this side don't have the density so we are more open in general. In fact, most of the functioning we do here is done by being open. So we have lots of practice. I must modify that by saying there is a great diversity over here and there are souls who show little evidence of being open. But generally we are more open here than you are on earth.

One of the frustrations of those who have passed over is that they initiate communications with their loved ones only to meet a closed mind that doubts or doesn't expect communication. Then it doesn't work. They try again. Sometimes after a while they get through. Often they don't. Then they get absorbed in being here and stop trying. This easily happens because it is fascinating over here.

I feel a need to emphasize again that wallowing in grief or letting yourself hunger for the past will close off communication. You must live in your *now*. You must engage yourself in your current life. You must participate in the things God brings into your life. Then and only then will you be open enough to communicate with us from this side.

This doesn't mean you cannot feel sad nor miss your departed one. It simply means you must embrace your life whatever it is and do your best to be grateful for it.

Exercise 53: Write your own evaluation as to whether you are living in your "now" or in the past or the unknown future (our fears usually are about the future). Your current life is very different now that your loved one is gone. Are you embracing your current life or retreating from it? No matter how you evaluate yourself, do not feel bad or guilty about it. The first step in solving any problem is to get to the truth . Once you get to the truth, you will have a much better handle on what you need or would like to do.

Chapter 55

Joy is the Sign of the Presence of God

May 20th, 1996 Along the Northern California Coast

I felt a need to get away for a bit so I drove to the coast of Sonoma. Being a former member of the Merchant Marine I have always loved the ocean. It feels timeless to me. I took some beautiful photos of the beach at sunset with a pink sky reflecting on the water and the wet sand. Walking on Wright's Beach and driving home along the river I felt both God's and Gail's presence strongly and joyously. Gail was sharing that overwhelming sense of joy and beauty with me. Some instructions came to my mind: "Joy is the most infallible sign of the presence of God." If I wish to feel Gail's presence, the key is to feel joy. And wondrously, I think it's true. Joy is without even the boundaries of death. What a wonderful healing of loss.

Dearest,

It is so nice of you to consciously share with me the perfection of your world and your senses with which you perceive it. Consciously sharing the enjoyment of your moment with us on this side is something anybody can do. In moments of beauty, joy and serenity, you may not only think of us but also openly share the satisfaction with us. This is much appreciated on this side. It moves us to feel your joy, gratitude and appreciation of your world.

You on that side are a monitor or sensing device through which we can share with you your experiences and which allows us on this side to learn, enjoy, and grow through them. This, of course, is somewhat the same as what we were doing when we were on earth with you but the format is different. However, it all works so much better if you are consciously aware of what you are doing.

Of course, it has to be this way because we are all *one*—**not separated. As you understand deeper and deeper levels of the** *All are One* **principle you realize that this sharing and communication are inevitable. But as each of us has free choice, we can** *choose* **not to listen. Not listening is the major cause of all the sadness and loneliness in your world.**

Right now, you are feeling that sense of sharing with me. Isn't that wonderful? Don't you wish everyone could feel this? All that sadness and loneliness is just not necessary. Why don't we both be still for a moment and let this strong sense of sharing—of being together—just sweep over us. I love you Buck.

Buck in the Merchant Marines, 1946.

Exercise 54: Look for opportunities to stop and "feel" the beauty of your surroundings. Be conscious that your beloved departed can and will experience that beauty through you—particularly if you invite them to join you.

Chapter 56

Gail's Birthday

May 24th, 1996

Happy Birthday Gail. Kind of foolish to say, may you have many more. But then you had that revelation in the kitchen which convinced you that you were indeed immortal and didn't have to die to become so.

GAIL, MY TREASURE

Gail you are my treasure,
Bountiful in memories,
Bountiful in love and joy,
Companion in my seeking,
Giving to my life resonance,
And now giving expression,
To your death and later mine.
God, I know you treasure my Gail.
You taught her love and gentleness.
You gave her that lovely femininity.
"You are God's symbol in my life."
I told her long ago
And so it was and
Continues to be.
I learned so much from her,
I grew toward her, toward God.
The lessons were the same:
Love and forgiveness the answer.

My Dearest Buck,

Thank you for your birthday wishes. Birthdays and death-days don't mean that much here except for the experiences they gave us. It is lovely though to be remembered and to be remembered fondly.

Exercise 55: Have you ever tried to write poetry of your own? Here is a chance to write a few lines—about your loved ones or some other topic. Give it a try.

Chapter 57

Incurable Romantics

May 30th, 1996

I have always prided myself on being a good problem solver. In fact I used to teach adult classes in problem solving. I learned to not seek the solution where the solution is not. How does it apply to the physical loss of Gail? The solution is obviously not in reuniting with her physical presence; it lies in uniting with her spiritual being, with God's being. When Gail gave up her physical body she also gave up her connection to my physical body as well. However, I am still tied to my physical body and must deal with that side of my experience and learning. She no longer places any demands on my body.

This applies specifically to my finding a girlfriend. I am sure that Gail wants me to find a loving female to share myself with. I'm also sure she wants me to use all that I learned in relating with her to make my new relationship that much better. And yes, I should have sex and enter into it joyously. It will be strange though after 47 years of fidelity.

Dear Buck,

As I have said before, if you wish to keep open communication with me then your robust engagement in your life, now, creates the right environment to make it happen. With my passing you realized that you had to have a new life style and to not try to hang on to the old one. Since you are basically an introvert this did not mean that you would become socially active. This would be appropriate for an extrovert. You are also considering, as you should, finding a special female friend. You and I both are incurable romantics. To live without this aspect would not be a full life. I know how loving you can be. I would feel it a waste for you not to find someone to give that to.

And yes there is room for you to learn and grow to be even more loving than you were with me. It does me no honor for you to place limits on yourself in how you relate to another woman. Particularly you should not think that your relationship with her must somehow be less than your

relationship was with me. Limiting yourself is not what you are about nor is it the wish of God that you limit yourself.

In truth, your relationship with her will be different than your relationship with me. This is as it should be. In your relationship with her you will be encountering new experiences, new personality traits. This in turn will stimulate a response in you that is also new and different for you. This is how you both will grow. Celebrate romance, and my dear, cherish every moment.

Exercise 56: Consider ways that you can ensure that you live a full life, even without your departed. Do not feel guilty—know that they want what is best for your personal growth and evolution. You could write to your loved one about your thoughts and dreams for today and the future. Most important, do not feel guilty for going on with your life. This is what you are supposed to be doing—and it sets the stage for a continuing relationship with your departed.

Chapter 58

Remembering Sacred Places

June 9th, 1996 In the High Sierras

June 9th, 1996 In the High Sierras

Every year, sometimes twice a year, Gail and I would come here to the High Sierras. We found the high altitude (8,000 feet and above) to be energizing and very beautiful. So now I am here by myself in my pickup truck, with sleeping gear and food, poking around at 10,000 feet on Mount Dunderberg. I feel a strong spiritual presence uncontaminated by people rushing around doing things.

Here I can see Gail everywhere and in everything. I feel it beyond the intellectual understanding of it. It is in my heart with grace and joy. We both are part of the One and to feel her I know I need to feel part of the One myself.

Dear Buck,

The Eastern Sierras are magical. We had so much fun exploring there. There are places in the world that are sacred in and of themselves. However this sacredness can be enhanced by the thoughts and presence of those who are attuned to it. In our travels we came upon many such sacred places and we felt their sacredness. We could feel it when we were alone that rainy day in the beehive tomb of Atreus*. The Kiva we climbed into at Bandelier** where the German was already meditating felt sacred. And our kopje*** there in the Sierras is a holy place.

Do you know what makes a place sacred? You can feel it but what is it you feel? There are some places on earth that are particularly congruent with the holy presence. If a person has within them a sense of the holiness of life and comes upon such a place, then they sense the congruency of their own sense of holiness combined with the holy presence of the place. This is a sacred joining and gives one that feeling of the infinite.

*Atreus: an ancient tomb in Greece. ** An Anisazi Cave in Bandelier National Monument in New Mexico. In kivas, religious activities, dancing and education took place. *** kopje: a natural pile of rocks large or small that sits on a comparatively level plain. It has a totally different habitat of flora and fauna than the plain out of which it protrudes.

A person who does not sense the holiness of life can come to that same place and feel nothing different than anywhere else. Although there are many energies that are flowing and ebbing about, you can't feel most of them any more than you can see the wind. But you can see their effects just as you do the effects of the wind. In some places these energies and the physical manifestations are congruent. They are in harmony with the All. This makes the place sacred. Thoughts also enter into this. Thoughts too can be congruent with the energies and the physical manifestations. It is congruency that does it.

Cathedrals become sacred places through the thoughts particularly of the builders. When we enter a cathedral we sense all of the energies and the thoughts of the builders those many centuries ago and then we add our own sacred thoughts to the cathedral.

Our ranch is a sacred place. There is harmony, serenity, and energy there, and it is good that you feel grateful for the privilege of being there. It is a place made sacred by our thoughts and presence.

There is another sacredness that you, dear one, are particularly aware of. You are very privileged to be so. It is beauty. This too is created by the congruency of the beautiful object and the thoughts of the observer who appreciates that beauty. Together they acknowledge the wonder of God's creations. It doesn't matter if the object of beauty is man-made like an ancient Chinese vase. Was it not God who created the clay with characteristics that firing would make porcelain? And the colors, where did they all come from if not God? The vase is a co-creation of God and man, is it not?

Exercise 57: Are there places that you have felt are sacred or that you have made sacred? Write a description of them.

Chapter 59

Choosing to Leave

June 18ᵗʰ, 1996

Gail, in choosing her time of death gave up a part of life, the elder years. But she just communicated to me, in my mind, that she got the center of the watermelon. She lived the best parts of a life and was perhaps spared the less tasty pieces. I think she is right, she did, and how pleased I am to have been a part of that.

Darling Buck,

You say that I chose my time of death. You know Buck, it could be interpreted that I committed suicide. In truth, it *was* my higher self that chose to die when I did. So in that sense I did choose my death time. Is this not what suicide is, when you choose your time of death? And though many don't believe it or understand it, everyone's death is a decision they make at some level. In effect, therefore, we all are suicides. This shows how unfortunate it is to pick on those who commit suicide as being in some way apart from the rest of us—having committed some act that we wouldn't commit. We are all *one* in life and we are all *one* in death. We are also all *one* in suicide. We cannot separate ourselves from ourselves.

It can be difficult to understand but for those who do, it will be helpful. The suicidal person is searching for his or her own truth. The suicide act itself has been chosen as a means to develop his or her own truth and as such it needs to be respected. As I have explained elsewhere, we are all here to develop our own truth. We each of us have our own path. It is not for others to judge the path we choose to develop our own truth. We need to give love and dignity—not judgment—when a person chooses suicide.

Marshall's note: According to psychic David Spangler, many of those who perished on September 11ᵗʰ, 2001 had made an agreement at the deeper soul level—or at the level of the higher self—to sacrifice themselves that day. The events of that day had a purpose to serve. Others, were drawn to the event for their own personal reasons and destinies and could not have avoided it. Yet others, who had not chosen to die that way and who were not bound by personal destinies remained untouched—sometimes for what appeared to be miraculous reasons.

Exercise 58: While it can be difficult to even want to understand, consider reasons—on a deeper soul level—that the departed might have chosen to leave when they did and the way they did. These would not be negative, fear-based or escapist reasons—but rather the reasons of the higher, more enlightened self. Write the reasons down in your journal.

Chapter 60

Lifetimes Together

June 19, 1996

I heard from Dr. Newton, the doctor who studies in between lives and he is willing to hypnotize me but he has a huge wait list—six months plus until he can take me. It is a 3 to 4 hour session and he does only one a day. I guess that in the in-between state I will see Gail again. We have had many signs that we have been together many lifetimes before.

Dear Buck,

Indeed, and many lifetimes to build much love. You and I have not only the love of this last life but the love of many past lifetimes as well. That love will always be. *A Course in Miracles* **is right when its says that, from the past, only love remains. This is a wonderfully large amount of love that we share. It is ours to have, to cherish, and to keep forever. Oh Buck I love you.**

Much of what you and I liked doing was because of previous lifetimes we had. For example, we loved being in Africa with those animals, big and small, 24 hours a day. Why did we think it thrilling and not frightening to have elephants, rhinos and hippos within a few feet of our tents while we slept? Why did we enjoy just standing there all by ourselves with elephants browsing and no fence or barrier between us? It was because of our past lives together as cave man and cave woman. We loved those lives. And we loved being back in that ambiance again. It was our territory and we belonged there. It was a dream come true for us, for both of us. We were fortunate indeed!

Exercise 59: Do you feel that you have had other lifetimes with your beloved departed or feel a strong connection to a place you have never been to? Even non-believers in reincarnation get that feeling—deja vue—about people or places in their lives. Write down those instances when you felt a strong sense of familiarity with another person or place. Or times when you felt a strong urge, for instance, to dance with a particular person to a particular type of music—or to share some other very specific kind of experience with them. One way to tap into earlier incarnations is by listening to ancient and ethnic music and paying attention to which music draws you.

Chapter 61

Communicating Heart and Mind

June 20th, 1996

Today I glanced at Gail's picture that I keep on my desk, wishing that I had some physical manifestation of her to reassure me. Just then, a thought came into my mind: "The only reality is the mind. Therefore normal communication between any beings is through thoughts." If this is so, then if Gail wishes to communicate with me it will be most likely through her inserting herself into my thoughts.

There are only a few people in this material world who can communicate with those who are unseen or dead. The same thing could be true, perhaps, of those on the other side. Perhaps there are some or just a few over there who can even manifest something almost material on this plane. So Gail may not find it easy to manifest something semi-physical to me at this time. I may also be blocking it in some manner. We shall see.

Dearest,

You reveal disappointment that I have not manifested in a visual form that would provide evidence that I live on. There is a reason why I don't appear before you. But I can instead insert thoughts into your mind. It is because mind to mind communication has been chosen for us since it is the easiest to accomplish for the largest part of humanity—both over there and over here. In other words, more souls can partake in mind to mind communication than any other and it is our task to help them do so. I'm talking about any mind to mind communication as well as inspired writing. For instance, your finding the black oak tree for my memorial service was a result of mind to mind communication. Many have some form of this mind to mind communication with the deceased already but don't give it credence. They dismiss it as their own imaginations.

There are certain conditions that make communication more likely. For instance, our communication right now is the result of what I like to call, "relaxed concentration." This is not the same as, for instance, the type of concentration you use

when you are at work. That type of concentration we will call "self-induced concentration." You were always very good at this. If you truly felt that something needed to be done you would set yourself into gear to concentrate on getting it done. You committed yourself. Your ability to do this is the reason you accomplished what you did in life. For example, you never doubted that you were the breadwinner in the family. You would do anything to fulfill that role. You brought to this task dedication and commitment. In so doing it became a wonderful and useful tool in your life. Mine too.

However, it can also be reversed where the task brings the concentration to you. In the self-induced mode, when you turn on the concentration, part of what you turn on is the necessary tension and energy to get the task done. Therefore it is different from relaxed concentration. Relaxed concentration can be more difficult to understand and to apply. However it is a tool that is very useful so it is worth learning about.

You and I applied relaxed concentration, for instance, in Africa when we would sit for long periods of time at a waterhole to observe the wildlife. We didn't really have to do anything. After waiting patiently for over an hour, we were able to receive the visual feast of a beautiful leopard. It would seem, therefore, as if relaxed concentration happens spontaneously without pre-conditioning. While this is somewhat true, it is not entirely. The proper use of relaxed concentration does come from knowing what you are doing. And it will enable you to do things that you could not otherwise do.

You can use the relaxed concentration tool to feel part of the *we are all one* principle. As a parallel experience, think of meditation. Beginners have difficulty because they tend to concentrate on not concentrating. It doesn't work. They get confused. Eventually they learn to do relaxed concentration. Then the higher self can bring to your mind a wisdom which you can now concentrate on automatically, just as we did the leopard. But, meditation is not the only place to apply relaxed concentration. As I said, our communication is the result of relaxed concentration.

There are times when you are not meditating, but you are busy with the rhythm of something totally different, when into your mind comes a thought, an idea or a message that begs for your concentration. Many simply dismiss it but it is best not to. Let your relaxed concentration allow the thought or idea to unfold.

You did this when you designed buildings. You gave over the data to your higher self, let it go, and then stayed open to your higher self's decision as to when to reveal the solution to you. This is so very different from tense concentration where you determine the subject to be concentrated upon. In relaxed concentration it is *not* the conscious awareness that turns it on and the subject is often a surprise to you. But you need to be alert enough to recognize it when it comes into your consciousness. Relaxed concentration is the doorway to the unexpected. And through it, great wisdom is available to everyone at any given time.

In essence, this is really the same as simply being "open." It is just a more detailed description of how to go about being open. If you simply tell someone to be open, they don't necessarily know what to do. It can be difficult. Our cultural way of learning things is to learn by following a recipe. We gather the ingredients, follow specific steps and lo, we have a chocolate cake. And it works every time. But, being open involves just yourself and no other ingredients. There aren't specific steps to take. It is more of an attitude. And you don't always get what you expect. Sometimes you get nothing. This is so different from your usual way of learning how to do something, particularly when you are feeling unsure of yourself. You wonder if you are doing it right. It is also hard to be relaxed under such conditions, especially if you want very much to do it. Therefore I feel it is important to introduce to you the relaxed component of being open.

I made reference to the *we are all one* principle but have not tied it into relaxed concentration. There is so very much of the invisible world that is unknown to most people. For instance, you are surrounded by love, by healing, by wisdom, and by communication channels. In fact, it could be said that the invisible is the abode of Oneness. The visible world, in contrast, seems to be made up of separate pieces. Therefore, to approach the Oneness you need to be open to the invisible. Relaxed concentration, in contrast to tense concentration, is a way to accomplish this.

Exercise 60: Experiment with being open—or using relaxed concentration. The more you practice, the better you will get at it. When thoughts, words and images come to you, or when you feel an urge to write, don't ignore it but relax and let it come through.

Chapter 62

Contacting the Inner self

June 24th, 1996 At Asilomar, California

I have come to the A.R.E. (Association of Research and Enlightenment, founded by Edgar Cayce) conference at Asilomar and curiously enough the speakers and the conference subject is about death. It seems that both *A Course In Miracles* and the A.R.E. are scheduling things just for me.

It is always nice to be around people who think as you do. The speakers were great. One was Dr. George Ritchie who wrote *Return From Tomorrow*, a book about his near death experience some years ago. His book was one of the first on the topic and it gave courage to many other people to share their own near death experiences.

I also went to a workshop with Betty Middlemiss who, now retired from this activity, once used her abilities to help the bereaved by communicating with the departed. She described what she did and some of the experiences she had encountered. I was impressed because she seemed to be seeking validation that what she was receiving was indeed what it seemed to be. I believe a lot of this stuff but also that it is important to stay somewhat skeptical and to discern the difference between imagination and true communication with someone else or something higher.

Asilomar at the south end of Monterey Bay is a lovely place and it affects me like the mountains. It is easy to get in touch with my inner self here. The ocean, the rocks, and the beach help.

My Dear Buck,

If only people realized how wonderful, how talented, how knowledgeable their inner self was, they would be very eager to communicate with it. The higher self has the additional capability of being the doorway to communication with so many other entities, places, and principles. Right now your higher self is the channel through which I can contact you. The higher self puts itself in neutral so to speak and opens its channel at both ends (also so to speak) and thus you receive communication from me.

Exercise 61: Write about what gives you a sense of serenity. Experiment with going to that place or putting yourself into that state and start to write. Your inner self may just speak to you!

Chapter 63

Finding My Way Out of the Maze

June 27th, 1996

When Gail was alive our inner selves spoke with each other as well as our outer selves. Now that she has gone, her inner self and my inner self are still communicating it seems. Only her outer self has gone silent. But at times it seems as if her outer self is here too.

Buck,

You are right. And in order to open a dialogue with me, you need to turn to your inner self. A very important by-product in the process of communicating with me is the ability you develop to contact your inner self. Even without communicating with the deceased, it is very helpful to know that the inner self is there for guidance.

For example, you will notice that when someone is upset and feels unresolved about something, they tend to repeat over and over again to the listener of their choice, that which is upsetting them. To the listener it is a puzzle as to why it has to be repeated so often. But it is no mystery to the talker. They feel like they are in a maze going around and around searching for an exit and feeling unable to find one. When you find yourself in this situation, turn to your inner self and ask for direction. How can you do this?

Begin to write, for when writing, as in contrast to just thinking, somehow deeper material comes into the written word. This deeper stuff is often from your inner self. It tends to throw new light onto how you feel, what you might do, or how others are affecting you.

This opening to your inner self can occur to your benefit with or without communicating with your loved ones on this side. As such it has value all to itself.

*Exercise 62: Write down unsolved questions that you have been carrying around. Then just allow yourself to write a response. Do not edit or evaluate what you are writing. Let it come out in an easy flow. It often helps to address the inner self as if it were a separate individual, like a very special intimate friend whom you

know and trust. When you have finished, you may or may not want to read it right away. Do as you wish. However do read it the following day. You will find it enlightening and edifying. You will see in it insights and meanings that you were not previously aware of. At this point you may feel the urge to write some more or maybe not. Go with how you feel. If you do write, use the same process, reading it over the next day.

In addition, after one week, you should reread again what you have written. If it is possible, read it aloud in privacy. You again will see in your writing new understandings. This contact with your inner self will at least lead you to a new part of the maze, lending hope that the exit to the maze will soon be discovered. It will also give you practice in contacting your inner self for the future. It is wonderful to be friends with your inner self.

Chapter 64

A New Pleasure for my New Life

June 28,1996

It is definitely a new and different life. It is time for me to pick out some new pleasures. As I said earlier, I have started some art courses that the local college offers to adults. Acrylic painting is one course—I want to learn the tools and language of painting. Drawing is another that I have begun. The drawing class involves sketching outdoors. It will be fun to be in the valley in the summer and I think I'm going to like this.

The fellow students seem interesting and I started a painting of the Marne Canal in France from a photo I took when we took our whole family on a boat trip in 1968. It was so peaceful there and I wanted to capture that in the painting. I put the horizon exactly in the middle to connote balance and lack of tension. Wouldn't you know that this is something you are not supposed to do in painting? At least in accordance with my teacher. Why am I always this way? I could be a good student and change it as she suggests but I know it is right for what I'm trying to do. So I went right on with the horizon in the exact middle. Don't get me wrong. I like the teacher. But I also like and trust that inner compass that I have always had that lets me know if I am going in the right direction. I am trying very hard not to be feisty about it but just quietly carry on my privately selected path. She seems to understand this and helps me along.

The drawing class is also great. We will go to various wineries and set up easels and sketch what we want. I did a drawing of a huge flowering foxglove that I liked. I also did one that turned out pretty well of an old stone winery building

Doing art work is very good for me—even if I never get really good at it. When I get caught up in what I'm creating I'm 100% there with it. All else is shoved aside including Gail's passing. It is like rest and recreation for the process I am going through and it really keeps me in the *now.*

Dearest,

We have discussed before the importance of your complete engagement in your new life if you want to maintain

communication with me on this side. This new undertaking will create the environment to help make it happen. Now you have started taking painting classes. And, as you noticed, while you were actually painting you were totally absorbed in what you were doing. That I had passed on was not in your thoughts or actions. This was healing for you. You also met and interacted with the students and teacher, which was good for you too.

Did you know you are co-creating with God when you paint? This doesn't automatically mean you do nothing but masterpieces. In fact, masterpieces have nothing to do with it. In contrast, the process of creativity has everything to do with it. It is your feeling that you are co-creating with God, using the tools that God graciously gave you to make things beautiful, that brings joy to your heart when you are painting. You feel congruent with God and His tools and sacredness results. Remember though, your most sacred place and process is that which is within you.

Also, you will try to create beauty with your artwork and by creating beauty do you attune yourself to perfection and fulfillment. And this, in turn, brings peace and serenity. Since I have passed on you have dearly wanted peace and serenity. So, where are you turning? To the arts. And what will you find there? Peace and serenity. This is how this cycle works. It will work for you.

P.S. The music on this dimension will blow your mind. It is so wonderful!

Exercise 63: Have you thought more about what new activities you want to take up? Write now about what you are doing or are planning on doing. If you haven't started, take your first step today.

Chapter 65

What Flows Out Flows In

July 8, 1996

We tune into what we seek. We see this in the material world with radar tuning into what it seeks. Our radios tune to the station we seek. This statement however has a much more powerful meaning when we apply it to the invisible, spiritual side of our lives.

One who seeks violence will tune into it and it will enter his life. One who seeks confirmation of his jealousy will find it whether it exists or not. We get confused on this however because we are aware that there are those who seek peace but do not find it and those who seek love and do not find it. This is because we build blocks of which we are not aware to the peace and love we are seeking. It is nonetheless true that you will tune into and receive what you seek.

Those knowingly on a spiritual path realize that much that goes on in the world is not due to material cause and effect, but because of the nonmaterial mental and spiritual influences. Edgar Cayce always said, "Mind is the Builder."

This morning I sought communication with Gail hoping she would give me some wisdom. I tuned to her and what I'm now writing is what I received. In this case my seeking was directed at an individual with no expressed subject matter. In most cases, however, it is the subject matter that occupies our mind that establishes what we are seeking. This tunes us to other minds that are both incarnate (in their bodies) and excarnate (out of their bodies—like Gail). This reinforces our own thoughts and can also give us insights and new understandings.

To be tuned into someone else's mind seems to be a rare event to us. In fact it is not. It is very common. We don't recognize it for what it is. Each of us is like a broadcasting station and a receiving station at the same time. We send out these vibrations that are picked up by others if their seeking is tuned into what we are thinking or broadcasting. If they are not seeking what we are broadcasting they will not receive from us.

Now this applies equally to advanced minds and beings. If we seek higher enlightenment we tune into the wisdom of minds that comprehend beyond our own. Thus do we advance our own enlightenment.

The reason we seem to be unaware of this is that these thoughts don't come labeled as to their source. It is the content and not the source that enters our minds. These thoughts, we tend to believe, are just our own thinking processes. And this is how it is intended to be. We all know that if we want to give someone else an idea the best way is to let them think that the idea is their own. Another aspect that helps to camouflage this thought transfer is that the sender has no idea of who is picking it up. It is like TV newscasters who, as they are broadcasting, have no knowledge who is watching them or listening to their words.

This system works both for high thoughts and low thoughts. It is therefore most important that you be aware of what you seek and consciously chose what you really want to draw to you. This is especially important to someone like me who has just lost a loved one. We must deliberately seek peace, happiness, and continuity. Most importantly, we must seek gratitude. This may sound peculiar but it is most germane. Gratitude is a great healer of loss.

Sweet Buck,

The proper understanding of thought is that it has the capacity and the potential to carry and convey feeling as well as thinking. Any good poet knows this. However words are not necessary to bring out the feeling aspect of thought. You can directly convey feeling in the very same manner as you would convey thoughts or ideas. On earth, feelings play a very influential role in behavior even though feelings are little understood and are often confused. Command and mastery of life will come through comprehending feelings, your own and others.

Your feelings tend to be specific both in their character and in what or who attracts them. You feel love toward this person and anger toward that person. To send out unspecified love seems pointless and powerless. Nothing could be further from the truth. This applies equally to other feelings such as gratitude, joy, acceptance, and awareness.

It is the love flowing out of you that causes joy to flow into you. There is no spiritual or mental vacuum. When the love flows out something else must flow in. What flows in? The law of congruency governs. What flows in is congruent with

what flows out. Therefore if you truly feel love and you let it flow out unrestricted as to whom the love flows, then you will have joy flow in unrestricted and unrelated to what seems to be happening to you from the outside. It is simple and simply elegant.

The reverse is also true in that if you let bitterness flow out of you then into you will flow bitterness or, more accurately, perceived reasons to be bitter. This in turn will attract to you apparent outside events that stimulate within you a bitter response.

Using the broader brush, if you let flow out of you separation perceptions and activities then flowing into you will be your own separation from the Oneship and from God. This is why Jesus taught us that our thoughts were so important and that love was the answer.

Your friends Nancy and Kathy express their deep compassion for the homeless and downtrodden of the city. And they wisely don't differentiate between what we judge as self-induced difficulties and externally inflicted difficulties. They are both the same. The homeless and downtrodden can benefit from our compassion. Nancy and Kathy both wish so much to be able to help them but recognize their individual inability to do so. They would feel much better if they only knew that the real benefit they can give is not limited to material help although that too is needed and appreciated. The greatest aid they can give is to feel joined with the homeless in the Oneship within God. You do this by sending out love with a sense of the oneness of you and the downtrodden who are both on the path of enlightenment. Avoid the separation thoughts that many use to dismiss the homeless and their problems.

You on earth are so absorbed in dealing only with the material, you believe the material is the only way to provide relief. If no material benefit occurs you assume no benefit has been achieved. This is untrue and greatly underestimates the power of the mind. This is strange because you well recognize the power of the mind but only when it results in a material change. The mind has tremendous power and effect that often does not manifest a material change. All of the many steps you individually take to return to God seldom involve a material event. They are mostly events within. It is true they may subsequently cause a change in your behavior that will show up materially but that is an aftereffect.

The other thing you greatly underestimate is the ability of one mind to reach another mind. When you see a drunk lying on the sidewalk and you send out to him inclusion in the Oneship and love, it seems to have no effect. The drunk is still out of it. But what you don't realize is that the inner self, the subconscious of the drunk does indeed register your joining. This is of great benefit. If you pay attention you will feel the response to you of the inner self of the drunk. It is a form of greeting that acknowledges the oneness of you both. Every time two or more minds join in the Oneship, does the Oneship strengthen. There is no greater labor or greater spiritual honor than in strengthening the Oneship. Do so consciously, deliberately and feel the results in your heart.

As I said earlier, what we do is not as important as what our thoughts are when we are doing it. In other words we can do quite a variety of things and it won't matter as much as the attitude with which we do them.

Right now as we respond to the events of September 11th and the war against terrorism, each of us has our part to play. It is more than just what we do consciously. Our thoughts are both *attracting* thoughts from others and *sending* to others. For this reason—if we are to further the cause of peace in our world—our thoughts must be elevated.

Exercise 64: Pay attention to your thoughts and feelings. When you find yourself thinking or feeling thoughts you don't want, try putting a big X through them and consciously replacing them with the kind of thoughts and feelings that you would rather draw in to yourself. It will become easier with practice. Write down the thoughts and feelings you desire.

Chapter 66

The Gift of Free Choice

July 23, 1996

I believe I received this from Gail this morning. I will write it down quickly before it fades from memory:

We are given free choice to manifest our divinity. Do you not see the perfection manifest in free choice? Did not God create perfection when he gave each of you free choice? Yet man in his ignorance attempts to make the world more perfect by limiting the choice of those he feels, in his judgment, are bad or are doing bad things.

God gave everyone choice. Man tries to make this world better by limiting this choice, given by God, to those with whom he disagrees. Man makes laws to curtail peoples options. He incarcerates to limit the activities of those he judges faulty. At the same time man even thinks he is doing so in God's name, to improve God's world. Man's thinking is backwards in so many ways.

Marshall: The first part of that I understand and think is very beautiful. The second part puzzles me and I feel I only get a glimmer of understanding, yet I feel it is very profound.

Exercise 65:   Ponder the notion of free choice.   Using the assumption that our beings extend beyond our physical bodies, how does our own death fit into the picture?   Consider the implications.

Chapter 67

Love Come, Love Goes, Love Is

September 2, 1996

Maybe Gail will write through me. I am sitting down to write to see what comes out.

Love comes, Love goes, Love is.

That's it.

Exercise 66: If you haven't already been doing it, try sitting down with nothing in particular in your mind—with relaxed concentration—and just write. See what happens. If nothing appears, do not be discouraged. Keep trying.

Chapter 68

Best Friends with God's Universe

October 4, 1996 (In our woods)

This is a serene spot. Gail and I sat here often and watched the deer walk and run by. Mostly they didn't see us. But we have been talking to them since they were fawns so they seldom spook.

Buried in the ground on each side of me are Gail's canvas hiking shoes. In these she hiked into Machu Picchu, across the Grand Canyon and so many private places in the Sierras. I'm going to try writing without thinking of what I write and just see what comes out. Here goes.

Trees are lovely and green. They grow, they blow in the wind and they make seeds. An autumn leaf falling to the ground is a lovely sight as is death when it is understood. We put Gail's ashes into the ground without a marker to parallel how a leaf falls from a tree where it will be of anonymous service.

So we have the symbolic perception of the leaf leaving the branch for earth. Does the leaf in so falling take the joy or feel our joy in watching its journey? See how the earth receives the leaf in simple acceptance. A model for us. A demonstration of acceptance.

Trees are a joining principle. They join the earth to the sky, the summer to the winter; their seeds join generation to generation. They harbor life, they feed life, they grow with life—all joining acts. This has always been their symbol to me. It is why I have always loved trees. It is why I planted a tree on our hill for Gail, nurtured by her ashes.

Divine heart, feel my beat in harmony with yours. May the rhythm be universal. May my heart be one with thine heart.

Gail I love you. You are with me. If you were not it would be impossible for me to feel this good. My five senses don't know of your presence but my heart does. I feel you here. It is good. As you asked of me I am content. Yours was a beautiful leaf that fell to the ground.

Dearest Buck,

Your loving attitude can and should be extended to the trees, weather, flowers, animals, fish and in fact, your entire world.

Why did you and I love the wilderness so? It was because all the life forms in the wilderness are following their own truth, their own nature. It created a vast ambiance of loving tolerance that we loved. Why did we so love wild animals? Why were we going to Africa on our own with those big animals right outside our tent? Do you remember the two big rocks twenty feet from where we slept that turned out in the morning to be two sleeping rhinos?

We have always been drawn to that and those who are following their own path, fulfilling themselves in celebration of life. This includes what the earth calls the non-living as well. Why did we delight in those magnificent thunderstorms in the Southwest? They too are living things that seek their own nature. All things are living or they wouldn't *be*. How can you look at the waterfalls, for instance, and not see that they are living? The vitality, the energy, the fluidity just flows endlessly. The water, like the leaf that falls to the ground, is also fulfilling its nature as given to it by God just as you are.

God's entire universe in which you find yourself immersed is worthy of your complete acceptance, respect, and love. You can be friends, best friends, with all of it. Walk your life in friendship with all that you see, hear, feel, smell, and touch. If you do you will know what joy is.

Can you not see the wisdom in this? Wisdom can be defined as finding God's intent. It is God's intent that you be friends with His entire creation. There is nothing that He created which you cannot be a friend with. You are among friends always. Being open will reveal this to you.

**Buck drew these alpine flowers at one of our
favorite places high up in the Sierras.**

Exercise 67: Think and write about all of the elements of nature that you would not normally extend a loving attitude toward. Send those elements your blessings and love.

Chapter 69

Stepping Through the Doorway

October 12,1996

Just moments ago I had a wonderful experience. Here I was at the computer working on my journal. I looked at Gail's picture and told her I loved her. Suddenly I could see her in three dimensions just as if she was there. The expression on her face was alive and I felt the frame of the picture was the opening, a window, into the spirit world and there I was seeing her alive and looking at me with love and welcome. She looked so good. I wept for joy. It lasted quite a while and even though my tears made it difficult to see, there she was. It was marvelous in the true meaning of the word. She told me by telepathy that I would be able to see her again like that, now that I knew how we could reach each other—and its true—I just looked again at the picture and there she was. I am so thankful.

My Beloved,

You can see from this that communication from this side involves what is happening to the individual on your side. Will they be sufficiently impressed to realize that something special is happening? Will they allow their minds to receive? Will the outside circumstance be quiet enough so the message does not get lost in the background noise? These and other conditions of the recipient are very crucial in our getting through.

Your ability to see the flowers in the waiting room of Dr. Ho's office in three dimensions in truly live color was a cooperative accomplishment. I can open the door but you must walk through it. We did it again with my photograph in your office. If you only realized the capabilities that are within your mind and your eyes you would be amazed. The phrase "in the mind's eye" is more powerful than you know.

Exercise 68: Write about any similar experiences you may have had. When writing, ask for the true meaning of the experience and then let your hand write the answer. Try to remain open to having similar experiences of your own.

Chapter 70

Saints and Sinners

October 13th, 1996

God created me perfect. I am an innocent child of God, immortal, guiltless, and one with God. However, I know I have tried to make myself into less. I am so encrusted with blockages, limited vision, boundaries, and limited understanding, that I do not recognize who God created me to be. This act of remaking me into this limited self is as close as I can come to sin. It is not sin however, only a mistake, which I can correct. One way of correcting is to forgive myself for making this mistake and asking God's help in correcting it.

Dearest,

Your higher self is here with my higher self and all the other higher selves of our teaching group. We all watch with wonder as the earthly portion of ourselves go about their lives. Your earthly portion of yourself truly has free choice. We watch with wonder to see what choices you make. We are constantly surprised and pleased. We are never disappointed because we see how what you think of as bad choices lead through God's laws to even better learning situations for you. It is ever fascinating to see how events unfold based on the choices you make. It is also fascinating how your path and the paths of others interact to bring about the best learning situation for you and the others too. One is not subordinated to the other. Both gain equally from every situation.

Although it is hard to accept (easier if you believe that we are all immortal), and particularly in the wake of the World Trade Center tragedy, it matters not whether the interaction is between two saints, two sinners or a saint and a sinner. Each is an equal participant and equal student in opportunity. They may not be equal in evolvement but they are equal in opportunity to learn their own special lesson. To see that from our perspective on this side is remarkable. If you can't see it outright, you can sense it from your earth's perspective. When you do, you will notice that your desire or need to judge is rendered irrelevant. You won't have to

discipline your self to stop judging. You just no longer have use for judgment. The Biblical injunction, " Thou shall not judge," becomes much easier to follow.

When it comes to the events of September 11th, God will not let so many die in vain. God in His infinite ability takes the thoughts and actions which we have selected with our free will and converts them into a learning stimuli which enhances our spiritual growth. Interestingly this stimuli acts not only on the surrounding people who are effected by the thoughts and actions but on the perpetrator of those thoughts and actions.

Take heart that everyone will grow from events such as these even though that growth might be so small as to be invisible to your eyes. There is a tendency to be impatient and demand visible, measurable results or you think nothing is happening at all. It is like you are building a huge brick wall just one brick at a time. From a distance the addition of one more brick is invisible. The pace at which individuals advance is up to their free will. It has already taken them many lifetimes. How many more will be needed? This will be up to them.

But those of you who feel more advanced than the terrorist need to wait for your brethren (the terrorists, for instance) to join you in developing your own truth which will bring you to God. This is hard but more effective than creating new terrorists by adopting vengeful retaliatory attitudes. The current vengeful violence can be traced back to prehistory in a long seesaw chain of perceived injustices. It is time to try something new.

We always come back to, *we are all one*. This understanding of equality discussed above removes another barrier you have erected to exclude yourself from consciously feeling the *at-oneness*. It's lovely isn't it?

Exercise 69: Think of all the victims in the world that you know of, and try to see them as students instead. How does that change your view of them? Write down your thoughts.

Chapter 71

Having Fun

October 14ᵗʰ, 1996

I remember telling Gail that if I went first she didn't have to prove or demonstrate her love for me to anyone by her actions or thoughts because I knew she had already proved her love to me.

After I was gone, I wanted her, above all things, to have a good, joyful life and I was confident she was the best judge of what that would be. If others thought that what she did or said didn't jive with the love we two were supposed to have had, then that would be too bad. It should not influence what Gail thought was the best thing to do. We two knew what we had.

She agreed and felt the same way. She expanded on the idea by saying we should not be afraid of our thoughts after the other died, especially those with which we might feel initially uncomfortable—for instance, thoughts about the times when were not at our best. Even thoughts about how it is now easier in some ways with the other not around. She was so wise. Any two people living together do many things to accommodate the other. After one is gone, the other no longer needs to do this accommodating. What Gail was saying was that the survivor should feel pleasure in those occasions when accommodating was no longer necessary.

If I was gone, one thing Gail would take pleasure in was in making a big purchase without asking me about it. It should be no surprise that I was more on the side of not spending than she was. Before you all leap to the conclusion that I was the controlling male on money matters, let me add that I would not make a big purchase without discussing it with her. Actually, we got along quite well on spending, particularly later in our marriage when we weren't just getting by.

After she was gone she wanted me to feel that all thoughts about her and our relationship were purposeful and in that sense good. Their purpose, as always, was to learn, to understand. I have tried to do this.

Dear Buck,

Not only should we not fear enjoying the positive aspects of being on our own, we should also not fear having fun. In fact,

God invented fun and humor and He is fun-loving. God gave us the gift of having fun and He delights in it. If you doubt this, watch young children having fun. You will then know it is a holy thing. In fact, watch anybody having fun and it is a delight. We tend to make life so heavy duty. We see all the misery in the world and think it is almost indecent to have fun. Think of how different the world would be if we reversed that and felt it was indecent to be somber or heavy duty.

Fun is very good for your health, for your mind and for your soul. When you are having fun you are much more likely to find your heart, mind and body in *congruence* with God than if you are somber. Being in congruence brings you into harmony with *the All*.

So, seek fun! Have fun! Share fun! Do not be afraid of appearing foolish. Rather, be afraid of *not* having fun. Enter into fun like you were jumping into the water on a hot day. Having fun will lift your spirits. It will give you energy to live.

Do you know we have fun over here? We do. We even have something that is like having the giggles. We see this as different facets of divine joy. We feel we are doing God's work when we have fun. I always thought work was a funny word to use for fulfilling God's purpose. Work seems to involve an obligation; doing something that you would prefer not to do. But God's work is fulfilling yourself. This fulfilling takes on as many forms as God has given you the potential to create. These forms are more appropriate to having fun and feeling joy than they are to being serious and weighty.

So when you are having fun be aware that the reason it feels so good is because it is you fulfilling your God given nature. Also be aware that those with whom you are having fun are joining you in a holy sharing. Knowing this will make it even more joyous.

You can even change other people's lives by having fun. Over here we discover that little episodes of our life on earth, episodes we thought of no particular import have deep meaning.

Do you recall the time our tourist bus stopped in New Zealand beside the road near a children's playground? We ran over and started playing on it. I was going down the slide and you were doing tricks on the rings. Then we both went ape style hand over hand on one of those elevated horizontal ladders. Here we were, two gray-haired people cavorting on children's playground equipment. I have learned that there was a lady on the bus who was younger than us and who marveled, unknown to us, at the child-like joy we were unconsciously displaying. Do you know that this inspired her to seek enjoyment in her life without trying to please others or to worry about what other people thought of her? I'm sure we looked silly doing what we did. But, that small stimulus she received from us cascaded to change her whole life. She is now married to a wonderful man and she realizes he never would have been attracted to her if she had not decided that she could choose joy just as we had.

On earth, we see very little of the ramifications we have in people's lives by the way we live ours, or the way we lived ours. Sometimes, it is just as well that we don't. On this side much of this is revealed as it is quite instructive, and I must say, surprising.

There are no boundaries or limits to what we can have fun with. We can have fun with sacred subjects. We can have fun with prayers or lovemaking. We cannot, however, have fun at someone else's expense. This separates us from the brunt of our humor. Fun is the essence of joining and thus is the opposite of separation. Our language, though beautiful, confuses us by giving too many meanings to one word. Anyway, have fun. I'm so glad in knowing that you are.

> *Let everyone that you meet be happier for*
> *having met you, for having spoken to you.*
> *This ye can do by spreading joy.*
>   **—Edgar Cayce**

Exercise 70: Think about ways that you can have fun—and ways you can bring fun into the lives of others. Having fun is one way of spreading joy. Write out a check list and get started.

Chapter 72

From God, Through Me, To Thee

October 16th, 1996

Over the years I seldom wore green clothing. I have no green pants. I never wore the green shirts I had. I wasn't against them I just never chose them. For some reason, since Gail's death I have been buying and wearing green clothes. Now I like being in green

In my paintings I notice I have been doing a series of abstracts all in different shades of green. I have had to push myself to bring other color into them. Today it just occurred to me that green is the color of healing. Maybe that is why I am finding it pleasing.

My Dear Husband,

Did you feel the healing that I gave you in the bathtub moments ago? Yes, I know you did. Your whole vision was filled with the lovely emerald green of healing. And it was one of the most vital healing you've experienced.

Actually there is only one kind healing and that is spiritual healing. However spiritual healing is so powerful that it spills out over into other aspects. One such aspect is your body. Spiritual healing will cleanse the body of imbalances. Be careful here and do not assume, therefore, that if your body doesn't heal it means you are not spiritually attuned or spiritually healed. Remember that karma, in its teacher function, will provide you with problems as tools for your en-lightenment. These problems may take the form of illnesses.

Another aspect that your spiritual healing spills onto is your blessing and forgiving of others. God's healing follows this path: from God, through you to your brothers and sisters. Hence the prayer:

> **From God**
> **Through me**
> **To thee**

You can use this prayer in your meditation. Spiritual healing can and often does occur in those who proclaim they

are atheists or agnostics. This may seem puzzling. Although your conscious mind does have some role to play in asking for and receiving spiritual healing, it is not the only player. This is because not all of each entity actually inhabits his or her body. Part of themselves—their higher selves—remain elsewhere. Buck, I know you liked to describe this as an inverted iceberg.

Marshall: Gail is referring to the fact that at sea, an iceberg reveals only ten percent of itself above the water. The remaining ninety percent is below the water and thus invisible to a ship's captain. Turn that whole thing upside down and you have an analogy of the conscious self and the higher self. Your conscious being, or the entity that is you has only ten percent of itself hanging down in this world as your visible self. The remaining ninety percent is above and invisible to this world. That which is above and invisible from here is your higher self.

Gail: With this analogy and in the case of atheists, their higher selves may call the spiritual healing forth. This healing may bring on a strong sense of brotherhood, or compassion in one who professes no belief in God. (Before we go much further I need to say that the analogy of the iceberg is incorrect in one point. Most often there is a much larger percentage of an entity visible in the material plane than just ten percent. There are few on earth that have only ten percent on earth.)

Why is this important? What can you gain by knowing that spiritual healing is not only available to everyone but can be received whether it is believed in or not? Several things. You can see how God's love is ubiquitous. You can sense the foolishness of judging others as to their goodness or lack thereof. Anything that can be done to reduce the ego's delight in judging is a step forward.

Healing is a gift from God to all His children. We would all like to be physically healed even though some of us have reservations as to whether we want or even need to be spiritually healed. What do we do to qualify, so to speak, to be healed by God? We both ask and give. We ask for healing, which opens us up to its presence. And we give healing to others which attracts healing from God to us. We cannot give what we don't have. If we have healing we can give healing. This sounds like cause and effect, which it is.

However, in this case, as is often true with dealing with the infinite, the cause and effect are simultaneous. In other words you can have healing and therefore give it. You also can not have healing but give it anyway and healing will be drawn to you so that you can give it. Both the chicken and the egg can come first or rather simultaneously. It is this that gives power to the six word prayer that is above.

Discover the pleasure in giving healing to others. In fact give healing to everyone without exception. They are all your brothers and sisters. If you are practically minded you may say, "What's the point? I don't see them get healed by my sending out the healing." In a narrow sense this is true. It is not true in the full perspective that I have referred to before. Earlier I described spiritual love. This is like the love, for instance, that you feel flow out of you for a child. You do not demand that the child return that love or respond in any given way. Your spiritual love is fulfilled simple by you letting it pour out from you. Similarly, when you send out healing there is no component of that healing that demands the healed to respond in anyway. They do not have to show you that they are healed, or even acknowledge your good intentions. Sending out the healing fulfills itself simply in the healing attitude you project.

When you do this with an open heart you will find yourself feeling spiritual joy that is most rewarding. At this point you will realize that this giving of healing is valid within itself. With this realization will come a glimmer of recognition that the healing you give out actually works, actually is healing. Yes, Buck, this is indeed because we are all *one*. It is yet another function of the *all are one* principle.

Exercise 71: You too can send healing to others—including the deceased—and in the process receive healing yourself. Relax, and in a prayerful, meditative state, consciously send out healing to whomever you choose. Repeat, "From God, through me, to thee."

Chapter 73

Relationships are Our Teachers

October 17th, 1996

In the *A Course in Miracles* on page 330 it says, "To forgive is merely to remember only the loving thoughts you gave in the past, and those that were given to you. All the rest must be forgotten. Forgiveness is selective remembering, based not on your selection."

I agree with the above but there is part of me that wants to be accurate and truthful. It insists upon me also remembering those things that both Gail and I did that were not our best moments. These don't bother me now nor did they when she was here. We were merely learners on the path. Our mistakes were our greatest teachers. We survived them and they were the sources of our deepest love. Yes, and respect too. You have to respect each other, and especially each other's mistakes. These you need to remember with a sense of sharing and not accusation. Sharing is really magic.

Dear Buck,

To share, to join and to communicate are all a means of loving. To create, to heal, to bless are all means of loving. To have compassion, to have tolerance, to have forgiveness will all lead to love. To know love is to know the Oneship. To know the Oneship is to know God. It all fits together.

Knowing that it all fits together gives you the wisdom to feel God in all things. To know this in your heart unlocks the joy which God placed within you. Now you can perceive that God has made a perfect world. You know this at the same time you realize many of the things of this perfect world could be better. Here is another divine mystery. How can this be? Yet it is.

You cannot limit God to being one way or another. Nor can you limit what He has created to one thing or the other. Analytical thinking is a very powerful and rewarding tool. The error comes in thinking it is the *only* tool. There are other ways to reveal and to understand the truth. The way is not one-dimensional. Feelings, intuition, and meditation are some of the additional ways to truth. Learn to use them.

Switch now to relationships. They are of infinite variety with infinite opportunities for learning. They provide a channel to express the very best and the very worst of who you are. For souls with free choice you couldn't ask for a better playing field. Relationships occur with one or with vast numbers. You also have a relationship with yourself—even within yourself. How do the different parts of your individuality relate to each other? How congruent are they?

The degree of congruency of our parts is the same as the degree of happiness in our lives and of our freedom from fear. This correlation—the more congruent you are, the less need for fear—is not immediately obvious.

Back to the Oneship. The Oneship could not exist without relationships. The individualities needs relationships to create the Oneship. Therefore, to know God is to relate to Him. Relationships then occupy a most vital and central role in all that is. This means they warrant your most dedicated efforts and energy.

Do you also see, that by definition, relationships imply the existence of two elements? Thus do relationships bring us to the individualities existing within the whole.

We humans choose to contribute to the whole—or to separate from the whole. In either event we are exercising our individuality. Our true nature, however, is fulfilled by being a part of the whole and not by separating from the whole. The separation choice leads to strife and all the other ills of the world such as the events of September 11th, 2001.

Part of the mystery is that individuality can be a separation identity or it can be a joining identity within the All. God's gift of free will lets you choose. God's laws are such that there are gentle loving opportunities to recognize that there is wisdom, joy and serenity in choosing harmony or love—to contribute to the whole. Do you see how this is?

Exercise 72: Consider how your relationships have provided you and your departed with opportunities for learning. Describe both the best and the worst they brought out in each of you.

Chapter 74

There is No Beginning and No End

October 27, 1996

I remember this day 47 years ago very well. Gail and I went to Xenia to get our marriage license. We were both nervous. We went into this lovely old stone courthouse which is still there and stood in front of a window. As the clerk was asking us all these questions and taking down our answers, Gail got the giggles. It embarrassed me. I kept whispering to Gail, "Stop giggling. They will think we aren't serious." That just made more giggles. Young people are very silly but that is part of their charm.

The day after tomorrow will be our wedding anniversary. I hear constantly how tough anniversaries and family holidays are after you lose your spouse. It seems I am always marching to a different drummer. I look forward to it as a special time when I may feel close to Gail and spend my time in reverie of all the great things we did. I suspect she will also come through to me in some way. Let us see.

One reason I have not been bothered by being depressed in my life is an experience I had in Poland right after World War II. We had just unloaded some horses in the harbor of Gdansk and were taken to a Nazi concentration camp. The people were gone but there were bones and ashes still in the ovens. There was a horrible great long bank of them. There were pallets of soap made from rendering humans. Two of my crew members took some of the soap for a souvenir. That bothered me. I couldn't touch it. Ever since then I have had difficulty in feeling sorry for myself.

Gail and I both would particularly remember the night before our wedding. It was a foggy light rainy night and we walked under the maple trees that dripped on us. It was magical and had an ambiance of timelessness. We both felt as though we were looking through a tunnel of time down our own path. It was nothing specific at all but it was as if we were given a great gift, that lovely path before us. We married ourselves to ourselves on that walk. And then it felt so good to get into bed and cuddle up with the mist outside the window. We never tired of it.

Buck,

I remember the magic of that night but it was far more than a tunnel looking down our own path. Our intellects had no awareness of past lives and therefore it didn't register with us. But our emotions and our hearts were feeling a long tunnel that went in both directions past and future. Our past lives together and what we had built with them made us excited that we had yet another lovely journey to take together in this life. Buck, recall if this wasn't the feeling.

Marshall: Isn't that strange. It *was* a feeling of no beginning and no end. There was a "we" feeling that was much more than the three months we had known each other. That's wonderful. It makes me wonder how many of our life experiences were greater than we thought.

**Gail at her high school graduation
2 years before we met.**

Exercise 73: Think back to the beginning of your relationship with your beloved deceased. No matter how it turned out to be later, write about the moment or the time when you first had an inkling that this person had a greater connection with you than this lifetime had provided. Do your best to write how you felt then.

Chapter 75

Our Anniversary and a New Way to Communicate

October 29th, 1996

Today is our anniversary. I do indeed miss Gail and very much wish she were here. But I'll wait to see if I feel her presence.

Many of our anniversaries we spent in Yosemite usually in our camper. Sometimes we would experience Yosemite's first snow. That was always exciting. We would take our roller skates (this was before roller blades) and skate around the upper end of the valley where they didn't allow cars. The paved trail from Mirror Lake to the Ahwanee was always especially fun as it sloped gently down hill for a long way. We would coast—not going too fast—past these magnificent tall trees and colored dogwood. Gail and I always took pleasure in how amused everyone else was to see us. Here we were two gray-haired people enjoying ourselves. We never saw anyone else roller skate there.

Gail and I always did things our own way. We decided to make our own wedding rings or more particularly that she would make mine and I would make hers. We wanted something very simple but made of gold. We were still going to college when we got married. Jan Walsh, a fellow student, was in charge of the craft workshop and she liked the idea and helped us make them. We bought some gold wire that was flat oval in cross section along with some gold solder. I think we bought two and one half inches worth. Jan showed us how to make the wire round and use the torch to solder the ends together. (Jan was the uneasy daughter of Pearl Buck who suffered greatly when Pearl wrote a book about Jan's childhood.)

Gail wore her ring until Rick took the ring off her lifeless finger the day she died. I kept mine on for about three years. In those days I was working as a carpenter. One day I was up on a roof taking off a long 2x4 piece of bracing. I partially pulled out the last 16 penny nail, picked up the 2x4 and gave it a heave off the roof. The head of the nail caught in my wedding ring. For a while I didn't know if I was going to be pulled off the roof or just my finger would be. Fortunately after giving my finger a great bruise the nail came loose and the 2x4 sailed off by itself.

I came home and told Gail about it. We both tried to pull the ring off but my knuckles had grown too big and neither ice nor oil did any good. I finally got out a hack saw and sawed it off. As you can imagine, this was not one of our better days of our marriage. I still have the rings of course. One sawed in two and the other small enough to fit inside. Those gold rings have unusual properties.

Many years later Gail and I were in Southern California at a beach festival with little stands set up selling all kinds of things. We wandered into a crystal booth. Gail found a lovely watermelon tourmaline crystal that was about an inch and a half long by three-eighths wide. It was a light amethyst in the middle and green at each end—thus the name "watermelon." It was nicely mounted in gold. I bought it for her and she felt good wearing it.

After she died I felt her ask me to get out both the rings and the crystal. Because I was into being open to any such prompting, no matter how nebulous, I did just that. I used the crystal as a pendulum with my elbow on the table and the crystal suspended from my fingers. I put her ring in the palm of my hand also steadied on the table, and held the crystal over it. Nothing happened, the crystal held steady. So I substituted my ring. Again nothing happened. Then I put her ring inside mine and put both in my palm. The crystal, which is not light, started to go in a circle directly above the two rings. Then it began to get energy and make an even bigger circle. I was dumbfounded as well as overjoyed. I feel she was telling me what we always believed, that we were indeed soul mates.

After watching fascinated for some time I wondered if I could ask questions that could be answered with a yes or no. Here was another surprise. I would ask a question and the ring would slowly stop and hover in the middle of the ring space. Then it would start to go side by side for what I assumed was no, or toward and away from me for yes. It would keep this up until I verbally acknowledged the answer as a yes or a no. Then it would go back to circle motion.

My scientific training, which Gail approved of, prompted me to find something fixed to rest my wrist on and see if it still worked. It did but the action was dampened somewhat. I then tried holding the crystal over a circular metal washer and see if I could deliberately, by moving my fingers, make the crystal go around in the same smooth circle. I could, but it was obvious I was moving my hand.

So now if I am undecided or want to feel assured about something I get out the rings and the crystal. Sometimes it will not answer me. Particularly if I am asking about the future. The ring will just stay motionless in the middle. If I then say, is that a question whose answer I should not know at this time, it will motion yes. I take it that these answers involve the lessons I need to learn myself.

Sweet Dear Beloved Buck,

A happy anniversary to you. I am so pleased you said today *is* our anniversary and not today would have been our anniversary. It *is* our anniversary. I am with you. There is no other place for me to be.

You are right about needing to learn your own lessons. As I have said before, we on this side cannot communicate to you information that would be the equivalent of doing your homework for you. You are still very much of the earth with your karmic lessons to be learned. We on this side cannot interfere with that. Often we have to leave you alone in your quandary because you need to figure out the lesson. This however does not prevent us from telling you principles of general wisdom that would apply to your particular quandary. Our giving you wisdom is different than you applying the wisdom. The latter is your job. Your application will demonstrate to you that you have absorbed the wisdom into your "own truth".

Our understanding on this side of the role of God's gift of free will influences much of what we do. We try to help you but never by interfering with your free will. You may be in the midst of what you regard as a trial and would like so very much to have your deceased one tell you what you should do. We see your dilemma and wish you the very best but cannot tell you how to solve that problem.

One very important instance of this is in regard to grieving. If you mire yourself down in grief and withdraw from your current life you will have created a problem for yourself. You should always engage in your current life as it is here that there are further lessons for you to learn. This is your homework which you should not ignore. When you choose to ignore it we cannot aid you in this avoidance. We cannot communicate with you if you will use it as an excuse to withdraw from life. Our communication cannot be substituted for living.

We *can* promote thoughts of applicable wisdom to occur to you. Whether you heed them or use them is up to you. *Only* by heeding them and seeing the result will you have an inkling as to where they came from.

If you *ask* for guidance and you are *listening,* we sometimes can be helpful to you. And if you were to ask for guidance whose primary purpose is to be helpful to others then we can very often be of assistance. I said primary because this can be mixed with wanting to help yourself. This is fine and does not diminish your desire to be helpful to others. When we give this kind of assistance it is often not obvious where the idea is coming from. We do this so you will feel it is your idea and will then incorporate this wisdom as your own. As teachers we want to have this happen.

Other times we allow our participation to be revealed to you. This is a function of how developed you are as a listener. It isn't so much that we allow it as it is a function of your individual ability to reach up and understand where it is coming from.

Exercise 74: Perhaps you can think of a way to receive messages from your beloved. All forms of communication can be valid. Different people respond in different ways. Finding out your way can be fun. Be willing to try each means at least three times before you give up on it.

Chapter 76

Picking Up Where We Left Off

October 30, 1996

All my widow friends tell me their anniversary is a very hard time for them. Strange, but it is not for me. I am thinking of the day we got married in Yellow Springs, Ohio. Gail had made her own wedding dress (It came down to just below the knee and was a beautiful russet color.) and we two had made our own wedding ceremony full of quotations from *The Prophet* by Kahil Gibran. My Uncle Ed (he was a minister) married us with avuncular concern for his headstrong nephew who insisted on marrying a three-month acquaintance, especially when his parents were away in Europe. He was a dear man and lived to see this marriage turn out after all.

When Gail and I first met, we were attending Antioch College in Yellow Springs, Ohio. Gail waited on tables at the college dining room. We noticed each other and started the usual small banter. I tried to sit at a table in her section so she could be my waitress. I asked my male friends who she was and they gave me her name. Furthermore, she was rich, frigid and a genius. They were dead wrong on two out of the three.

I called her up for a date as we did in those far away days of the late forties and she was busy. I tried again and she was busy. I decided to try one more time and if it didn't work to conclude that I had struck out for whatever reason and should move on. The third time it took and I was to pick her up at 6:00 to take her out to our local tavern for dinner. I was in her dorm at 6:00 sharp and I waited and waited. I have never found waiting easy and in those days keeping me waiting made me grumpy.

Yet thirty minutes later when she came down the stairs it flashed through my mind that I would marry her. Never had I had such an inner message before. She had been late because she had been delayed at work. She was working her way through college. Later I was to learn that she was a very punctual person.

She would insist that I also tell you about my wearing socks. At that time in my life, I usually wore tennis shoes or sandals with no socks. To my practical mind, socks just added unnecessarily to that difficult-to-get-done laundry list. The girls in Gail's dorm had decided that if I called for her not wearing socks my interest in her was casual. But if I arrived wearing socks that would mean I was serious about her. Totally unaware of this litmus test, I came wearing socks. When Gail came up the back door from work the girls all told her; "He's wearing socks!"

That first date was very interesting. Although we were each practiced at that game of presenting ourselves in our best light to a new date, we did just the opposite. We both went out of our way to reveal the truth about ourselves to the other. It was as though we wanted the other to know our true private selves in contrast to our public selves.

After our dinner we walked in the lovely spring dusk in the Glen, a semi-wild park adjacent to the campus. There I told her how much I liked animals and had worked with them. My favorite animal was the snake. Gail said she liked snakes too and as a child had had several for pets. Right then I knew we had something really good going. Three months after that date we were married and we did live happily ever after—even with all the arguments, disagreements, and fights.

Dear Date,

Do you know when we really got started? You found me wounded in the berry patch where I was attacked by a bear. You carried me to your tribe and your shaman stopped the bleeding and infection. I got well much to the surprise of the shaman. He told you I was one tough lady. You asked me to "become us." I still think that sounds better than asking "Will you marry me?" as people do now. Strong but gentle men were not in abundance so how could I resist? In fact you were the only gentle man I had ever known. When things didn't go well between us all you had to do was see that long scar below my neck and you would feel grateful I was alive. That lifetime gave us many lessons in being grateful. It got us off to a good start. And now there you are grateful that I no longer have any backaches. You are a dear.

Each succeeding life we have together we just pick up where we left off. You remember when I came down the stairs for our first date and the thought came to your mind that I was the one you would marry. This, in spite of my tardiness which was a real no-no for you. That was us picking up where we left off.

Exercise 75: If it feels right to you, pick up your pen and write about how, when and where you and your beloved first set eyes on each other. Did you feel something special right away? A special connection? Can you imagine any other lifetimes together with them? Describe what you think they might have been like.

Marshall at his high school graduation—age 17.

Chapter 77

In Between Lives

June 17, 1997

Tomorrow is the long awaited day when I am going to see Dr. Michael Newton. He will hypnotize me into the spiritual realm between lives. I'm concerned about being a good subject. Yes, I know, the more concerned I am the more likely I will be a poor subject. I've got to let go, be open and just let it happen. I can't imagine what it will be like. I understand that I will be able to remember afterwards what happened. I surely hope so. Anyway, it will be on tape.

June 19, 1997

Wow! What an experience. Here it is a day later and I still feel somewhat other worldly. Driving home from Dr. Newton's I felt kind of a super consciousness although I had no difficulty driving. It was just as if my awareness now included so much more. Things looked as if the light came from within them as well as reflecting the light of the sun.

The session itself was some three hours long. A good part of that time was spent taking me into what must be deep hypnosis. Dr. Newton said I was a good subject so I passed that test.

First he took me to my last life as a farmer in Sweden. I described my family with three boys and three girls and my wife Aida. I blurted out that I had tried to organize the farmers and what a waste of time that was. He asked me to go to the day I passed out of that life. I can still recall visually being in a hay field with a horse drawn wagon loading hay. I had had a heart attack and lay on the left side of the wagon rapidly dying. I was only forty.

I tried to communicate with my wife Aida (it was Gail) that I was going. She was in the kitchen but I couldn't get through to her. I then sent my thoughts upstairs to my eight-year-old daughter, Julia, who always had a feeling for the unseen. She was playing with her doll that I had made for her. She looked up immediately, heard me and rushed downstairs to her mother and brought her running out to the hay field.

I was already floating above when they came, falling down over me weeping. After several attempts I was able to communicate with Gail (Aida) that I was leaving. I told her how thankful I was to her for our life and that from the other side I would look out for her. I did this by projecting my thoughts in a beam to her third eye location on her forehead.

I sped away up through a golden glow. There were little points of light forming and disappearing around me, some quite close. One ahead of me grew larger and I flew to it. I soon saw a robed spiritual being. He looked at me with love that swept over me with rejuvenating energy. It felt wonderful. We moved off toward a group of people who greeted me. One was my guide. There were others there but no Gail! I was disappointed. I suspect my conscious mind had intervened briefly.

I should explain that Dr. Newton and others indicate that when we reincarnate, all of our energies do not come down to earth. There is part of us that stays in the spiritual realm. Some have called this our over self or over soul—Gail and I call it our inner self or higher self. So, just because Gail had survived me in Sweden, it didn't mean that she would not be available to meet me on the other side at the same time. We coexist in both realms.

Later I realized her not meeting me was validation that it was not my imagination that was telling me what was happening. If my imagination was at work Gail would have greeted me as I was expecting it.

It was Julie, my daughter at the time, who first greeted me as I passed over. And there was also a tall bearded man—I was unsure who he was at first. As it turned out, it was my inner or higher self and I merged with him. At that moment I felt a resurgence of energy and power.

I then went on to identify a number of those I was meeting, none of whom were Gail. It is strange how you know who someone is even if they look different and are of different age. It is very much like the dream state in which you just know where you are or who the other person is even if they don't visually look the same. The appearance is secondary.

Dr. Newton asked me what my spiritual name was. It was Hallus. I didn't like that name when I said it under hypnosis and don't like it now. I have no explanation for why I have a spiritual name I don't like. If my imagination were in charge I wouldn't have picked it out.

Our group drifted off in the direction of what I could see was a city. It was actually more like a town with spires and towers.

Some of those who greeted me moved away to do something else while my guide led me off to the side to a kiosk sitting in a woods. I entered to see a dozen others already seated around the edge. There was room for me to sit at what I described as 1:00 o'clock.

This was my soul group. We souls had worked and reincarnated together for quite some time serving an assigned purpose. Dr. Newton asked what this purpose was. I told him that we were together to learn, to be teachers.

He instructed me to try to identify each one in my group, tell their soul name, and see the color of their auras. There were members of my family including Grandma Stocking. She greeted me with the comment; "Didn't I tell you?" She had a deep yellow aura. Her spiritual name was Mowena. Others had names like, Mishwa, Lamda, Wansa, and Pomanda with auras of light yellow, yellow with emerald green, light blue, aqua blue, and blue with a lavender tint.

I had great difficulty in identifying the person at the 11 o'clock. Here is the transcription.

MN: Are they male or female?

MK: Male

MN: What color are they projecting?

MK: They are projecting a gold light that is not metallic. It is translucent, a yellowish gold.

MN: I take it this does not come through as a being who is in your current life or this past life in Sweden. Am I correct in this?

MK: Yes.

MN: But you have incarnated before with this individual?

MK: Oh yes.

MN: Go back to the life in which the two of you were together.

MK: It was in Rome. He and I served in the army together.

MN: Tell me this, Why has it been so long since the two of you have worked together in a life?

MK: It hasn't been. I've had other lifetimes with him. (Interrupted)

MN: But obviously it has been at lest two centuries, hasn't it?

MK: Yes it has.

MN: Are you absolutely sure, Hallus that he is not anyone in your current life? Take your time with this. Could he have been someone with whom you had meaningful contact? Search your mind for this.

MK: Hmmmm. (A long pause). Robert Stirling, my piano teacher!

MN: Very good. Why do you think he chose that body to be with you while you studied piano?

MK: He wanted to open my mind to the creative impulses that are within all of us.

MN: Good. There you go.

This was very strange because I hadn't thought of Bob Stirling in 40 years. He was my (only) piano teacher for two years. I can thank him for introducing me to Bach among other things. I really liked him. When he would be practicing for an organ recital I used to come to watch him play. His work on the foot console just amazed me. The organ sound of Bach in the empty church was celestial.

I would go to his house for the lessons and often stay after the lesson to have tea and conversation. He was Scottish and proud of it. We would talk of many things. It is only now that I realize that his role in my life was to introduce me to the arcane. He talked of the Scottish rites and temple meanings. He opened my mind to this kind of thought although I did not take it seriously until much later.

When Dr. Newton asked me who was immediately on my left at the 12:00 position I choked up and started to cry with joy. It was Gail! I hugged her. She looked so good. Dr. Newton let me enjoy that for a while and then asked me what Gail's spiritual name was. Alleusha I replied. I think that is a beautiful name. Her aura was purple lavender. Today I discovered that this is the aura of great advancement, primarily in wisdom but love and tolerance also. Dr. Newton wanted to know what percentage of Gail's energy she had put in her incarnation as Aida. This is the transcript. I include this to show that I didn't necessarily go along with his suggestions, but countered him if it was not what I was seeing.

MN: Tell me Hallus, how much of Gail's energy, who after all is Aida at the moment in terms of the life you just left, was left behind. And how much is in her body in terms of percentages? What are we seeing?

MK: Oh my, she's just a small percentage down there in Aida, very small.

MN: Really. In other words like (interrupted)

MK: Most of her is up here.

MN: She's only about 30% down there?

MK: Even less than that, 10%

MN: Really, Really (surprised). Maybe it would be more accurate to say 15%.

MK: It seems like only the small 10%.

MN: It is. Is it possible she's living in another body on earth at this time, where her energy is off somewhere else?

MK: I wouldn't think so.

MN: How much of your energy Hallus did you have as Ayoh in Sweden?

MK: I had more than she did—like 15%

MN: More like 15%. Now, why do you think there are those differences? Why did she leave more of her energy behind? Why did you feel it was necessary for you to take a little more of your energy to earth?

MK: Well I think it was because I had more to learn?

MN: Okay. Good.

When my soul group finished with the Kiosk we moved off toward some buildings on the mountain which looked like the monasteries in Tibet. They are kind of an outgrowth of the mountains themselves. They were beautifully sited—beautifully sited! The message they emitted was that they were all *one*, united, that man and nature together are *one* and they build as *one*.

I was taken to the Council of Elders. This council is a group of spiritual beings. " Once or twice between lives we visit this group of higher beings who are a step or two above our teacher guides." Their number varies but is likely to be between seven and twelve. In Destiny of Souls, Dr. Newton writes, "The Council of Elders is not a tribunal of judges nor a courtroom where souls appear to be tried." "Members of the council want to talk to us about our mistakes and what we can do to correct negative behavior in the next life."

I seated myself in front of seven elders sitting at a semi circular table. They were dressed in diaphanous robes that I noticed had no shadows in the folds. They emitted a soft purple light that shifted in color and intensity. My guide was standing behind me. I felt in no sense that I was being judged but welcomed and helped. I felt we all shared, myself included, this objective but loving interest in how this being, Hallus, had done in this past life. They seemed interested in my mistakes, not as something to be reprimanded or even changed, but as a measure of where I was on the path.

Dr. Newton asked if the center elder had an emblem hanging around his neck. He stated that if I could see it that would mean that I would know its meaning. The elder did and it was a fattened triangle with the point down. The two upper points of the triangle represented aspiration. The whole emblem symbolized completion. In the middle of the triangle was a carved piece of amber with an abstract figure that I couldn't make out, other than it was oval shaped. On the top of the triangle was an emerald. He asked me its meaning and I replied that the amber represented life on the material plane and all the planes above it that had not reached the Godhead. The two points represented the aspirations of the amber to reach the Godhead. The emerald was the healing that occurs upon unification of the soul with the Godhead. Thus the overall meaning was "completion."

Dr. Newton asked if any of the elders was telling me anything. Indeed they were. In the past I had not trusted my inner self enough. I was now learning to do that. I will advance more rapidly now. They are promising that once I open the door it will move fast. They advised me not to be afraid of it.

I was advised that I needed to work on acceptance and letting go. There was no need for me to try to make the world into what I thought it ought to be. Through acceptance will I find perfection. The elder whose principle was acceptance pointed out that all of our lives are but learning situations so what difference did it make what exercises I or anyone else had to go through? Instead, he said, pay attention to what it is they are trying to teach us. Why be a rebellious student?

I needed next to realize that I harbored too much concern about what people will think. I am afraid to move forward with the instructions I have received because people will think that I made all this stuff up.

Dr. Newton asked if the elders felt I was enough of a risk taker to get past that. "Yes, they do. That's why they chose me for the task." (I didn't know what task they were talking about. Only now do I realize it might be this book.)

Promising to come back to the council of elders, Dr. Newton took me to the projection room where one chooses the next life. In this case the life that I am now living. I chose my parents because "my father was traditional and practical and this provided me with a pedestal to reach for the creative which was my mother's virtue." I thus would receive both influences.

It was understood that Gail was to be my wife for the "continuity of loving each other and to stimulate each other in our spiritual growth and patterns." Alleusha would be encouraging me to be patient and I would give strength and creativity to Alleusha. This was very integral to our relationship and we knew this from the beginning.

We went back to questions about the activities of my soul group—we were making music together, music that we were composing as we went along. Dr. Newton asked what kind of music it was. I said it was much like earth music with lovely melodies but it was all played without the emotions of earth music (such as nostalgia and longing). It had only high aspirations as you sometimes hear in Bach's compositions.

This led Dr. Newton to ask if there is an emotion of the soul or is the soul emotionless.

MK: "The soul does not have earthly emotions. We have a love that is altogether different."
MN: In what way is it different?
MK: It makes no demands. It does not require the satisfaction of a response from the other person. It is love that you give out and that is all you need. It is complete in and of itself. It does not require the other person to respond, although they do. It is very warm.

We went next to other soul group activities. It surprised me when I said, "We meditate to contact our higher selves even here." Dr. Newton asked me some questions about my teaching creativity and asked what idea was I most gifted in conveying:

MK: Structure. Structure on earth is just an outward manifestation of the inner divine structure. When they talk about God being the grand architect of the universe the word is chosen wisely. He has structured the universe in a most intriguing, complex and wonderful manner. It is beautiful to see how it is structured so it all fits together without any voids, any errors. It is lovely to see, beautiful to see.

Next we returned to the Council of Elders:
MN: Did you feel a "presence" there beyond the elders?

MK: Yes.

MN: Describe it to me.

MK: It is God in all his glory

MN: Can you tell me why God, who is already perfect, needs to create imperfect beings in order to evolve toward perfection?

MK: God is love. Love is creation. So therefore God has to create just as we have to create when we get there. It all fits together.

At this point I choked up. I went off on a journey of my own which I recall with great vividness even though it occupies only a few seconds on the tape. I went up to a high elevation where I felt I could see forever. I felt like I became part (part is the wrong word but I can think of no other) of the All that is One, observing the dynamics of the universe. I was overcome with the knowledge of how it all fits together to perfection. It seemed like what some might call "cosmic consciousness."

Very little of this got on the tape. As I listened to the tape later, I realized that under hypnosis you do answer the hypnotist's questions but that much else is going on of which you are aware but don't articulate. Sometimes you tell the hypnotist about it but most of the time you just experience it without vocalization.

Dr. Newton brought the session to a close by asking if my inner self ever went to other places, other universes, other realms. I replied that I loved going to the planet Uranus. I described it as a very spiritual place from which one could view much more of the universe. I described it as a portal from which I could and did travel to many other worlds.

I hardly know what to make of all that. I recall the entire session quite vividly. I recall the surprise I felt when my mouth was uttering things I didn't expect or were contrary to what I had previously thought to be true.

I am impressed with the fact that at times I seem to be agreeing easily to what he suggested and other times when I just plain wouldn't accept what he said and came up with my own independent statement. He suggested that the amber in the emblem on the elder represented strength and courage. I disagreed and said that it represented all of the planes below the Godhead. This, of course, is a totally different idea. Once I remember telling him flatly that he was wrong. So I conclude that what transpired was neither Michael Newton nor my conscious mind. It was something else.

Dear Buck,

Your home is really here in the spirit world. When you go to earth or some other venue it is as if you have gone off to boarding school and have left your home and family behind. This is ameliorated somewhat by the fact that some of your family members go with you. By this, I mean that members of your spiritual group also reincarnate and weave in and out of your life. You don't recognize them specifically but you feel a rapport with them.

Like at boarding school, your sojourn on earth has the purpose of learning. You have teachers who are especially trained to teach. You are put into an environment that is designed to promote your best learning. The good students enter into this fully and learn a great deal. However this does not change the fact that the school is not home. Home is home. So too is this spirit world home. You feel this strongly when you pass over. It is a real homecoming. As with summer vacation from school you remember your friends and may even write or call them—but you are home.

While you are home it gives you a chance to digest the data and information that you learned at school. When it is time to go back to school, hopefully you feel refreshed and ready to go back and learn even more. The school is a place that provides you with unique learning opportunities. It is true you can learn at home as well but you learn different things at home than you do at school.

Your lives at school are like your lives on earth. Your experiences on earth provide you with the stimulus to grow in a manner that is unique and unavailable generally here in the spirit world. This is why I ask you to cherish your moments on earth. When you come home you will have the opportunity to amalgamate the experiences you gained into your total being, into your higher self.

You do eventually graduate from boarding school and no longer need to return to it. In time however you may elect to go back to the boarding school as a teacher. This too parallels what occurs. Some are chosen and choose to return to earth to help. These are advanced beings with specific roles to play. They may or may not appear to be outstanding people. It depends on what best serves the roles they play.

Here we should leave the metaphor because in this earth/spirit world life each teacher and each student are not clearly separated. They are all *one*. At this time of the millennium there are an unusual number of these advanced beings who have reincarnated. There is much to be done in a short period of time. There is considerable concentration of beings and thoughts to carry out the transition to what we call the "new millennium." You can take heart in this.

You can also take heart that you will be returning home yourself and that this homecoming will feel good. You can also feel a bit of your home while you are on earth. The rain that you hear if you are quiet and still, will induce in you a feeling of what it is like to be home, home on this spirit side. There are a number of sounds that will carry this same feeling of being home. A sense of beauty as in contrast to viewing a specific beautiful thing will also bring this appreciation. Sometimes you can be in a group, a family or otherwise, and sense a great feeling of oneness that is without threat or tension. This will give you a great sense of home-ness.

Everyone has sensed a restlessness within them that they don't understand. It is simply homesickness— homesickness for your spirit world where you belong. You need to be patient and do the work the boarding school requests of you. You can, however, seek and feel the wonderful sense of being home that is available to you.

Let's also talk about family. We all know what a family is on earth. However there is further meaning to the word family. It is true, as it is written in many places, that we tend to reincarnate with the same group of souls. Seldom is this done in every lifetime but nonetheless it occurs frequently. The reason for this is that the preliminaries in forming a relationship are already done. The souls then can get right to the higher level lessons and experiences that are appropriate.

This association of souls can be called your spiritual family. Within that family you will find a number of special purpose groups. You and I belong to a learning teaching group. It would not do to have the spiritual family be composed of just one group. You need a variety of groups each with their own special contribution to the advancement of the spiritual family. Again using the body analogy, the body needs muscle, bone and stomach. All stomach wouldn't work. These group representations within the spiritual family fluctuate as the need in the lifetime episodes changes.

By the way, why should you now not like your spiritual name, Hallus, that for quite sometime you lived amicably with? It is because you have in this lifetime transformed yourself into something beyond what you were. Your spiritual name is no longer appropriate. You already have a new name. Hallus was from after your last life and before this one and therefore is not necessarily your current name.

Have you ever wondered why we have such a fascination with names? Names of course are labels. We give labels a power they *don't* have and then we don't recognize the power they *do* have. We think when we label something that somehow we know it when in fact we only know it very superficially. On the other hand labels and names do carry a power.

There is a vibration between a name and the thing named. One affects the other and back again. We all either like our names or dislike our names. The simple explanation is that someone who dislikes his or her name really is saying they don't like themselves. There is some truth to this but it goes beyond that. Sometimes you outgrow your name and are ready for another.

When one tries to integrate with their name but it doesn't work, it is often because they are trying to stretch the name too far to fit their person. It is then best to adopt another name. Often people will choose their middle name rather than their first name. Or they may just make up a name they would prefer to be called. This is a good thing to do, to choose a name with which you feel compatible. It is important to feel harmonious with your name.

If you pick another more appropriate name for who you are, you will find that you have increased power. This will manifest in you feeling and being more effective in what you want to do. This is why most people love their nicknames. They feel themselves truly recognized for who they are when called by their nicknames.

I felt much better with my last name when I took yours. It was of course partly romantic but it also felt like a dress that fit very well. I felt in harmony with it the rest of that life. Now I am back to my spiritual name—Alleusha.

Exercise 76: Ponder the possibility that life on earth is similar to being at boarding school. How does that change your view of what happens to you and the important people in your life? Write down your thoughts on this. And if you do not like you name, consider what name you would choose for yourself instead. It could be you have grown out of it.

Chapter 78

Ashes to Ashes

July 22, 1997

It was time to take Gail's remaining ashes up to the Sierras. I asked Gordon to go with me because since he had been in Poland, he had been left out on Gail's dying day. We loaded sleeping bags and food into my pickup truck and took off. We were headed to that spot where Gail and I often went. We had both agreed that we would like our ashes left there when the time came. It was at a kopje—a South African name for a large pile of rocks and soil that stands out on a relatively level plain—I know of no English word for it.

This kopje is about sixty feet high at its highest point. It has quite a number of ancient western juniper trees on it. These trees grow to be very old like the bristlecone pine. They also look like them but not as exaggerated. They have similar dead weathered branches on the living trees. By ring count, one three-inch diameter branch was determined to be four hundred years old.

The place seemed timeless. It was also off the beaten path so it should remain undisturbed. Carrying Gail's ashes in the wood box I had made for them, Gordon and I climbed up to where Gail and I often sat and meditated. It was a small sheltered flat spot with nice rocks to lean against.

After sitting quietly for some time, we placed Gail's ashes and then took turns speaking of our memories of her. It was tearful. After more silence we left with a longing in our hearts.

My Husband,

I remember when we first saw the kopje, we just had to climb on it. I stopped to hug one of the venerable western juniper trees and immediately felt the presence of a wise old Indian. It seemed as if he welcomed me to his sacred place. I felt honored. We then climbed about and found that small level spot, where we sat down in the warm fall sun and meditated. Remember how holy it felt? We went back there many times afterward and always felt the special vibrations. One time higher up you found that spot under the branches that made a fine lookout for hunting. You climbed in there as if you had

done it many times. You looked and acted like an Indian, your eyes darting everywhere. I felt my love go out to you then. I had a deep but vague sense of the many wilderness lifetimes we had had together.

Perhaps that was why we decided that the kopje was where we would like our ashes to be when the time came. The ashes themselves are meaningless but the mind is always the builder. If we put into the ashes a meaning, a symbol, a love— then it is so—just as it is with our other illusions. Thank you for taking my ashes there. I enjoy the little animals and birds picking through my ashes for the minerals they contained. I am glad to give my bones as mineral supplements to those dear little beings.

We made that place sacred by our thoughts. In truth the place was already sacred by the thoughts of others previous to us, including Ha-tee-she who was the old Indian who greeted me. There are many sacred places in the world, made so by souls that loved them. That sacredness can be felt by others who are open to feeling it. However, it does require that you feel your own sacredness in order to attune to the sacredness of others and their sacred places. May you walk in peace.

Marshall: When I went to the kopje a year later I noticed that Gail's ashes had been stirred up with little beaks and paws. The creatures left the larger pieces. Gail painted these little birds below.

Exercise 77: Is there a place that you and your departed one felt was especially yours? Write about the first time you were there and realized that it was in someway in harmony with you both.

Chapter 79

A Conversation with Gail!

November 12, 1997

I have just come back from another A.R.E.(Edgar Cayce's Association for Research and Enlightenment) conference at Asilomar. I had a chance to talk to Betty Middlemiss (see Chapter 62) about having a session to see if we could contact Gail. Betty is a very nice lady and we set up an appointment for the first part of January after the holidays.

January 13, 1998

Tomorrow is the day I go to see Betty Middlemiss to try and contact Gail. I'm excited about it. Gordon, our oldest son, is going with me. I am trying not to have expectations but it is hard. I need to let happen what will happen.

January 15^{th,} 1998

Yesterday we went to Betty's. It was fascinating. Different than I expected. She let us tape it. There seemed to be quite a time before she sensed anything. Finally she felt like Gail or someone was near and asked us if we felt it too. Gordon and I both answered yes. I did feel Gail's presence come just like a soft breeze.

    I transcribed what was said. Betty spoke as herself and as Gail. It was not difficult to tell which was which. Here are some excerpts. Gail's words are in bold. If I couldn't understand something I put in a series of periods. What is in brackets identifies the speaker or was added later.

[Betty] It is January 14, 1998 with Marshall Kent and his son Gordon.
[Some time passes with nothing happening.]
Do you feel the emotional energy right now? Do you feel the emotional response?
[Gail] **What JOY, What JOY I feel.**
[Betty] I'm assuming this is Gail. You can respond if you want to.
I'm overwhelmed with this feeling of joy. Welcome. We hope that you have something for us—will make us all happy and will be

helpful. I'm again just overwhelmed with this feeling of joy. Are any of you picking up on this? Wonderful, wonderful. Well we are assuming you are here Gail. Your thoughts are here, which if you're not better correct us.

We'll turn the floor over to you and if you want to speak through me I will be happy to send the message. If you want to send personal thoughts that's okay too. The advantage of speaking through me is that it gets onto the tape. I'm telling you this is one powerful lady because she sure has some strong energy and you don't always feel the energy this strongly. (Betty told me later that in all her years of doing this work she has never had a communicating entity express such joy.)

[Gail] **I have been with you so many times and I have watched you, and loved you, but this is a special occasion where we can hear. The sound of speech is so PRECIOUS. We don't treasure it enough, consciously anyway. Oh please speak to me, let me hear your voices addressing me.**

[Gordon]: I'm so glad you're here Gail. It's wonderful.

[Betty] Thank you Gordon, thank you—and Marshall?

[Marshall]: I remember the Theilhard de Chardin quotation about joy that we loved: "Joy is the most infallible sign of the presence of God." Gail, I love you.

[Gail] **I love you too. I do. I always will forever. ...I am very active here. It took me a while to adjust to the manner of communication and accomplishment but I am working and I'm busy. And I'm learning. Isn't that exciting to know that we can learn? You know how much we loved learning.**

[Gordon] Yes it is. [Marshall] (microphone not picking me up)

[Gail] **We learn together. While you learn I learn and hopefully now you can learn from me too. This is indeed a meaningful purposeful existence. It's not just a happenstance. It's meaningful. Everything is purposeful, meaningful and so rather than get bogged down in regrets, joyously embrace the experience as meaningful, purposeful. These words are very, very familiar to Betty. She uses them in her work. But I want to emphasis them for you and also as a little gift of validation for her.**

[Gordon] Thank you Gail. I've often thought about that since you died. It's nice to hear you confirm it .

[Gail] **We do get very attached to the physical body, the physical plane and that is as it should be because we can** function better when we're really invested in the experiences that we're having. But we should always keep the little objective witness in our minds that is telling us this is not all there is. There is so much more.

We ARE spiritual beings. I'm telling you this now from actually knowing it not just from believing it, but *knowing* it. And the physical experiences we have are ones that we are unable to have sometimes in the other dimension. So treasure everything, every experience you have, everything you learn, every relationship. Treasure all those things because that physical vehicle that you occupy is what allows you to have these experiences. What I experience here is very fine but it is different. So don't rush yourselves through the physical experiences in order to get to this dimension. SAVOR EVERY MOMENT.

And now I'm going to borrow from Betty again because another word she likes to use is giving your consent— another phrase. Give your conscious consent for the experiences you have, even the painful ones, something you really don't want. Give your consent to work through that experience. It totally changes the energy. Now Betty don't get nervous because I am using your words.

[Betty]...........I like her.

[Gail] Well it's really nice to have had a physical experience and all those you've left behind telling you they love you.

[Betty] She really hasn't left you behind. We are all part of this life, this one life and we're all part of it but sometimes we use an earth-suit, like they use a space suit when they go to the moon. Our bodies are like our earth-suits. We couldn't function without them.

[Gail] This is a wonderful, wonderful experience of life. I am even more overwhelmed with it where I am now than when I was in my physical suit. It's just overwhelming to try to understand or even see how it comes to be. This life experience in the physical body and then the transition back into spirit without the physical body. But I still have a body, I want you to know that. I have a spiritual body and sometimes when we get very advanced on this plane we can even show it. It takes a lot of energy but we can do that. I don't know whether I can do that or not. And I need to use the energy I have right now in reaching out to you. So I'm not going to do a lot of experimenting. I may do that later. I'm so grateful, I'm so grateful that I can reach you. ...

[Betty] Oh Gail, Thank you for coming. I appreciate it very much too.

[Gordon] Me too because many times I've thought all the thoughts that you said today. I felt they were true but I wasn't always 100% sure. But everything you've said today, Gail, is confirming something that I've thought...

[Gail] **Marshall here is a thought for you. When you have a...**

[Betty] Did she used to call you Marshall?

[Marshall] No.

[Betty] Because it didn't seem comfortable to me.

[Marshall] No she didn't.

[Betty] I wanted to check that out because I'm calling you Marshall but it doesn't seem like her way of doing it. Okay...I don't know if I can find out what she called you. Don't tell me. Maybe it will come up. I feel her energy is waning a bit now.

[Gordon] I love you Gail, thank you for all you've done for me.

[Marshall].....................

[Gail] **I couldn't have had a more wonderful experience than this last one. When it comes to family and being responsive and loving and having a strong desire to grow together. I look forward to the time when we WILL be together again but I don't want you to hold off on anything waiting for that. I want you to go ahead and live the rest of this life and any other lives you have with gusto, with commitment, joy and confidence because when we do come together again it will be as though no time has passed.**

So the time seems long while we're experiencing it now but remember it is just like the blink of an eye. ...Oh Betty, thank you, thank you and thank you...Thank you Betty for making this possible.

Exercise 78: Imagine if you were to have a conversation with your departed loved one today. Write down how you think it would go. If you stay open, perhaps they will reveal themselves to you.

Chapter 80

Seeking Validation

January 15, 1998

The session with Betty was wonderful. When we were driving home, Gordon said it seemed as though Gail was addressing him more than me. I agreed. I had the same sense.

I confess that I was hoping to have a hard validation that it was Gail. If Betty had been able to hear from Gail that my nickname was Buck, I would have been blown away. However, she didn't. But for me that doesn't invalidate what was said. That Betty even sensed that Marshall was not what Gail called me was a pretty strong piece of soft validation. I don't think we should expect an imitation of our earthly verbal communication. We simply have not learned how to communicate with the other side with the surety of a phone call.

Some of what she said we had talked about when she was here. I certainly felt the thoughts expressed were Gail even if at times it seemed the syntax was more like Betty than Gail. This latter is to be expected.

I was very pleased with the results. I liked the statement, **"We learn together. While you learn I learn and hopefully now you can learn from me too."** I hope that means that in future sessions with Betty I can ask some deep questions. (Buck's Note: Remember this is several years before Gail started writing through me.)That is just as Gail would have said it. It is also an idea that she would very much want to convey to us.

It seems to me that communicating with those on the other side involves overcoming that threshold that is between us, the veil. Being a negative skeptic would increase the height of that threshold. Other factors can increase or decrease that threshold. Betty's talent obviously decreases the height of the threshold. Transmitting soft validation has a lower threshold than transmitting hard validation. I suspect that if one has a great need for comfort from someone who has passed on this would decrease the threshold. Also if one does not have a great need for comfort that it can in effect raise the level of the threshold. Applied to myself I already feel a great deal of comfort from Gail and in truth do not feel that she is far from me. This may explain why there was not hard validation.

I know that scientists, in general, don't support the concept of psychic phenomena. This has always struck me as being very unscientific to assume something is not simply because it has not been scientifically proven to be. After all, every day reveals new knowledge that we did not possess yesterday. For instance, throughout most of mankind's history electricity was not proven to exist. To conclude it therefore didn't exist is foolish by hindsight.

My Dear Buck,

You on earth do not know how psychic events are made manifest. From a scientific point of view it is all very fuzzy. Being so fuzzy, all sorts of true and false events are hard to separate. Because some people act as if they are psychic when they are not, some scientists like to throw the baby out with the bath water and call all psychic events fraudulent.

Let us compare your five senses to the four forces [as in physics]. First you can say that sight and the electromagnetic force are associated by their common use of the photon. The comparison is only an analogy, not an attempt to connect the senses and forces in some way. We will use feel and taste as sharing some of the characteristics of the strong and the weak nuclear forces. If we could not feel, the material world would not be of much use. Also the strong nuclear force is what makes the material world manifest for us to feel. The sense of taste like the weak nuclear force is very important but it comes into play only in special circumstances. Similarly let us associate the sense of sound with gravity because each is very sensitive to distance.

Now we have a problem. Where does the sense of smell fit in? At present there is no force left over to associate it with. This is where the analogy begins. If we had no sense of smell how could we ever figure out how to make a detector to be sensitive to smell? We wouldn't know where to begin. Not being able to smell, we wouldn't know what smell was. We would have no idea there was such a thing in our universe.

This analogy points us to the question, if there is another force or two out there but our limiting sensing devices are not "smell" sensitive, how are we ever going to find out about those forces? Dark matter or dark energy may consist of particles that respond only to, say, the fifth force, much as the

neutrino only has eyes for the weak nuclear force. We cannot detect those particles because we cannot conceive of how to build a detector to detect them.

Now this problem of there being more forces than four is not new to scientific thinkers. Nor is the conundrum of how to build a detector of this force if you don't know what you are trying to detect. But here I would like to pile another analogy on top of this one. Psychic events of all types share this same difficulty.

Just as it is hard to grasp a new undetected force, it is hard to understand how telepathy works when it seems to do so outside of our normal purview. But it does work and some open unbiased (either way) investigation would be most enlightening. However, it needs to be understood from the beginning that your current procedures and methods are inadequate and off the mark to bring light to the problem. This is why psychic events are currently regarded as being unproven scientifically. They are there; it is just that the scientific apparatus and scientific procedures are not adequate for what you are trying to detect.

Science would be well served if they were more open to what has not yet been proven to be false. All areas in which human knowledge can be expanded are worthy of scientific examination without prejudice as to the outcome. To understand the dynamics of psychic events would be a great boon to mankind. It would provide a whole new group of tools with which to communicate, discover, and utilize.

Exercise 79: If you have trouble believing in psychic phenomena, ask yourself why you don't believe in it. Write down all the reasons why you think it is impossible. Then write down all of the underlying assumptions you would have to have that would make psychic activities impossible.

Chapter 81

Whose Thoughts are We Thinking?

January 28th, 1998

Since my meeting with Betty Middlemiss, I have been thinking a lot about all of this. With all these channels, messages, and even statements made under hypnosis, I think that there is an unintentional alteration of the message by the receiver. I think God designed it that way so that we can take nothing from somebody else as pure truth. We must seek our own truth. We cannot abdicate that responsibility by getting truth from outside of ourselves. We can and should get suggestions, stimulus, ideas, and potential directions from others. These we must reject or assimilate as we become aware of our truth. Our path, however, is our own.

The same thing would apply here to the reading with Betty Middlemiss. It would also apply to what I believe I am at times receiving directly from Gail.

The main point here however is not whether we have 100% absolutely true information from a superior source. It is the content of the message that we must receive with an open mind. We must appraise its value to us and others and absorb the truth it contains for us. We should withhold judgment on that which we don't find so compelling and see if later experiences reveal further truth to us.

This brings up the issue of source versus content, which many people have difficulty with. In today's information age we are inundated with information on top of information. People competing for our attention to buy their product or to give them this or that further bury us. One of our greatest tools in getting through all of this and selecting that which we need or want is to look at the source. If it is a source we have learned to have some trust in we will pay attention to what this source provides. Otherwise we are reluctant to seriously consider those other clamoring voices.

While this approach is very necessary to live in today's world, it has its costs. When our judgment about things becomes too dependent upon its source then the actual content of what we are considering takes a back seat. We forget it is the quality and truth of the content, not the wrapping it comes in, that determines whether what we absorb from it is beneficial. In other words, we need the peel of the banana to tell it is a banana but we shouldn't forget that it is what is inside without the peel that nourishes us. Ideally we should evaluate only the content for its wisdom, irrespective of its source. We cannot necessarily do this with ease, but we should nevertheless keep in mind our true goal.

If the focus on the source ends up unduly controlling our thoughts, we become close minded and deprived of new ideas from other new sources. One way out of this dilemma is to first realize that we are becoming source-dependent and that this is a good tool most of the time. However, we want to realize that those areas of our thought which are important to our life require that we deliberately look to new sources with an open mind to receive the stimulus we need to grow. We cannot evolve or learn if we will not bring new things into our thought processes.

Those who like to debunk psychic phenomena use the logic that if you disprove one part of an event then the whole thing is false. Thus if I suggest that some of the above is Betty and not Gail, they would say it disproves it all. This is not scientific. To prove that one star does not have a planet does not prove that all stars are without planets.

The fact that it appears to me that some of what comes through Betty is more Betty than Gail in no way counters other material as being pure Gail. We just don't have much understanding of what is going on.

[Marshall's later note: According to Sidney D. Kirkpatrick's *Edgar Cayce, An American Prophet* (page 255), even Edgar Cayce's "source" indicated something similar. In a reading Cayce stated, "Edgar Cayce is in the state of being guided by the individual who makes the suggestions, and so long as the suggestions are in accord and the mind of the individual is kept in accord [the information will be correct]." In other words, he was saying that what was held in the mind of the person conducting the reading and the person requesting the help or information would effect the result.

My Dear,

To understand psychic phenomena, it is necessary to understand that all of your thoughts are actually dual as to their source. You think your thoughts are solely yours, generated only by you. Only on special occasions such as this

do you feel that someone else is entering your thoughts. Right now my thoughts and your thoughts are going through your mind. So here you have thoughts that have two sources, yours and mine. Surprisingly, this is true of all thoughts that you have and that anyone else has—all of the time. It does not occur only on special occasions.

In truth, all thoughts have dual sources. The first source is the thinker who generates an idea, a thought form, or a simple thought. This thought by its very nature attracts to it similar thoughts that have been generated by others. These can be higher thoughts, if the thinker's original thought is so attuned, or unfortunately, lower thoughts, if the original thought is so attuned. The second source of thoughts we will call the contributor.

Although the two sources sharing the thinker's thought do not necessarily go by percentages, it nonetheless helps illustrate what goes on. Right now, for instance, we are having a 50-50 dialog. I'm doing the talking but your half involves following what I'm saying with a comprehending thought. If you were to do inspired writing I would be contributing more like 80 percent of the thought. This is because you would be starting the writing with a blank agenda so that I can take over with the subject and where I'm going with it. Your thoughts continue to be in the low twenties because you make no attempt to understand my overall message. You only try to set down the words and the phrases as they come to you in small segments. As we begin to practice this inspired writing we will get better at it. Getting better at it means I am contributing a still higher percentage and you correspondingly less.

As I said, percentages are not a complete analogy. There are times when my contribution hits a resonance in your thoughts. Then your thoughts and my thoughts are one and the same. In this case you cannot say that it is your thought *or* my thought.

Scientists, some of whom would blanch at the thought, also have the same duality in their thoughts. They have their own generated thought which then tunes into thoughts that are out there and they come up with new and better ideas. Since all thoughts share this duality of source, we therefore haven't known anything else. Thus we regard this as the normal thought process—which it is. There is no way we can compare it to a non-dual thought because there is no such thing.

This all follows as a natural consequence of our *oneness*. Our thoughts have to be part of the One. Being *one*, we are sharing our thoughts all the time and don't even know it. Since we are all *one* with spiritual beings as well as human beings we can also share the thoughts of these spiritual beings. In a way that is what you are doing with me right now.

People who are psychic are those who are able to diminish what their own mind contributes and allow other entities, thought patterns, etceteras to come into their thought process. Most psychics and channelers cannot get their thoughts to be 100% from another entity. It may be 95% or 80% or even much lower like 60%. When it gets down to 30% the message is pretty contaminated with the thinker's own viewpoint and wishes. This latter explains why there is much out there that is not very high-grade material. But do not judge that harshly. They are all trying. They need practice and show courage in trying to develop themselves. It does, however, point out the wisdom that you never should accept someone else's truth. You should evaluate the contents, accept what seems valid and reject the rest, thus creating your own truth.

And there is another reason for working with content versus source. I know that you would like it if you knew for sure that what is contained in these inspired writings was one hundred percent me with no inadvertent altering by you. If you were sure of this then you could just accept completely what is written as the truth. If the source were pure me then you would adopt it without much question. But this would be short-cutting your own truth-finding process. This is not the way to develop your own truth.

All spiritually inspired ideas and writings are contaminated to a greater or lesser degree by the receiver or the channel. This serves a divine purpose of bringing the student back to searching and evaluating the content.

What our group over here is working on is how advanced teachers can provide a learning environment that will cause the student to receive, to digest, and to create his or her own truth. How can the material be presented so that simple adoption is not substituted for true learning?

Teachers can't just lay out the teachings, hoping that the students will pick up what they feel advances their own truth, because the students have a problem. They have a tendency to accept "wholesale" the teachings of a teacher they respect. Such short-cutting does not build one's own truth. It attaches another's truth.

You have, therefore, this strange situation wherein the greater the teacher the more likely the student is to respect their views and adopt them simply because of their source. But it is the content that needs to be digested. Digestion properly infers a process that is not instantaneous. It is by digesting the teachings that they become your own just as it is with food.

This long process will create within the student his or her own truth, which is far stronger, far wiser than would have been the quick adoption of the thoughts of a beloved teacher. The long process will leave the student eager and ready to pursue the next level of learning. The short process will result in the student being confused and discouraged by the next level of teaching. Do you see this?

Exercise 80: Have you ever experienced times when you discovered that other people were having the same thoughts and ideas as you, right around the same time? This certainly helps explain how different scientists can be coming up with similar discoveries at the same time. Perhaps they are tapping into the same thought source. Write a description of an event that sticks out in your mind as a good example of dual thinking.

Chapter 82

Through a Glass Darkly

March 15th, 1998

I have long considered how it is that our mind works. It seems as if it breathes. We have our own home-made filter which determines what we breath in. We also have a self-created grid that shapes what our mind breathes out. So we have a filter/grid system through which we relate to the outside world. It determines who we are. If we change our filter/grid system we change ourselves.

I think it functions like this. As I receive data from all sources and from all my senses, my filter automatically takes over and excludes some data and allows other data in. For example, my political beliefs will welcome that data which supports my views. It will pass through my filter with no trouble. However that data which does not support my views I am more likely to filter out.

Based on what I have allowed in and how I have digested it, I now impose it upon the world and say, "This is my understanding of my world and my place in it." This understanding of my world is my grid, which I impose upon the world. Like the filter this is self-generated and uniquely me. The world that I feel I act in is in fact this grid. For a quick example, a paranoid person has a grid that tells him the world is out to get him specifically. This is not the actual world but his grid that he imposes upon the world and stamps it as true. We all do this, each in our own way.

The two facets of the filter/grid system work like this. We breathe in data, filter it and this affects our grid. When we breath out we impose this grid on the world which then affects our filter and what we next allow ourselves to breath in. The result of our filtering now affects our grid. So we constantly cycle the filter affecting our grid, the grid affecting our filter and our filter affecting our grid continuously.

So why do we need the filter/grid system in the first place? The truth is that we are constantly inundated with too much data. We would be in constant overload if the mind did not have the marvelous ability to filter out the innumerable non-essentials that are conveyed to us by our senses. This is done so automatically we are unaware we are even doing it. I am not talking only of the recent technological overload of information. It has always been with us.

If I were to describe what is now in my field of vision without this filter in place and functioning, I could go on literally for hours. We are swamped with sentient data. We could not function as an organism without this wonderful filter protecting us from overload and allowing us to concentrate on the matters we wish to pursue. So our filters are very valuable to us and what I am about to say should in no way detract from their necessity and desirability.

We must recognize that at *no time* are we using *all* of the data pertaining to any decision or action that we take. We are always selecting some data and rejecting other data. We are not aware of the immense amount of data that we are rejecting because of our automatic, unconscious filter system. This inevitably gives us a bias. We cannot escape it. Not being aware of the data we have removed leaves us ill informed as to our bias and leads us to think we are objective when we cannot be. The philosopher John Locke gives as one of his three reasons for man's faulty thinking, *"We seek but in part and know but in part."*

These unavoidable biases are revealed when intelligent and educated people come up with very different opinions and views when presented with the same data. Identical history will teach clear-cut but opposite lessons to those with opposite filter systems. Thus the filter becomes a stabilizing mechanism which will continue our present beliefs. Only a massive batch of contrary data will suffice to overcome this threshold of built-in inertia. This is both good and bad, stabilizing and bigoted.

Given this situation of unavoidable bias of some kind, and even seeing the positive stabilizing effect, what can we do to bring our perceptions closer to the actuality of what's out there? The fact that we can never achieve actuality does not mean that our striving in that direction is useless. On the contrary, the closer our filter/grid system comes to actuality, the better our lives become in all aspects.

♦ First, we must recognize that we have a filter system in place all the time and we do not have the option to disengage it entirely, no matter how skilled we may think we are at being "objective." There is an "actuality" out there but we will only know "our realization" of it. This will make it seem "real" to us, but it is only our "realization" of that actuality.

♦   Second, we must try to take the filtering system out of
     "automatic pilot" and deliberately discern the filter being used.
     It may be necessary to redesign the filter to bring our
     realization closer to actuality. We are in control of our filter.
     We created it in the first place and therefore we can change it
     if we find it is not working for us.

The complementary system between our filter system and our
grid system is necessary. To make sense of the world and to act
reasonably in it we must have some idea of the environment we are
in. We cannot start from scratch with a blank understanding in
responding to the ever-demanding circumstances of our lives. We
may or may not be correct in our understanding but nonetheless it
provides us with the basis of action.

Grids are not only necessary but helpful. One very familiar
grid system used by the human race consists of the latitudes and
longitudes used in geography. If you were in need of rescue
somewhere in the middle of the Pacific Ocean, you would have no
way of radioing your position to anyone without this grid.

We need to recognize, however, that this grid is an
imaginary thing that we impose upon what is external to us and has
no existence in the actuality. No one, for instance, has yet bumped
into the Equator.

If we wish to bring our realization closer to actuality we
may need to modify our grids which we have artificially pressed
upon that actuality. We did create the grid probably for a good
purpose. Nevertheless, we need to analyze the grid that we
imposed to see the manner in which it distorts our view of the
world and of any problem that we want to solve. This is essentially
the same deliberate, conscious discipline one uses with adjusting
the filter system.

A fascinating demonstration of this involves a Chinese
friend of mine, a fourth generation American. He was raised in the
Chinese community of Oakland and speaks with an accent. He was
the eldest of five brothers. At age 12 he left school to go to work as
money was needed to promote "the family." Times were better
when his younger brothers came along. Each of his four brothers
grew up to became doctors, while he, in no way inferior
intellectually, worked all his life for the government at a lower job
scale. His Chinese cultural grid system imposed upon these
circumstances a sense of pride in the contribution and the sacrifice

gladly given to advance the well being of his family. He is as pleased with his brothers, their accomplishments and financial success as any parent would be. His filter system removes the data that would encourage jealousy and passes through the data that enhances his pride. The grid and filter system converts his life to one of self-esteem and satisfaction in his contributions.

In the same circumstances another man might have employed a more typically American grid system, the main tenet of which is that it is unfair that the older one had to sacrifice his education and job opportunities for the benefit of his younger brothers. His filter system would have allowed through that data that proved to him that he was a "victim," that he had been treated unjustly. This same filter system would have blocked out the data that would give him a sense of accomplishment achieved through his brother's success. The data which would encourage resentment would come through instead and that data which discouraged resentment would be filtered out.

The point here is not to extol one cultural grid system over another. It is to show how different grids can give different results from the same experience. In living our lives it is essential to be conscious of both our filter and our grid systems. We must accept the responsibility as architect of those systems and recognize that we have the power to change them to suit the circumstances in which we find ourselves.

Dearest,

You can only have spiritual growth by moving your mind into a different context and viewing something over again. You used to say that what you see depends upon where you are looking from. This is true, of course, and it implies a very useful corollary: if you wish to see things differently put your mind in a different place.

Let's repeat the obvious. If you wish to grow you need to see things differently. Otherwise you stay the same and do not grow. To see things differently requires that you put your mind in a different place. Now the different place can be physical—a result of travelling or changing residence, or it can be a mental and/or emotional place that is new and different. Many of the experiences that are given to us are for this purpose, that is, to put our minds and emotions in a different place. Thus do we then see things anew and subsequently we grow.

You and I both knew that was one of the reasons we loved to travel so much. As always with travel, it opens the mind because you are placed in a different context and therefore you have to see things differently. Travelling is quite a spiritual thing to do.

And you and I were drawn to the third world in particular because it required that we see things very, very differently. We drew many spiritual understandings from our travels. We saw demonstrated that *we are all one* even though our outer circumstances were so different. We saw that the inner part of each of us was indeed so much the same that it was humorous. Remember in Mombasa, the heavily veiled young lady with only her eyes showing that nonetheless conveyed that she was boy crazy? Or the old Greek couple I photographed in Corfu who just loved to sit in the sun in front of their house?

Books are wonderful for the same reason. Do you remember how anxious we were to get our kids hooked on reading? Learning to read is such a laborious task, but lo and behold, there came a day when we found each of them reading something we didn't tell them to read. I remember tiptoeing away when I discovered it to avoid disturbing them.

Reading is an avenue to many, many things. Reading dissolves boundaries. Because we are such boundary makers in our pursuit of separation, our inner self desires and urges us to break out of our own constructions. This is what reading does for us. Reading a children's story takes the child's conscious awareness into a different time and a different place. The child's imaginative mind creates an ambiance so real that the child is there, in it.

We all love to be taken out of our boundaries. This is why books, movies, and TV are so compelling. We all recognize them as not real—rather as imaginary and make believe—but we nevertheless treasure them and seek the experience. Even those who read non-fiction—whether it be history or the Scientific American—are seeking to be taken out of their boundaries and carried into new worlds. Those who love history would be surprised at how much their past lives play a part in their consuming interest. Why do you think our friend Richard so loves the history of the Civil War? He is eager to shed light on forgotten and therefore unknown aspects of that time because his sub-conscious remembers them.

The larger perspective, which I always like to go to, would show that there is within each of us a very strong desire to break out of our boundaries. The very fact that we created these very same boundaries does not diminish our wish to get outside of them. It is a duality of the material existence.

Part of us also strongly resists the breaking down of our boundaries and underlying this resistance is fear. We feel that our boundaries protect us. We are not sure from what but that is part of what we wish protection from: the unknown. We mistakenly see this as an either/or choice. Either we stay within our protecting boundaries or we go outside of them into unknown chaos. This either/or construct is a separation device to separate the either from the or. It is simply another boundary we create that denies the *we are all one* principle. We do not need to choose one or the other. We may choose both. This realization will reduce the fear in venturing beyond our created boundaries.

This is also why we love books, movies and the TV so much. It allows us to choose both. We can move out of our boundaries with confidence because we know we will return to within our boundaries any time we want to set down the book, leave the theater, or shut off the TV. We are in command and therefore fearless. We have the best of both worlds.

The thing we don't realize is that we always have the best of both worlds, as there is no either/or choice about it. If we had the courage or the inspiration we could and would leap out of our boundaries and fearlessly look at and experience what is out there for us. We are, as I have said, invulnerable. To sense and use this invulnerability to go beyond the limiting boundaries of self is a great joy.

Let us look at death with this in mind. To die is certainly to venture outside of the boundaries of life (as you view it in your limited way). Certainly you greatly fear death for the very reason that it goes beyond your boundaries. You even call it "the beyond". If death were like a movie, which you knew would end and you could then walk out of the theater back into your normal life, you would not fear it in the least. But that is just the reason for your fear: you cannot come back to your normal life. Or can you? This all depends on how you define normal life.

If normal life is being back in the specificity of where you are now in that house that we built on that lovely hill, then you cannot come back to that normalcy in the physical body you now have. If, however, normal life is the journey of your soul through it's immortality, learning, loving, and living, then your normal life is restored. Restored is the wrong word because your normal life was never taken away to be restored. Your normal life continues the cycle through death to where I am, to rebirth and in this process, it is never taken away from you. If you but realized this you would no longer have any use for fear.

Your love of books, movies and TV is but an apprenticeship exercise for you to practice and experience removing your self-created boundaries and move beyond to enlightenment and its joys. Death too is a journey past boundaries to enlightenment and joy. Buck, you and I suspected it, but now I *know* it.

Exercise 81: Write down the ways that you know of for opening your mind to new and different viewpoints. Think about ways you can expand your mind. How does it change your view if you see death as going home? To learn to set fears aside try something new that you have never done before. Afterward, evaluate whether your initial fears were valid or merely imprisoning.

Chapter 83

Dogma

March 20th, 1998

With Gail's death, my filter/grid system came very much into focus. It forced me to determine what I really believe. There are many who simply adopt a traditional religious belief system, and others who choose to dismiss the concepts of God or the afterlife completely. Both sides have their filter/grid system in place and some would call this by another name: dogma.

Let us examine this question by trying to eliminate the grids the various groups have in place. First, there is the grid held by some religions that the subject of an afterlife is solely the province of religion and no one else should invade this territory. This is a limitation that has no objective actuality. We all have free will and a mind to go with it. This mind can cogitate on whatever it chooses.

Second, there is the assumption (a grid) that unless something has been proven by science it does *not* exist. But if an afterlife has not been *proven* by science it is equally true that it has not been *disproved* by science.

Understanding this, we can now build a new grid system based on what we know. First, the concepts such as the existence of an afterlife, psychic phenomena and reincarnation which are advanced by various religions are theories. You can choose to believe the one of your choice and really believe it. It is a theory but since it has not been disproved you are not burying your head in the sand to believe it.

There is another theory: that there is no afterlife. This theory is no better and no worse than any other theory. It has neither been proven nor disproved in a scientific manner. If all of the religious concepts of the after life were eventually proved to be wrong, it would still not make the theory of no after life the correct one by default. There may be another theory that has not as yet been put forward which may be the correct one.

We can see that in the matter of an afterlife, all we have are theories and beliefs. However, no matter what we believe, each of us will one day be confronted with the truth—and what we believed will probably not make much difference in what happens to us after we die.

Dear Buck,

You are right. The death process is immutable as is the birth process, whether you want it to be or not. So, in this sense, the belief or non-belief in what happens after death is not relevant. However, once you get to this side there are tremendous variations and choices as to what happens to any one soul.

Far more important than what one believes or does not believe is what lives in one's heart. Beliefs and convictions tend to be intellectual activities whereas the heart is what you truly are. It is true that if you believe there is nothing after death your mind will try to create nothing, a difficult task. If however, you have a loving heart, this will not last long and you will be drawn to the love that you are and which is part of all of us. Thus you will join with the *all that is us*.

On the other hand, if your heart is hard and you do not believe in an afterlife you will go into kind of a slumber that can take quite some time to heal. If your heart is hard but you do believe in an afterlife it may not be to your liking.

You have observed yourself that there are people who declare themselves to be on the spiritual path and yet their understanding of spiritual principles is not demonstrated in their lives. Just because they say things in the spiritual vocabulary does not particularly help them when they come to this side. Again, it is what is in the heart. And there are people like our friend Don, for instance, who get very uncomfortable with any mention of spirituality, yet they are kind, open, and treat everyone with dignity. Their kind hearts will do well for them on this side and it will be much to their surprise. We both felt Don's kindness was all the more impressive because it was not motivated by trying to create good karma for himself as some on the spiritual path are. Do you see how this works?

Exercise 82: With honesty, write about what lives in your heart. Include the virtuous along with the less than virtuous. This can be quite an experience and very helpful in determining what our next direction in life will be.

Chapter 84

Five Steps to Communication

March 31st, 1998

Part of our cultural hypnosis—whereby we act and react according to how we have been hypnotized to behave—is to believe that we *must* commit ourselves either to believing something or to not believing something. We believe that to not declare on one side or the other is to be indecisive, which our culture regards as inexcusable and weak. The O.J. Simpson trial is a fine example. All of us all across America *knew* if he was guilty or not guilty even though all of us had very few facts and data to make that decision. Our lack of evidence however didn't intimidate us in the least. We knew him to be guilty or not guilty.

In this same way we get involved in whether we believe in an afterlife. "Do you or don't you believe?" our peers demand. What we don't realize is that as soon as we decide either way we are closing our minds. Once we make a decision our filter/grid system will change. It will allow in what reinforces our beliefs and will filter out contrary evidence.

If we want to stay open-minded it would be best to not make the yes or no decision. What do we do then? We can say that we *think* that there is an afterlife because we see evidence that it is true. Therefore, we will currently act on the hypothesis that it is true, knowing that further evidence may later change our view.

I am hoping skeptics will accept in the same way— tentatively—what I am honestly trying to convey. Just live with the hypothesis that what I am saying is true. Through living with it you will either get a sense of it being your truth or you will not. If not, then reject it as not being for you. The final determination of what truth or untruth you will bring into your life is yours. It is not my decision or anyone else's. It is yours.

Dearest Buck,

As I was dying you were immediately open. You didn't know to what. And that is the key to being open. In the spiritual sense it means being receptive to what you don't know or expect.

If you choose to be open, not closed, you will receive guidance from many sources suggesting that there is an afterlife and that the afterlife has received your loved one. Further, remaining open, you will be getting communications from your loved one. At first the communication will likely be fuzzy. Here you will have choice. You can dismiss this fuzziness or, in other terms, close it down and it will disappear. Or you can choose to be open in which event you will learn to communicate better with practice.

It is not important to believe in the afterlife. It is not important to believe that you can communicate with the dead. All that is important is that you remain open to what *might* be, including these two possibilities.

It does help to know what to expect when you try to communicate with us. First we need to remember there is great diversity. This is one of God's great accomplishments. This diversity applies to the very wide range of communications types between the material world and the spiritual world. You, the recipient, therefore must be open to receive communication in such form as is appropriate to you. For some it will be like taking direct dictation. It will come through word by word. Automatic writing can occur. Others will hear a voice. Some may see an apparition of sorts who will communicate telepathically. By far the most common and the easiest for us to do from here is to insert our thoughts into your thoughts.

This mind to mind communication is the first form available to us when we come over here. It requires less energy. The frequency gap between your world and ours is bridged with less effort. That is on the plus side. Although, when it is received on your side, it is more tenuous, more subtle because of this lower energy requirement. This results in it being harder to recognize by you at the receiving end.

What can you expect then in communicating in this most common way? We need to start with the realization that you are a material world oriented thinker. You feel best and most confident when you have a material demonstration of what you are seeking. In the field of thought you seek precision and definitiveness. This gives you confidence in what is happening. This is characteristic of the *doing* approach. We need to shift this to a *being* approach. You must allow things to come through which are not definitive and precise. I will try to illustrate this in a seeming round about way.

Intellectually you know that you should be forgiving. Yet emotionally you find it hard to do at times. So there is lack of congruity between your thoughts that are precise and your emotions which are not. When it comes to actually forgiving there is no doubt that the imprecise emotions carry far more weight than the concise thinking part of you. This illustrates that your heart, your emotions are the seat of who you are.

We on this side address this heart side of you. It is received by the heart side of you in the imprecise form that the heart is used to dealing with. This is essentially true but not totally true. We can at the same time address your intellect but only after we have connected with your heart.

What all this means is that when we communicate with you it starts with a gentle nudge asking you to be aware that we wish to communicate. You must recognize this and open up to the communication. Then our message can be received and understood. This nudging is often not recognized for what it is by the receiver. He or she pays little or no attention to it.

In sum, if you wish to communicate with us, you need to:

1. Believe it is possible.
2. Believe that *you* can do it.
3. Be open and receptive to it.
4. Understand that what you receive will be subtle. It will not come in an envelope with a return address on it. It will not be labeled so that it can be believed without a doubt.
5. Be willing to take a chance and be open to these soft nudges.

In doing all of this you will be able to ascertain for yourself the quality and meaning of what you receive. You can decide in your mind and heart who it is communicating with you.

Exercise 83: Write about any fears you may have about remaining open. Try to understand where those fears are coming from. In doing so, you may find them diminishing. Look at the five steps above and examine where you stand for each of those steps. Then work on them from there.

Chapter 85

Cast Adrift

April 25, 1998

Yesterday I had my second session with Betty Middlemiss. I had prepared a bunch of questions which I hoped Gail would answer. But the session came out very differently than I expected. Betty couldn't contact Gail. She felt that Gail had already moved on to other things. That shook me up. I really don't want to lose contact with Gail. I was hoping this would be a way we could continue to learn spiritually together as we always had and loved to do.

I was upset because it was like losing Gail again, a pattern in which fear predominated. While Gail was alive and particularly as we got older I greatly feared losing her. This fear was a significant part of my emotional life and the love I felt for her. And now it felt like losing her again. In addition I was upset because I was losing what I thought was a wonderful channel through which to receive spiritual insights.

Beloved Buck,

I am always here. It cannot be any other way. I feel what you are going through and I wish I could help in more ways than I am. You have always been brave and strong. Rely on that.

We've said this before but it bears repeating. When you feel disturbed you will notice that your perspective has been reduced to the narrowness of the unpleasantness you are dealing with. To regain peace, broaden your perspective to include all the other aspects of your life. The latter of course is the truer picture. Always you need to come back to the fundamentals.

Do you remember when you heard yourself at a board meeting spontaneously saying, "The fruit tree doesn't like to be pruned but nonetheless it will produce more fruit"? The other board members would have been astonished if you had told them that you had just received that statement from your inner self. You had not previously thought about it, or composed it, it just came out whole all by itself. It was then topically appropriate. But it has a more universal application.

As we souls go through our many lives there are quite a few things that happen to us that we do not like, particularly as they are happening. We feel unlucky, unfortunate, undeserving and like to feel sorry for ourselves. We think we would be better off if these things did not happen to us. In fact, we go to great effort to try to make sure that such things do not happen again in the future. We even mistakenly think that is our goal in life: to achieve happiness by eliminating "bad" things in our life. Yet bad things continue to occur. Problems may change but they never go away, it seems. New ones crop up to take the place of old ones.

What we don't see in all of this is that we, the fruit tree, are protesting the pruning without realizing that it is happening for our own benefit—so that we can produce more fruit. And what is the fruit that we should be producing? We are to develop our own truth to fulfill our nature as given to us by God. More specifically, we are to develop the wisdom within ourselves to understand that we are perfect creations of an all-loving God. Our fruit is that wisdom.

Seen in this manner, the pruning we experience makes a good deal more sense. If these "bad" experiences in our lives bring us the opportunity to develop wisdom then we can see the "good" in them.

This understanding will also bring about a change in our goals. To achieve happiness by eliminating "bad" things in our life is neither achievable nor desirable. To achieve wisdom however is both possible and desirable.

If we realize this, what effect will it have on the fear in our lives? We have already stated that it is in the future where our fear lies. We are fearful of what the future holds for us. Behind all our fears is a huge dark backdrop: the inevitability of our death or the death of our loved ones and our separation from them. This backdrop casts a pall on all our other fears. If all things that happen to us are for our benefit then what is it we have to fear?

We have also written that fear promotes separation in all of its forms, particularly separation from God. Therefore the *we are all one* principle and fear cannot survive together. All of this suggests that wisdom could be described as the realization that you need have no fear. If your goal is to gain wisdom, the corollary would be to shed fear.

If we, the fruit tree, recognize that the pruning we are experiencing is actually helping us gain in wisdom, then what is it we have to fear? Previously we were fearful of the pruning and had the goal of trying to prevent any pruning from taking place. With this new understanding that the pruning is for our benefit to fulfill our goal of becoming wiser, the fear in our lives is then greatly reduced. In this seemingly counter rational way do we achieve happiness. The world has so many things backwards. We thought that happiness would be achieved by eliminating the pruning. Now we see that happiness can be achieved by accepting the pruning and thereby diminishing the fears. Happiness is to live without fear and to gain wisdom.

Exercise 84: Think about and write down the ways in which the "pruning" you have undergone has lent you wisdom.

Chapter 86

Some Help From Gail

April 26th, 1998

Significantly, the evening of the day of my disappointing meeting with Betty Middlemiss I went to the local A.R.E. study group*. I walked in the door and my friend Richard Zoll handed me a book called *Conversations With God* by Neale Donald Walsch. He thought I would find it interesting. I had heard of it and had vaguely been thinking I would read it.

I took it home, read it and I was overwhelmed. I feel that Gail arranged to provide me with that book as a source of spiritual understanding. And she did this the very same day I felt I had been put adrift.

For Gail and I, *A Course in Miracles* had always been the best spiritual book we knew. It had helped me greatly in the first months after Gail left. Nonetheless parts of it I never felt like I truly understood or felt comfortable with. For example, I felt that illusionary as this world may be, I didn't think it was useless nor that it should be ignored. It must be serving some divine purpose.

The *Conversations with God* book addresses these issues and resolves them in a way that intuitively I felt right about. I thank Gail for bringing this book to my attention and in such a timely manner.

I am now rereading parts of *A Course in Miracles* and find that when reading more deeply between the lines there is no conflict between *A Course in Miracles* and *Conversations with God*. In *A Course in Miracles* Jesus says he uses exaggeration as a teaching tool to clarify the principles. I now see that both books say the same thing but from a different point of view and with a different emphasis. This pleases me.

Both books say that every decision and action that we take is based on either love or fear. *ACIM* says that the love we experience on earth is of death and destruction and it is so typical of the ego thought system that we don't even recognize it as such.

*The A.R.E. (Edgar Cayce's Association for Research and Enlightenment) has study groups all around the world which study Cayce's *Search for God* books which are considered by some to be his greatest legacy.

I had a hard time with that. It seemed that the love I experience on earth is very fine. But now I see this differently. I opened this entry with how my love for Gail was mixed with my fear of losing her. This certainly gives credence to *A Course in Miracles's* view that earthly love is contaminated with death and destruction.

When I sought out Betty Middlemiss I was carrying this same love pattern forward. I don't need to do this. In fact, it is counter productive to do so. The true essence of my love for Gail, stripped of its fear of loss, is with me and is being continually created and recreated by me all the time. I need not fear losing it because I cannot! Gail is an integral part of me that cannot be removed. This includes her vast influence on who I have come to be but also her essence too. I can and do love her with no fear, which means that I have no sense of loss. This is pretty amazing to me.

Dearest,

Love is my favorite topic. It is both much more and much less than what you on earth think it is. It is much more because it is really the basic energy of the universe. It is the energy with which God makes everything both material and spiritual. As I said before it is that which is referred to as the first cause.

It is everywhere. It is on all the planes of existence. It is in all the parallel universes. It is therefore available everywhere to be used to create. One of the magnificent aspects of love is that it can be used to create an infinite variety in both the material and non-material worlds. There is nothing that love is not capable of creating.

Yes, it is love that is the universal force of which electromagnetism, gravity, and the like are but subordinate aspects. It is the umbrella under which all things exist. God is the generator of love. It is His basic tool, which He makes available to each of us.

Love is at the core of all things. If God withdrew His love from you, you would cease to be. Your very life depends upon it. And yet you recognize it not. Love comes to you from God pure and constant. It comes out of you distorted and in jerks. It takes work and energy to change the love energy that comes into you into the distorted form that you give out. It

takes no work nor energy to just let it pass through you as love unadulterated.

Love on earth is given many meanings, some of which seem very beautiful. Take for example the love given to a child by its parents. They truly do love that child with genuine love. But then in school for instance, the parents are so very pleased when their child is the best in the class. This love then becomes a put down for all the others and a means of separation. Similarly, a man can be so pleased with his beautiful wife. Part of that is that he appreciates her beauty for what it is but another part is that he regards her as more beautiful than the others. The latter is again a separation concept.

So much of earthly love is conditional. This makes it like a contract. If you fulfill these conditions (your part of the bargain) then I will love you (my part of the bargain). And then there is the corollary, which says I withhold my love because of what you do or don't do. Further I will continue to withhold my love until you straighten out and comply with my vision of who you ought to be. As an extreme example, you withhold your love from Hitler because of what you judge as unacceptable conditions of his person. But we really don't have to go that far to find examples. Many a husband, wife, parent or child have at times withheld their love until such time as the offender has come back in line.

But love does not come in pieces. You cannot give a piece of love to this person and withhold a piece of love from that person because in your judgment they are not entitled to it. God has entitled all. Don't argue with God. Don't argue with love, just give it.

Exercise 85: Consider ways in which you both give love and withhold it. Write these down and then imagine giving love unconditionally. Consider how your world would change. Write that down too.

Chapter 87

A Letter From Gail!

May 24, 1998

Today is Gail's would-be 70th birthday. It has been one month since my failed session with Betty Middlemiss. I still feel Gail's loving presence frequently but I so much want to have a dialogue with her—to continue the process of learning together that we so loved. I think I will ask her to write for me. What else can be done? I even feel that she is asking my permission to use me in this way. I am so pleased to say yes. My dear Gail, please use my pen so that we can continue the joy of learning together. Gail please go ahead.

Dearest!

I am with you. I cannot be any other place. Onslow* was right. Do not doubt. Do not fail to trust that I am here communicating with you, helping you and helping myself. Be yourself, accept yourself and thus you will be accepting of the *oneness* that we share together and with everyone else.

Yes, I'm busy, busy in my work, which is teaching. *A Course in Miracles* is right; teaching and learning are one and the same. This is all for now but we have started and I ask you to do this again. I love you. *Do not doubt.* Doubt and acceptance cannot be together. Choose!

You are asking for a sign. You just read how in prayer you need to ask nothing and accept what you have already been given. I give you signs. Just now I found your *A Course in Miracles* notes for you. You also are fond of judging by content, not source. Your desire for signs is an attempt to establish a source when your attention should be on the content. (She's telling me to practice what I preach.)

Remember, all is but acceptance without boundaries.

*Onslow Wilson, a friend of ours, and I taught in adjacent classrooms. We felt a rapport that we carried into other activities and friendship. It was Onslow who strongly urged me to keep a journal .

When you feel this you have peace and communication. And you know how dear communication is to my heart. Truly you need but ask and it is given.

Marshall: Gail I ask now that you help me write the book that will serve as a hopeful, joyous message to our truly beloved brothers and sisters. Help me.

Gail: I will. Keep yourself open. Do not judge. Do not judge yourself or myself as being unable to do this. I love you. I must go but I will soon be back. Enjoy this day in the *now*. You have nothing to fear. The world is bountiful.

Hold my hand as you hold my heart. I am yours forever. As you are mine. There is no other way. You are a builder and we built a relationship. There is no person and no thing to tear it down. So it is there and always will be. *A Course in Miracles* says that in this illusionary world, love is the only thing that is saved, that is eternal. What we have built with love is a beautiful structure that will last. We both can use it all the time. You sleep in it every night. Till I come again.

Chapter 88

A Final Exercise

Have you yet overtly invited your beloved departed to communicate with or through you? If not, why not give it a try? This last exercise has three parts.

1) Write a summary of where you feel you were when you started this book.

2) Next write a description of where you feel you now are in your perspective, understanding, and success in communicating inwardly.

3) Write a dialogue with your inner self, your lost loved one, or anyone you wish to go with you on your journey.

Begin the dialogue by greeting your chosen correspondent and stating what you would like revealed to you. Then express a willingness to accept and appreciate the gifts that await you. You may even want to write of the excitement or other feelings you have about this adventurous journey. When it feels right, let your correspondent write using your fingers. Do not stop or be concerned if it starts out sounding like you. The two of you are, after all, drawn to each other through a commonality of outlook. With a bit of warming up, your correspondent will find his or her own voice.

If at any point you sense your correspondent asking a question, pay strict attention. It is now your turn to respond to the question. Or, maybe you will feel you would like to comment on what he or she has said. If so, do so. In this way the dialogue can continue. It can also stop and then be picked up at a later time. This dialogue can lead you anywhere. Nothing is impossible. Continue to be open and let it come.

A word about validation. In this work we would all like to have something come through that would validate conclusively that we are indeed communicating with someone who has passed over. This may happen but is very unlikely at the beginning. Furthermore, the validation you receive will probably be of a very personal nature which will not offer much objective proof. I would like to illustrate this with an early example of mine.

In one session, Gail was writing about the difference between *doing* and *being*. To illustrate her point she wrote. **"You have the golden rule of "do unto others as you would have others do unto you." This uses the verb *to do* and reflects the earthly emphasis on *doing*. It is, however, but an earthly modified version of a higher spiritual law. This higher spiritual law recognizes the surpassing importance of your *being* as in contrast to your *doing*. This law states, *Be unto others as you would have God be unto you...*"**

When I was writing this and came to this last part, **"Be unto others..."** my mind immediately completed the sentence as, "as you would have others be unto you." And although this was what was in my mind, my fingers wrote, **"as you would have God be unto you."** That was a concept I had never thought of before and as I read it I was impressed with how profound it was. Gail had actually improved upon the golden rule which has been around for centuries. I know for certain that this wasn't me. Anyone else who might have been watching me write this down would have witnessed nothing very different than a man writing and then describing a subjective feeling. To me, it was personal validation of a very high order. This is what I mean by *personal* validation. You will find your communication easier if you don't get side-tracked in trying to seek objective validation. This is counter-productive. Let come what comes.

Gail and I wish you the very best in this adventure in self-knowledge. It is not impossible that one or both of us may join you in this dialogue.

Part Four

Sharing the Wisdom

Dear Reader,

Finally, after many, many months of feeling Gail's presence, receiving mental messages and just knowing she was with me, I have finally been able to communicate directly with her. I must confess that when I originally wrote and reread this "inspired writing," I was not very impressed. There was nothing in it that I didn't know or that my imagination couldn't have easily put there. I was also concerned at times that the syntax—the pattern of language that I was using—was too similar to my own. Gail explained my concern with the syntax of the inspired writing being too similar to my own in this way:

It's as if you, Buck, have a giant typewriter keyboard in your head. Instead of having letters on the keys it has phrases that you like to use. It also has some words that you like to use. When you talk you punch these keys containing all your favorite ways of saying things and your syntax comes out.

Now when I or anyone else from this side communicate with you, it is with difficulty. This is why such communication is unusual. Such communication requires energy, congruency, and something else for which you have no word, but it is something like a lock where all the tumblers have to be in a certain configuration to open it.

When I communicate with you my main goal is to transfer the content of ideas. I try to do so in the most energy efficient manner possible. This allows me to convey the most content. Do you now see why I use the keyboard that is already in your head rather than try to remake your keyboard into mine. This latter alternative would be a waste of energy and would also create some incongruities.

The reason the syntax bothers you is that you wonder if it isn't you doing the writing, not me. That is a luxury you do not need. Besides, I know you, and you would much prefer to have more exciting content than you would my phraseology. Be satisfied with the content with the way it is. Accept. And you

know that sometimes my syntax does come through in little flashes. I feel this happen when I am communicating with you.

Maybe in time we will get better at this. In the meantime, as you have so often expressed it yourself—the validity of the communications comes from the content. Is it new to you? Is it a new point of view on otherwise familiar concepts? Does it stimulate you to new insights? You know these communications do all of this and more. This is where you get your validation.

Even though one may not think so, I was a skeptic and as such, originally I dismissed this writing as just my imagination just providing what I wished to read. This is a good example of me not being open in spite of thinking that I was. For this reason I didn't try it again for a couple of weeks until once more I felt a soft urging from Gail to write.

I was more impressed with my second session. Not that I completely believed it was from Gail. It seemed too good to be true. But I was convinced that there might be something to it. I decided to try the inspired writing every day and see what came of it. After getting seven or eight of them I sat down and read them in order. It was then that I was truly impressed. Not only was I amazed with the wisdom the writing contained, but I realized that they were organized in their presentation. And I knew it wasn't me who had organized them. I had just written down whatever came to me, without any consciousness as to what direction I was going or how the writing would end. I have been good at organization all my life and I know that organization is never a matter of chance. It has to be deliberately conceived and executed by somebody.

So this rereading convinced me that somebody was organizing the material. Each writing made a point and came to a logical end. I further realized that each inspired writing was related meaningfully to the next one and then the next one. Again, this was something of which I was totally unaware while I was writing them. I noticed (with some humor) that these writings were short and succinct—usually only a page. I, myself, tend to go on and on and would have great difficulty in saying so much in so few words. This again strengthened my belief that this was really Gail writing to me.

As this writing began to accumulate, my belief in it was reinforced time and again. Wisdom came through that was totally new to me. New and insightful ways of looking at things were written down. With 20 or 30 of them I began to see that Gail was using the spiral method of teaching rather than the more commonly used linear method. The spiral method takes an even greater organizational effort.

Linear teaching involves covering the preliminary material thoroughly before you go onto the next stage, which you again teach thoroughly in preparation for the next stage after that. Universities use this approach with all the required courses you must take before you qualify to take the advanced courses.

Spiral teaching, on the other hand, gives you a brief but enticing bit of observation or fact that is understandable in itself but leaves open the greater ramifications. Spiral teaching then goes onto another observation or fact and treats it briefly. This continues for a while until we come back to the original subject which is now elevated to a newer broader understanding based on the various other subjects touched upon previously. It is thus that you see the relationship of various facts that may have seemed unrelated.

This spiraling around and returning to previous subjects was present throughout the series of "inspired writing." In this next part, I share with you a few choice "inspired writings" that touch on subjects still not addressed.

Chapter 89

What is it Like to Die?

Good morning dear Gail, I am home again after a nice stay at the ranch. Please use my fingers as always to write what you wish.

Beloved Buck,

The question was asked, what is it like to die? We have all experienced it many times. When you really get into it—dying that is—you realize it is something that you have done many times and you feel very familiar with it. You have this strong sense of coming home.

Everyone realizes that when you wake up in the morning after dreaming, that the dream quickly fades from your memory. This is why, when you keep a dream journal, you are instructed to write down your dream immediately upon awakening. This is typical of dreams but very atypical of your memory. Most people have little difficulty remembering what they were doing or thinking five minutes ago. Yet five minutes after awakening you cannot recall your dream. It is as though you were one self doing the dreaming and that you set this self aside when you awoke and stepped into another self. Actually this is what is happening.

Now when you die you also set aside one self and step into another. This new self is larger and more consciously inclusive than the one you left behind. It has, however, shed the body. It is as if you reversed in time the memory pattern from the dream state to the awakened state. As you die, your memory opens up instead of closing off to who you really are. You step into the invisible (from earth's view) world that is suddenly all so familiar to you. You remember it well. You meet your guide, your higher self, and so many, many others. In sum you feel you have returned home, which of course, is what you have done.

And yet through all of this you have not been cut off from earth. You have sense of what is going on with those you left behind. You are aware that you have the ability to convey to those you left behind ideas, thoughts, healing, and other communications. Although you also gently recognize that it is the free choice of the recipient as to whether they receive them or not. I say gently because you do not wish to intervene uninvited. You recognize the vast importance of readiness on the part of those with whom you wish to communicate. You accept that if they are not ready they should not be forced to receive what you wish to give. This is why we want so much to convey the idea of openness on the part of those on earth who are grieving.

Again I need to add that there is great diversity in the death experience. The above was my experience which is shared with many others. Based on the readiness of the individual there is, however, a vast variety of death experiences. For this reason there is real benefit to the individual on earth to bring himself or herself into readiness for the transition to this side.

Now that does not mean that you must think about death and dying. What it does mean though is that you should have those attitudes of openness, realizing that we are all *one*, and that you are children of God. Inasmuch as these same attitudes are ideal for living your life on earth in the *now*, you have nothing to lose by bringing these attitudes into your current life. By doing so will you experience joy.

Chapter 90

Death Changes Your Life

July 18th, 2001

Hello darling, today is Gordon's 50th birthday. Can you believe that little baby who peed on Doctor Burley when he was born is now the big 5-O? Please write to me as you wish.

Dear, Dear Buck,

We have very pleasant memories of all our babies. They were such treasures. I'm proud of them because they have all contributed to making the world a better place.

Today I want to open with this statement:"Going through the death experience changes your life."

If you but think of it, the death experience is a huge event in your conscious awareness. If you didn't believe in an afterlife your entire life long and then are confronted with the fact that you still are, it has got to change your basic thinking. Even if you had hoped there is an afterlife and are then received with this engulfing love and now know for sure there is an afterlife, again your life view has got to be fundamentally effected.

The point of all this is that the survivor on earth tends to believe that when the deceased one comes to this side they remain basically unchanged in their views from when they were alive. This is almost impossible given the magnitude of the death experience. Death makes you modify, often quite radically, your views on life. This spills over to include a change in their attitude toward those in a past life with whom they had significant relationships.

These changes in attitudes tend to be toward greater understanding, greater tolerance, and greater love for those in their past lives. Those who found living with the deceased somewhat difficult should not assume that the deceased remains so difficult when they come over here. Quite the contrary, often the deceased finally gets it—that is—he or she finally gets the message that you have been trying to get them to recognize in their life on earth. At last!

Therefore, after they have passed over, often the deceased wants—badly—to communicate with the surviving one that, "Yes! Now I do understand!" They *do* appreciate what you were trying to do. But then often they find the communication channels cut off. The channels are cut off for a number of reasons that we have already discussed but a review would be in order since this is so important.

Channels are cut off because:

♦ First and foremost, the surviving one is trying to live in the past and is not partaking in the *now*. They fail to understand that they are still on earth because they have lessons to learn. These lessons cannot be faced by looking backwards. They must engage in the *now,* looking forward. One of the lessons they need to learn is that they *can* communicate with their departed one. The dissolution of this separation is a vital part of the God's grand plan to heal the Oneship from separation. This is obviously holy work and you have your part in this holy work. And it is not accomplished by looking to the past! Communication with the deceased can *only* occur when you fully engage in your *now*.

♦ Second, communication blockages occur because the survivor does not believe an afterlife is possible, or if it is possible, the deceased must be completely separated and hence incommunicable. Again, I want to say you do not have to believe in these things completely but you need to be open minded to believing they are possible. You need to be willing to try it out for yourself. This book is to show you what you can do to try to find out.

♦ Third, there are those who think that all of this is possible but that they can't do it themselves for any number of reasons. You can do it. But you certainly won't if you never try it.

♦ Fourth, discouragement is also a shut down. It comes in many forms. Discouragement is hard to turn off, but to succeed it need not be turned off completely. It is sufficient if you just pick yourself up and try again with the understanding that all worthwhile things require persistent effort.

♦   Fifth, loneliness drains the ability to communicate. It is sad that the very thing that can relieve loneliness is handicapped by loneliness itself. Loneliness too is very hard to turn off but you can give it a back seat.

So dear ones, do not be discouraged, open your minds, and be willing to try to achieve something that will become very dear to you. As you already know, it is easier to do something for someone else than to do it for yourself. Realize that in communicating with your deceased you are not only doing this for yourself, you are doing it for them and in fulfillment of God's wish to dissolve the separation between your realm and ours. You are doing holy work.

Gail and her twin, Bud, taken a year or so
after their mother passed.

Chapter 91

Death is a Lesson in Fear

March 24th, 2001

Dear Gail,

Yesterday was the 5th anniversary of the day you passed on and I didn't even realize it. I don't know whether to be ashamed or pleased. Ashamed because I forgot that day that was so important to us or pleased because I am letting that fall behind me. Please write for me.

My Darling One,

Be pleased. You never showed much talent for remembering anniversaries and the like anyway. I always felt this was because you were always so engaged in your *now*. And the *now* is what you should still be engaged in.

Neither you nor I will forget that day I came over here. It was a most powerful experience. That experience is now part of our being. There is no need for an anniversary remembrance to highlight its value. It's already part of us.

You wonder why it was so important to me as well. Many reasons. Here are a few of them. It was a lesson about fear. The fear of an anticipated event or condition is often worse than the event itself. Often the fear of a future event is a mistake in that the fear is unjustified. The actual event can be good—not bad.

My mother dying of TB when I was ten made me fear death. All those health nurses warning me about getting TB made me more afraid of death. Then as you know, when we were raising our kids I worried that one or the other of us would die, leaving the other one alone. That made me fear death. Also I loved you so much I feared losing you. All this made death frightening.

Then when our kids left for university we started traveling. We managed to get into several death threatening situations like the time we were in Tienneman Square during the demonstrations. We got quite fearless in looking death in the face. Remember walking across those wet mossy logs on

our trek into Machu Picchu with a three thousand-foot drop under our feet? Then I also had that revelation in the kitchen that I was immortal.

The result of all this was that I had mixed feelings about death. You do too right now, I know. I had no idea how I would feel when death actually came. When it came, I knew it. And there was no fear there when I realized this. In the beginning I was concerned about the effect on the family, particularly you. But then somehow I was not fearful for you or the family either. That was strange. All my life I have been concerned with the well being of my family. I had been willing to devote much energy promoting their well being. Yet here I was feeling calm when I knew my passing would be a trauma to you all.

The reason was that my perspective had widened greatly. I could see clearly that my death was a lesson each of you had chosen. Furthermore, each of you could grow beneficially from the experience. I also felt each of you would. This made me feel pleased in a way I had not experienced before as a wife and mother. The word *Godspeed* had a whole new meaning for me. It meant I could lay down my concern and active participation in your lives and give you over to God. He and I would speed you on your path. Godspeed.

My passing was also a lesson for me in *being* instead of *doing*. In the death experience you are much more a passenger than a driver. In this, it is similar to the birth experience.

I understand that those of you who are compulsive *doers* often have difficulty in the death experience because you feel frightened by the loss of control. In this sense the understanding and practice in *being* is a good preparation for getting the most out of your dying experience.

After completing the dying experience you do return to a mode in which you can elect to be the doer. It is a different kind of doing from what you do on earth. Nonetheless the doers of earth will like it and adapt to it quickly. I tell the doers this so they need not be frightened.

Time for you to go Buck.

Chapter 92

Let's Talk About Death

June 28th, 2001

Dear Gail,

Let us talk this day.

Gail: Yes let's have a dialogue. We will talk about talking about death. Many people on earth are afraid to talk about death whether it is their own or a loved one's. Contrary to their professed belief in a religious based afterlife, this fear comes mostly from the deeply held belief that after death there is nothing. This is so scary to them that talking about it can be impossible.

Marshall: Perhaps, it would help these people if they understood that the idea that there is nothing after death is but a hypothesis that has been neither proven nor disproved. Further, if the Christian heaven (or any other afterlife) seems impossible, it does not mean that there is no afterlife by default.

Gail: Once you become convinced that reincarnation is probable you can see that death is but a process or station in the journey of life. As such, it does not need to terrorize us. Reasonable talk about death then becomes possible. In truth there is no death. There is a transition that people of earth call death, but there is no end to the soul's existence. Buck, you say what it meant to you—that we had talked about death when I came over here.

Marshall: I cannot describe how important it was to me to have talked about death with Gail before she left. In those talks we covered a lot of ground. All during those talks I was assuming I would go first as men usually do. I very clearly knew that after I was gone I wanted Gail to have as happy and satisfying life as possible. I knew I didn't want her to be defeated by my leaving. I also knew that I had great faith in her abilities and competence particularly in being discerning about people. I therefore trusted her to do what was best for herself. Especially I knew that she would not allow herself to be depressed for any extended period. Since she and I were both romantics, I hoped she would find a nice man to share herself with. I'm going on about how I felt as I remember it so well. Gail agreed with those feelings. It convinced me after she left that I knew how she felt. I strongly felt her encouraging me to get the most out of the life that I have left. She wanted me to live without self-imposed limits as to how happy I could be or how deep a relationship I could have with another woman. The result is that the joy I feel with my life now is in no way a disloyalty to the beautiful life I had with Gail. Right now I feel Gail encouraging me to be in a romantic relationship.

Gail: As important as all that is to Buck's happiness now, there is much more that is gained by being able to talk of death with your beloved ones. The immediate aftermath of losing a loved one is a very difficult period indeed. It tests severely all your beliefs and understandings. You perceive the inadequacies of your self and your beliefs. As Buck has written elsewhere, there is more than one way to deal with this period. You are in command. Therefore you can select what fits you best to respond to this tragic event.

Buck and I chose to use that high emotional energy that death would prompt to seek greater open connection with our inner selves. The beauty of this is that your strength is in your inner self. Therefore being in closer communication with your inner self is the same as reaching your inner strength for which you have great need.

There are other choices you can make and if they feel right, take them. During this grieving period, as well as all other periods of your life, your task is to develop your own truth. You should choose the alternative that you feel will advance your own truth. Experiencing losing a loved one is a crash course in developing your own truth as your own truths are seriously tested. This process, if properly done, will result in great strides in creating your own truth at an elevated level.

I watched my husband go through this and tried to help him find his inner strength in his inner self. I tried to point him to thoughts that would aid his creation of his own truth. I think he did very well. I wonder if I could have done as well. I probably would have with his help from this side. I'm pointing this out because I want our readers to know that their

departed one is trying to be helpful and to provide strength and wisdom. It is important to be open to this so that you can receive it. This is true even if you had difficulties with your departed one. Once the departed come to this side they have a broader perspective and feel a resurgence of love for those they just left.

Marshall: I cannot describe how much it means when you are swallowed up by the departure of your loved one, to feel that loved one encouraging you, wanting you to be happy, wanting you to gain wisdom, to live the life you still have left with greater understanding. When your loved one dies it is so easy to feel alone and so difficult *not* to feel alone. To feel the encouragement of your departed one just dissolves that loneliness. What a balm that is! Somehow, in ways I do not understand, the discussions Gail and I had about death really helped me feel Gail's presence after she died.

I have written about Gail prompting me to look for the black oak tree. This was two weeks after she passed on. In the nursery when I found the tree I burst out laughing. The other people shopping at the nursery looked at me queerly. They would have looked even more queerly if I told them I just recently lost my beloved wife but was laughing nonetheless. They would really know I was weird if I said Gail had led me to that tree and that was why I laughed. For me it was a message from heaven. What more could I have wanted?

Gail: Yes, what more could you want in a time of great need? There *is* an afterlife. In fact there are many afterlives. You have lived through them and you *will* live through them again. You need not be afraid. Nor do you need to worry if you are afraid. All will be revealed to you in time. What will be revealed to you will gladden your heart just as finding the oak tree gladdened Buck's heart.

When you lose a loved one you're not alone even though you may feel so. You have chosen to feel alone by refusing to believe it possible for you to receive help and love from the departed one, from your guide, and from kindred spirits of the Oneship. Open your mind to receive. Open your mind to the truth that we are all *one*. This makes it impossible for you to be alone. That is, unless you choose to be alone and make that your truth. You are in command of yourself. Choose to open doors. Do not close doors. You have too many closed doors in your life already.

The reason Buck feels that our talking about death helped him feel my presence after I passed on is simple. Talking about death is an exercise in being open. If you practice being open, it is easier to be open in the future. This helped Buck be open to my presence. So, be open. It helps in so many ways.

Marshall: People deprecate this kind of thinking as obviously untrue—that it simply represents wishful thinking. We would like it to be true so therefore we think it true. The truth is, wishful thinking neither creates nor negates the truth. The truth exists independently of our wishful thinking. Gravity went right on being gravity whether we believed in it or not. It will carry on whether we wish it to or not. So too with the truth. It will go on whether we wishfully desire it or wish to ridicule it. We should not make the mistake of thinking that if something has not been proved to our mind it therefore must be false. There is far more to this universe and to God than we have any idea. Our knowledge is not only quite small but much of it is wrong.

Gail: That is true if a bit harsh. There is much of the universe that you do know about but are not now remembering. Opening doors is a good means to remembering.

Chapter 93

We Are Among the Chosen

August 9th, 2001

Hello sweet one, back to our foggy mornings before the sun burns it off. Write to me as you wish.

Dear Buck,

Today I would like to talk with you about the barrier between your world and mine. Both worlds belong to each of us, as we exist in both—often concurrently. Right now I have no part of me incarnated on earth. You, however, have that self on earth whose fingers are typing away as well as your higher self over here with me. Everyone on earth has their higher self on this side. The reverse is not true. There are many on this side, besides myself, who have no incarnation on earth.

From this it can be seen that the existence over here is more fundamental. This is also borne out by the fact that life on earth is very temporary while life on this side is infinite. Your immortality is assured by your life on this side—not your life on earth. In fact, your lives on earth will result in your spiritual evolution to such a degree that you no longer need to return to earth. Thus it is seen that your immortality is not tied to earth but elsewhere.

The above concept is not new. Most of the mystical (metaphysical) systems and some of the religious systems support this view. My point is that if this is the case, the importance of you on earth being perceptive and communicative with this side becomes apparent. You may regard your attempts to communicate with your deceased loved one as your affair, which it is. However, it is also of importance to mankind as a whole because it diminishes the separation between our two worlds. This helps raise the consciousness of those on earth for the new millennium's emphasis that we are all *one*.

This realization should bring about within you an evolved attitude. You are trying to communicate with your loved one over here not only for your own self-centered reasons but to help dissolve the separation. "Dissolving

separation" is another way of saying "bringing love" to the earth. Yes Buck, it all fits together and that is the wonder of it all.

Let us carry this idea one step further. As communication opens up with those on this side, so too does the wisdom flow from the wise to the less wise. In spite of what you might say, when I was on earth you and I were equal seekers of wisdom. In some areas I was more advanced than you. In other areas you were more advanced than I was.

However, when I got over here three important things occurred that changed that. First when I got here I was able to review in great depth the experiences that I had just had in that lifetime on earth. That review allowed me to see it all with a much broader perspective. For example, I could see how actions I had taken had effected others. This is a real eye opener as you can imagine.

The second thing is that I have ready and easy access to the wisdom of others. On earth I also had access to wisdom but how I could go about accessing it was a good deal fuzzier. Coming here, it was almost like suddenly discovering how to use the library.

The third thing is that my mind is no longer cluttered up with the requirements of living in a material world. As you put it, no diapers to change or mortgage payments to make. This makes a tremendous freedom to pursue wisdom directly and in depth. To lessen misunderstandings, I must remind you that there is great diversity here and the mind is the creator. Thus if someone comes over here totally engaged in the material world, that person will likely create with his mind a similar world here to place himself within. In so doing is the access to wisdom postponed. There are many, many variations of that.

Buck, you and I were fortunate because we had long ago come to the realization that learning was the purpose of our being on earth. It was not difficult therefore for me to come here and continue to pursue learning. When you come you will delight in discovering our wonderful library with its most helpful librarians.

Your role and my role is to help open the communications between this world and the earth. With the channel opened I can reveal to you much of the wisdom which you and I on earth sought so dearly. It gives me great pleasure that you are receiving it, understanding it, and being thrilled by it. Our learning together that was so much fun on earth is continuing and at a much higher level. When I was on earth I had no idea this could happen. It wasn't that I disbelieved, it was just that it didn't occur to me as a realistic possibility.

There is a lesson in that for both of us. (I remember my Mother using that phrase when I was a child.) You will be much closer to wisdom if you stay open and think all things are possible, rather than assume so many things are impossible or unlikely. Assuming things are unlikely closes your mind. Gaining wisdom requires the opening of the mind.

Take my hand and rejoice. We are among the chosen. The fact that everyone else is among the chosen in no way diminishes the wonder of our being chosen. On the contrary, it enhances it.

Chapter 94

Being Versus Doing

May 19th, 2001

Dear One Close to My Heart,

Here I am sitting in the same place you sat so often. This is where you sat when we meditated with me beside you. I like being in this very spot. The doe with her two newborn fawns were right outside while I was eating breakfast. They are such a symbol of the serenity of this place. Please write to me whatever you wish this moment of *now*.

Beloved,

Serenity is indeed a precious state of *being*. Notice that serenity is not a precious state of *doing*. It is a precious state of *being*. This tells us something. Our western cultural hypnosis convinces us that our response to all things should be an act of doing. If we perceive an injustice, if we have difficulty in a relationship, if we wish to maintain our health, if we wish to be caring, all these circumstances, we think, require that we *do* something. The problem is, we think, to simply decide *what it is* that we should do.

There is another menu choice that the above system ignores. You also have a choice to just *be*. Our rational mind immediately bristles at this and logically points out that injustices will not be corrected if we do not do something. We feel that *being* will not achieve anything. We react this same way toward all situations that we believe require us to do something. The history of mankind is a history of people *doing* something. The result is that we have a never-ending set of changing injustices, difficult relationships, and other chronic problems. Would it not be reasonable to conclude that our "*doing* something" response to the world's ills is not effective? Would it therefore not be reasonable to try something else to see if it works better?

That something else to try is *being* instead of *doing*. I agree that it is counter-intuitive to think *being* is an effective solution. But we have seen this pattern before—that true

wisdom often seems counter-intuitive. By the way, I feel the need to point out that *counter-intuitive* is a very poor phrase and that counter-rational would be better.

Let's look at what a *state of being* might bring forth. In a state of being you are left with your thoughts. If you now understand that your thoughts are dual with a thinker, you, and a contributor whom you may invite to join in your thoughts, you will have opened a door. Your focus is now away from your outside circumstances, the very ones you feel need correcting by doing. Your focus now is inward. Looking inward brings you all of the wisdom of the inner self or the higher self. Further, it brings you serenity. You have now entered the state that is most likely to broaden your perspective. As I have said many times, broadening your perspective will bring you understanding which will become your guide to living in this life.

This is in contrast to doing. It is the very nature of getting ready to do something that you limit your focus and your attention to a narrow perspective of what it is you're going to do. This shuts other things out. As a general rule then we can say that *doing* narrows your perspective while *being* widens your perspective. This leads to another higher generalization and that is that narrowing one's perspective is a device of separation. Widening one's perspective is a tool to get closer to the *we are all one* principle.

This gives us a hint of why the *doing* response does not bring peace to the world. The *doing* response separates. At the same time that we have narrowed our focus to what we intend to do, we are usually separating the good guys from the bad guys or the good behavior from the bad behavior. If you think about it, you will see that there are further precepts of separation that cascade from these. You thus are facing and going in the wrong direction. Difficulties in your world will therefore persist. Is it not reasonable to abandon that which doesn't work in favor of a new way of responding?

I understand this is a very difficult concept to understand. It is even more difficult to change when your entire life training has been to the contrary. I hope that at least you are beginning to realize why what you are doing isn't succeeding all that well and that you can see an alternative to try.

I should add that there is a purpose and value in *doing* but I will not go into it now, as it will just confuse everything.

Chapter 95

Gratitude is the Attitude

June 15th, 2001

Dear Gail,

Here I am at the small rock pile in the sagebrush desert we discovered years ago. I am totally by myself. God seems so very near and the world so perfect. I hear God's voice in the wind through the pinyon pines. Write to me as you wish.

Sweet Buck,

What could be more perfect than the butterfly that just jiggled by? Perfection is everywhere you give gratitude. It is only by feeling gratitude that perfection reaches your perception.

Again the world has it backwards. They withhold gratitude until they see perfection or something close to it. They feel it would be a grave error to give gratitude for something that they feel doesn't deserve it. It is as though gratitude was something scarce that should not be spent willy nilly. Gratitude *is* a precious commodity, not because it is scarce, but because is it so powerful.

Perfection does not bring forth gratitude. Gratitude brings forth perfection. I know you know this and reap the rewards. Others would receive a great gift if they would try it and see that it works. Gratitude is not something you need to conserve. In truth the more you use the more you have. It is not a crime to give gratitude for something that on the surface appears undeserving. Gratitude will let you see deeper into its perfection. This is particularly true of the adversities in life.

You feeling gratitude was very key to your response to my death. You kept returning to the gratitude you felt for me sharing my life, my love, and our learning with you. This gratitude brought to you a perception of the perfection of my passing. Having gone through it, the word perfection is not too strong a word for me to use with you. To others it will seem a gross exaggeration. So let's describe it differently.

When I died there was an ambiance of great sorrow. You, in your gratitude to me for spending my life with you,

brought forth therefore a positive, loving presence into that soup of sorrow. This, in turn, brought healing to you and through you to our family. Although this might be hard to understand, this is perfection in action.

Perfection is not a static state. Therefore perfection in action is not an oxymoron. It is how it is.

Marshall: This ties in so well with what Betty Middlemiss says about giving our consent to whatever happens to us. Gail, I know you said this through her but you acknowledged that you were using her words. You didn't worry who got the credit when you were here. Presumably you care less there. (This is a family joke. Gail did many, many things that other people were given credit for. It happened so often that it became a family joke.)

Gail: That's true. Wanting credit acknowledges you have a lack that receiving credit could fill. But somehow receiving credit is always smaller than the hole you want it to fill. You would think this would cause people to try a different and better way.

As always the solution lies in broadening your perspective. When you realize there are other ways of feeling your own self worth that work better you can take or leave the credit that comes to you.

One such way is to know that you are as God created you. You are God's child. This in itself makes you worthy. No one has the power to make you more worthy than that.

Marshall: Gail you are right. I have great gratitude to you for living this past life with me. I also have great gratitude for the wonderful way you offer wisdom with such clarity and simplicity. I have great difficulty in doing that. Thank you. Thank you yet again.

Chapter 96

The New Millennium is Underway

April 30th, 2001

Dear Gail,

Please write for me as you wish.

Dear Buck,

The new millennium is well underway. Many don't see it yet because much of it is still in the preparation stage. There is a lot happening that is not reported in the media so it remains largely unknown. But nonetheless much is occurring which can bring satisfaction to the spiritually minded.

There are those who are repairing this troubled world. There are those who are healing. There are those who are counseling the separated. There are those who are teaching the ageless wisdom. There are those who are filling the earth with beauty. There are those who are nurturing the children. There are those who are opening hearts. There are those who are just *being*. These are all sacred endeavors. These all fit together into a vast pattern to bring this earth to an age of love. If you knew of just one tenth of what is happening you would feel very much encouraged.

Each of you can be a contributor to one of these purposes. Look within and you will be guided to your place in the resurrection. You are surprised at my use of the word resurrection. Don't be, for the world is being resurrected and you are a participant along with many, many others who are bringing this resurrection about. You will be guided by what you like to do. Do not feel you have to participate in all of the paths. Having found your path, rejoice in it. Again turn to your inner self and let it instruct you as to what you can do. You will find your fulfillment in working in the vineyard.

In knowingly working in the vineyard you will feel the energies of all those others who are working with you not only in your area but all areas. You probably will not know specifically what is being done but you will sense the energy and the devotion of your sisters and brothers who are with you. You will also feel the at-oneness that comes when you are in a joining state doing holy work. I have written often of the power and the all-pervasiveness of the invisible. It is the invisible that will let you feel all of this. Do not doubt it, just feel it.

Along with all the other things that are needed to bring about the resurrection, there is patience. Patience is much easier if you recognize what is happening and that great progress is being made. You have been given a great gift in being allowed to be a participant at this special time in this great and holy effort. Give thanks not only that the world is being healed but that you have been given the opportunity to be its healer.

Buck, you and I are joined in a love unit to work in our area of learning/teaching. What we are doing right now is our contribution to this massive pilgrimage to love. Isn't that exciting?

The other day I asked you if you felt others working through you. You replied no. Try to pick up on this again. I say this not because you need to feel others working through you but because you would like being aware of what is happening. Others are working through you now so it doesn't require that you be conscious of it. This same thing is true of other people on earth. Whether they are aware of it or not, many are getting help to fulfill their own path of contribution. It is like one vast orchestra which plays together to create the magic of music. One cello is helping the other cello to sing its part. The cello section helps the other strings to play their part and so on. Consciously seek to hear this concert of effort. Don't worry so much about knowing the specifics. Instead feel the energy.

Marshall: What are the ones who just "be" doing?

Gail: Remember the difference between doing and being? You just asked what those who are being are doing. In truth they are *being*, not *doing*. This is not a play on words. They are two different functions. What would you guess the function of those who are *being* is? This is the question you meant to ask.

Marshall: In *being* are they radiating their thought level, their understanding to be picked up by others. Are they somewhat like the magnetic north pole radiating out knowledge (where north is) but being unconcerned with how many compasses are detecting this knowledge?

Gail: A clever analogy. However unconcerned is not the right word. Not interfering is the right thought. They radiate wisdom that guides just like the magnetic north pole and they will not interfere with those who use this guidance or who don't use the guidance. They *are* concerned, however, with their brothers and sisters. Do you not detect an echo of God in this? Is this not the way God relates to us? He gives us guidance when we ask for it. He does not interfere with our free choice. He is concerned with us and loves us, but lets us do what we *will* with his guidance.

Marshall: That leaves out the immense blessings he gives us doesn't it?

Gail: You could say that. But truly the blessings come only if you ask God for them through your awareness of the gifts and your gratitude for them.

Chapter 97

Infinite Patience

October 6th, 2001

Gail, my friend, I feel you wanting to write more. Do use my fingers as always.

Yes Buck I do. You know patience is a very many layered word when it comes to its understanding. Patience is a godly attribute. It is found in all layers of evolution right up to God Himself. To give you free choice as God did, it would require Him to have infinite patience. He allowed us to choose anything—good or bad, evolved or stupid—anything—when giving us free will. And He obviously needs a great deal of patience as He observes how we choose to use our free will. Our misconduct, if you want to call it that, however, does not cause God to rescind free will. If He didn't have patience He would probably be tempted.

As above so below. We, who participate in the recycling of life on earth, also need patience. We all know what it means and think we have practiced it any number of times. However I want you to think of patience and forgiveness. Generally most religions, spiritual systems, and many people believe that forgiveness is a virtue to be emulated. We may not be as forgiving as we wish but we strive toward that goal.

Patience enables us to forgive. To forgive by just forgiving doesn't seem to work too well. If, however, we view our sisters and brothers with patience, forgiveness begins to seep into us. Further, if we view our sisters and brothers as inept rather than mean, cruel or self-centered, patience becomes even easier and we can expand our forgiveness.

People on earth, especially you Buck, tend to want everything perfect by 9:00 o'clock tomorrow morning. If others fail to contribute to that perfection by that time you will tell them in detail what they are doing wrong. You fail to note the improvements they are making, in favor of seeing why it still isn't 100% right. This impatience is fostered by the assumption that we have only this single lifetime to create utopia. We must, therefore, hurry and get it done.

There are a number of religions which teach that God gives us only one chance, this one lifetime, to pass the test of righteousness. Fail in this single appearance and it is too late. This causes a great deal of impatience in our world, which in turn causes a great lack of forgiveness toward those who appear to have transgressed. Then comes a great separation into the good and the bad, the saved and the unbelievers, and the chosen and the unworthy. But separation of the Oneship is not Godlike, even if done in the name of God. Do you see how impatience gets in the way of forgiveness? If you truly want to be forgiving, try finding a deeper meaning in the word patience.

Chapter 98

Make Friends With Your Higher Self

October 11th, 2001

Dear One,

What will it be today? I am here to write whatever you wish. Please use my fingers.

Yes Buck,

I am here too. Have you ever thought about karma and your higher self? You think in terms of karma being what you have done in relationship to someone else, someone outside of yourself. In contrast, your higher self is something that is within you. Again you have an assumption of separation when there is none.

Karma, in fact, is largely what is going on *inside* of you. It goes well beyond simply the karmic accumulation or debt that one must resolve, pay back or make up for. The center point of karmic action is within. To expiate Karma does not require that someone outside yourself do to you what you did to someone else. For instance, you were cruel to a friend. The simple view of karma is that you now need to experience cruelty from a friend. In this view that friend is obviously an outside agent (other than yourself) fulfilling karma. This incorrect thinking makes you see karma as outside yourself, as something that impinges upon you and something which, at this point, you have no control over.

Karma is not only within you because we are all *one* but because this is the place where karma is incurred as well as cured. Going back to what we said earlier, karma is a teacher. As a teacher, karma is trying to bring about greater understanding *within* you. This makes the goal of karma within you not outside of you.

When you are cruel to a friend the stimulus for this poor behavior is due to what is inside of you—your attitudes— and most importantly your ineptitude. So, you can regard karma as the teacher who is trying to evolve your ineptitude

into enlightenment. Again this is addressing what is within you.

This brings us to the higher self. The higher self can also be defined as that which is within you. The first part of what is within you is your conscious awareness. Beyond that is the sub-conscious which blends into the higher self. The higher self is also your teacher. And what is it trying to teach? It is trying to bring about greater understanding in you. It is trying to convert your ineptitude into enlightenment. This is hardly different from karma. In fact it is not.

Karma and your higher self work as one to achieve your growth. How is it that you expiate karma or escape its debts? The question itself is based on false understanding of karma but can nonetheless be answered by saying: you do so by learning the lesson contained in circumstances. By learning the lesson (or becoming less inept) you rise above the karmic debt and by God's law of grace are free of it. All this is done ideally within you and without any outside agent—in this case having a friend be cruel to you.

If, however, you are deaf to the teachings of your higher self and karma and persist in remaining inept, then you will experience something in the same pattern as a friend being cruel to you. And you will continue to receive (attract) similar episodes, which will, incidentally, get progressively more difficult, until you pay attention, listen, and learn. So would not it be sensible to try to communicate with your higher self to begin with and listen to its urgings? It makes sense to make friends with your higher self.

Chapter 99

Karma is a Balancing of Cause and Effect

February 28th, 2001

Dear Many-Times Wife,

Please use my fingers to write what you wish.

Dear Buck,

Let's talk more about karma. It is not a balance between good and bad or reward and punishment as many conceive it. Karma is not a system of justice and it is not an accounting system. It is a teacher. But, it is also *more* than a teacher. It is God's means of balancing cause and effect. It is a balance between two parts, which are neither good nor bad. It is a tool whereby things remain related to one another because we are, after all, *one*.

You always liked the duality of centrifugal and centripetal forces that keep the earth in orbit around the sun. They are, of course, the effects of momentum and gravity. Neither is good or bad nor are they opposites. They are just two principles that operate together at times to produce a single effect. Stripped to its basic, this brings two things together into a oneship. Karma too brings two or more things together into a oneship, or more accurately, brings them within the pattern of the One.

This bringing together is a most important aspect of God's natural laws. Think of all the spiritual concepts that share this function although each in its own unique way. Love brings together. Forgiveness brings together. And meditation brings together. It brings you to your higher self and your higher self brings you to other higher selves and to God.

Karma also brings together. It allows different parts to relate to each other in a vast variety of ways. When the parts seem against each other it allows them to work it out and eventually brings them together as *one*. Karma is therefore closely related to patience. In the long run, patience and karma succeed as God intended. Notice that during such an interchange, no matter how acrimonious or prolonged the

conflict between the two parts may be, they are always in a state of relating to each other. Yes, you are right, it is but yet another layer of the wisdom contained in the understanding that *all is but one.*

In fact, we are all related to each other at all times. This is because we are all *one.* Our first introduction to karma is not unlike being introduced to the boogie-man. If you don't do right he's going to get you. Then we discover good karma and open up our bank account and launch a savings program. This helps because now we are trying to do good albeit in our own self interest. This should introduce us to the joys of doing good for itself alone and eventually does. Then we start loving and forgiving without thought to our karma simply because it feels right to do so. To love is salutary to our awakening being. In forgiveness we experience giving up burdens we realize we don't want. As we do this we become conscious of the Oneship with God.

A clearer view of karma allows the joy that one has when he or she sees how all things fit together and relate together to achieve the harmony of the cosmos in its grandest form. This leads us to a new understanding between *doing* and *being. Doing* is local, finite and temporal. You cannot reach the All through simply *doing* no matter how virtuous you may feel your *doing* is. This does not imply that what you do doesn't matter. It matters a great deal. It is simply the wrong tool with which to sense the infinite, the universal and the everlasting *now.* To come to this realization you need to *be,* which is not local, not finite, and not temporal. After all, you live forever. Or put another way, your *being* is forever. Your *doing* comes and goes.

See how this makes clear that it is our beingness that returns us to God. And if we let our beingness thrive, our doingness will happen automatically. In turn, our karma will be instantaneously cleared. Karma will not be gone but will manifest in its purest, uniting form of allowing us to relate as God intended us to do. Do you see, my love, how much wisdom can be contained in a few pages?

Marshall: I do. It amazes me. I start to write for you and the word karma comes to my mind. Immediately I think it is wrong because we have written a pretty thorough description of it. Therefore I think I am not yet attuned to you. But dear one I am learning. So I trust you and myself too, I guess, and go with karma and wonder what kind of a rabbit can you pull out of this hat. Right away you go into how karma is a balance which I never ever thought about or read about before. Then you go onto the spiritual principles and how they relate in ways I never thought of. And then you seem to jump to another subject of doing and being. I have never seen anywhere a better differentiation of the two. Then you pull it back to karma like it was the easiest thing in the world. All that organization about which I had no inkling as I wrote. And all in a few paragraphs. Wow! Gail I thank you so much for letting me do this and for exposing me to this marvelous wisdom. Michael Newton (author of *Journey of Souls* and *Destiny of Souls*) was so right when he said you are "a very, very advanced soul". I just hope and pray that I can do my part in this larger thing that we must be doing, whatever it is.

Imagine, when I sat down I wondered if anything would come. Now here I am blowing my nose and wiping away the tears from being overpowered with—what can I call it? I don't know but it is awesome. Gail, before you died I seldom used the word awesome. Your transition was awesome and I have had quite a few awesome experiences since then. What gifts you have given me.

Chapter 100

More on Karma

March 5th, 2001

Dear Gail,

I have been reading Bob Smith's book, *Misdiagnosed*, about his wife, Jane, dying of cancer. I can't read very much of it at a time as it is so sad and tears come to my eyes. It makes me wonder at the way you chose to leave this world. Quickly and painlessly. There was a threat that I might have to take care of your vegetable self. The threat was short lived, thank God. How lucky we both were. And I know luck had nothing to do with it. Luck doesn't exist. But what a blessing. If your higher self had decided it was time to go you also chose the very best way to exit. I am confident I too can exit in such manner.

Dearest Buck,

I wonder if people realize the nature of karmic principles when we ask "How do bad things happen to good people?" Karma is a teacher along with other things as we have discussed. We advance through levels. The lessons we are given are at one level and our ability to learn them or rather our learning of them comes right up behind them to join at the same level. What happens at this point? You are given more lessons and those lessons are at a higher level still. And what form do you suppose those lessons take? They appear as problems as they always have. These problems do not appear because you have not expiated bad karma. On the contrary, they appear because you have graduated from a lower level and are now at a higher level where the homework is more difficult. When you show competence and graduate from sixth grade you now become eligible for seventh grade work. Again this is not bad Karma but the opposite; you are being rewarded for your advanced learning.

Here again we get back to perspectives. The narrow perspective says this is terrible and so unfair, so undeserved. The wider perspective sees this as an advance along the spiritual path Those intellectual arguers who think taking

things to extremes is enlightening will say, "Therefore the more we advance the more difficult life will be for us as our problems will continue to get worse and worse." Taking things to extremes blinds the mind rather than enlightening us. There is a seed of truth here but fortunately we have a God who mixes it all with kindliness. Along with this function we have other abilities that come to us as we advance. Serenity and joy are easier to have with advancement, for instance. Love becomes more real and understanding becomes ours with patience. These more than makeup for the increased difficulty in the lessons. Poor Bob went through some horrendous emotions which would make the most spiritually advanced feel despair. And he is advanced. He is now beginning to feel a broader sense of what was going on.

On earth there is a great temptation to judge people as to their spiritual level. Bob judged Jane as advanced. Even when this appraisal is correct it still has no proper function for the person so judging. The judging person is immediately thrown into further judging that therefore what is happening is unfair, or undeserved. Acceptance is the key principle here. And as we have said before, acceptance is much more than passivity. By habit, our perspective is way too narrow for us to be able to use judgment of these matters with wisdom. Instead our judgment can lead us into error.

Do you remember how I disliked the word "deserve"? When you would use it I would call your attention to its inappropriateness. You learned eventually not to use the word but better yet you learned not to think the word.

Marshall: You're so right. Now I see that to even use the word implies a judgment has been made that will lead away from God and not toward Him. One of many things I can thank you for.

Karma is not over when it has been expiated and your so-called karma has finally been worked out. On the contrary, Karma at that point has been fulfilled and is in its purest form.

Chapter 101

Free Will Versus the Oneship

August 25th, 2001

Dear Sweet Gail,

Another lovely day with bright sunshine. Margarita is all excited about getting married. She remembers you so fondly. Please use these fingers as you wish.

Yes Buck,

It is a lovely day. It is a lovely *now*. It is a lovely *always*. Let us talk about free will and also prayers, healing and times when others are trying to help us. It is well understood, as the farmers used to say, you can lead a horse to water but you cannot make him drink. Here we understand that you can offer people your help but if they choose not to accept it then it remains unaccepted. Free will trumps the offered help. This is quite clear when we talk about the visible world where we can see the offer and see either the acceptance or rejection of that offer.

However, when we deal with what goes on invisibly we are not so sure. What happens when someone prays for another? Does the prayer's stated wish take precedence over the recipient's free will? No. And in healing does the healing power of the healer bring about changes that are against the will of the to be healed? No again. Understanding this allows you to know how to be helpful, loving and healing to others including your deceased. Do pray for us on this side. Do send us healing and other loving thoughts. We will choose to receive them and appreciate them. They will help us feel the Oneship of all of us and the oneness of just we two. The dissipation of separation is holy work and benefits both sides.

Dear Beloved One,

It is Sunday, bright and shiny, a wonderful day. Please use my hands for writing what you wish.

Good Morning Dear One,

The question needs to be asked about the free will of each individual and the Oneship. We are involved in the new millennium where the awareness that we are indeed all *one* will become paramount. This will be accomplished by shedding the attitudes and practices of separation which have so dominated earth's history. If we are to relinquish these separation notions how can that fit into what I have been saying about free will?

Have I not been saying that each person's free will is separate and within their own separate jurisdiction? I have further extolled how one should respect and not be so quick to try to interfere in someone else's separate free will choices. This seems to extol separateness at the expense of oneness. How do we resolve these two positions?

You can appropriately use the word separate to describe each individual's free will choices. God gave you and all of us free will. He also made us such that we need to relate to each other and to our environment. Our nature, given to us by God, is gregariousness—although some are more than others, but all of us feel the need to relate to each other. It is by bringing our individuality, including our free will, into relationship and, hopefully, harmony with each other, that the Oneship is fulfilled. You could say that the free will and individuality is what each of us brings as the bricks with which the one wall is built.

It is God's mystery that we can be both individual and part of the One at the same time. Light is both a particle and a wave, another seemingly impossible pairing. This pairing is both mysterious and of amazing potential. Quantum mechanics has discovered part of the vast phenomena and powers that are given birth by this strange coupling. However, what can be accomplished by the congruence of the individual within the Oneship is even more phenomenal.

To understand this at our level you could say that God's plan is as follows: God in and of Himself was One. He created us and worlds for us to live in to develop our own individuality, our own small One. Once we had created that, we were, by our nature, desirous of accepting the invitation by God to join, or rejoin, the One which is God.

This grand plan has been told in allegory by many religions in many ways. It is the fall from grace in the Garden of Eden. It has been distorted into the original sin as if Eve and Adam were sinful in fulfilling their nature given them by God to become individual. This individuality can only be described as sinful if it is regarded as a final completed state of being. It is but one very necessary step, which needs to be followed in bringing this individuality back within the Oneship.

It has been recognized on earth that you need to love yourself before you can truly love someone else. This same pattern holds that you need to be an individual before you can truly join the Oneship. Your individuality is formed by your free will. Do you see how this is? Even without really understanding how you can be both individual and *one* at the same time, you nonetheless can see the process through which we are going.

It is so exciting to be at this time when a huge transition is being made by earth to leap forward toward the realization that we are all *one*. This does not mean we have to discard our individuality. Just the opposite. Our individuality is the gift we bring to the Oneship. What some of us see only dimly is that our individuality can be harmonious with other individualities, with all individualities. Most seem to feel that individuality requires confrontation, control, dominance, and other grossly separating devices. We fail to see the potential within the individuality to bring congruence and harmony with other individualities. The new millennium will manifest this potential of harmony. It is a giant step for this earth.

Chapter 102

Free Will and Universal Laws

November 14th, 2001

Hello Gail.

Our rain is still with us. Yesterday I got around to picking the pomegranates. As usual I didn't pick them soon enough and a number of them were split. You always had a hard time getting me to pick them at the right time. Please write to me with these fingers.

Hello Buck!

All that happens is in accordance with God's laws (including pomegranates splitting if you don't pick them before the first real rain). This confuses some people because they feel that it means things are already predetermined. But they are not predetermined because one of God's laws is that each of us has free will.

Free will does not mean, though, that you have free choice to do absolutely anything. You cannot expect to jump off a seven-hundred-foot cliff and also choose to survive. You cannot choose to breathe water like a fish. There are, however, very many things you can choose. This is particularly true within your mind. You can choose what to think. In fact your mind is the center of your free will.

There are many things that influence your decisions and your view of things. This, however, is different than *determining* them. I have talked about the influence of names. There are other influences such as karma, genetics, past lives, and culture.

Let us look deeper at influence. Influence is a result of the *we are all one* principle. If we are all *one*, then all parts inter-relate to all other parts. This is the same as saying that all parts influence all other parts. This is why chaos theory is such a giant step for science. Chaos theory acknowledges that a small change in a beginning set of conditions can result in a vast change in a subsequent set of conditions. This is the influence of the small upon the large. Although, even when all

parts influence all other parts, some influences are greater than others and some influences are immediate while others delayed.

It would be impossible to be aware of all the influences to which you are subjected. But it is possible, with wisdom, to be aware of the major influences acting upon you. This awareness will allow you to make better choices with your free will. The influence of the law of karma is an excellent demonstration of this. If you are unaware of the delayed aspect of the inevitable law of karma you may take advantage of another person and feel clever and rewarded for doing so. This is your operation of your free will. Nonetheless the influence of karma will be such that you will have this lesson to learn at some later date. Another person being aware of the influence of karma would not be so foolish as to intentionally do this.

There are other influences that are not as inevitable as karma. Astrology is one such. It describes your tendencies in how you act and how you view things. Very importantly, it also describes the tools you have to practice your life. If you live on automatic pilot, these tendencies will *become* you. However, your free will allows you to develop beyond these tendencies and grow into something more, which fortunately, many of you do.

We can describe the same thing in another way. Within the supreme pattern of the One are sub-patterns. Influences are sub-patterns. Your individuality is another sub-pattern. These patterns are joined and inter-relate. They influence each other in a wide variety of ways. When two raindrops hit the calm surface of a pool you can see each wave pattern cross each other—but are little changed. However, when those same waves collide with the pool edge they bounce back in a new direction. Wisdom lies in learning what influences are the most active and in what manner they act upon you. For those without this understanding, these influential patterns are unknown and life seems to be a matter of Lady Luck just giving and taking away.

Those who have mastery of their lives know what influences are acting upon them and how. Understanding these influence patterns allows the use of them to build what one wishes in his or her life.

Chapter 103

You are an Enchanted Oasis

July 25th, 2001

Dear One,

Another beautiful foggy morning making this place seem like an enchanted oasis. Please use these fingers as you wish.

Dear Buck,

You *are* in an enchanted oasis but those externals are there just because they exist inside of you. *You* are yourself an enchanted oasis. Every soul is. The meaning of this oasis is not that you are all alone in the middle of the desert but rather that you have within you all that you need—water, sun, greenery, sustenance, and a cohesiveness of being.

When you realize that God has given you all you need, many good things come to you. You have less to fear and you feel good about yourself. You feel capable of pursuing your life fulfillment. Perhaps most important, you feel gratitude for what you have been given. Gratitude opens the door to so many other good things.

I have written before about things that happen to you that may appear at first to be unwelcome. If you can feel gratitude for these events this will strip away the outer covering and you will see the perfection that is there in the experience. Part of this perfection is that you will see the opportunity to develop greater wisdom which will in turn bring joy to your life. Seeing this opportunity for what it is, leads you directly to knowing what you should *do*. That is, to learn the lesson so presented to you by God. Thus do you change an awkward situation into something from which you derive direction.

Knowing the direction of your life is highly satisfying. It will do wonders to diminish the ever-recurring problems in your life to much more manageable proportions. In fact it can even convert them to exciting, joyous challenges.

If you observe your world you will see that problems are always there. As old ones are removed new ones present themselves. Individually, we seek to solve our current problems. We are hoping to finally arrive at a problem free state that we would call happiness if we ever got there. And of course that problem-free state never arrives. New problems come into our lives and it is easy to see this as unfair or pure bad luck. We would be much better off accepting the circumstances for what they are.

In so doing we would shift our goal from trying to achieve a problem-free life to one of learning how to solve the never-ending stream of problems. It would be the same as learning your trade—for that is what it is. You are given a bunch of lumber and your problem is to build your house, the one you will live in. So instead of wishing for a completed house would it not be more sensible to learn the carpentry trade? And how can you learn? You learn by participating. And how can you learn most rapidly and skillfully? You do so by eagerly pursuing your apprenticeship and feeling the joy that comes from learning something useful.

It is all in the mind. The mind is the builder. With it you can construct a world much more to your liking than what you have so far. It can all come to you simply by perceiving the world as it truly is. God has given you so much power yet you have covered it up by limiting your perceptions. As you begin to truly see who you are, so will you see how glorious it all is. All life on earth is singing but you have turned the volume so low you can't hear it. Turn it up and listen. There is so much more for you to see! There is so much more for you to hear! There is so much more for you to feel! Welcome these into your life.

Gratitude leads to perfection
Perfection leads to wisdom
Wisdom leads to joy
Joy leads to God.

Part Five

September 11th, 2001

Dear Reader,

The "inspired writings" that we have shared with you represent just a portion of the almost 300 that Gail and I have done since that wonderful day that we got started.

As we were writing this book, the horrific events of September 11th, 2001 occurred. I wondered if Gail would comment on them. Indeed she did and as usual came up with some new ways of looking at things.

In the past century we have seen our civilization seriously threatened many times and we have had the task of mobilizing our efforts to overcome those threats. Reading Gail's comments I get the idea that the World Trade Center tragedy is another one of this pedigree.

We also are in the midst of other kinds of threats to our civilization as we know it. The pollution of our world, whether causing the greenhouse effect or toxic waste could also change everything. All of this puts the World Trade Center tragedy into a wider perspective—one of Gail's favorite approaches.

I include here excerpts from the September 11th writing, done over the weeks that followed. I think they address not only the tragedy of 9/11 but also other continuing major problems of our world.

Chapter 104

Free Will in Action

September 11th, 2001

Gail,

Hours ago terrorists attacked the World Trade Center, the pentagon and other targets. America now has become aware of its vulnerability. It's hard to see how this fits into a spiritual path. Use my fingers as you wish.

Dear Buck,

It is a most difficult time to digest as to its meaning. The world has in it many people full of hate who are nonetheless your brothers and sisters. They perpetrate these acts with a full feeling of righteousness and vengeance. They do not see their victims as they see themselves. They have exercised their free choice in their own way.

To understand it requires, as always, a wider perspective. Those thousands of deaths in the World Trade Center are now on this side. They too live forever. So they are not the tragedy. In fact there is no tragedy: there is only an opportunity to react in a new and healing manner. Whether this will be done is of course yet to be seen. To graduate into the new millennium will require a new higher level of response. It should be no surprise then that this higher level will have to be a response to a higher level of difficulty. It is similar to school homework: the higher the grade the more difficult the work.

Although it is not easy to look at it this way, this attack, though very devastating, is better than World War Three or a nuclear war, threats that you have also lived through. It pinpoints the crux of the earth's evolvement. It also allows a wider menu of response than would a world war or nuclear exchange. Thus it provides an opportunity more pregnant with an enlightened response. Again, you must wait and see what the response turns out to be.

Be steady. Nothing can happen that cannot be turned into an opportunity for the advancement of the All that is One.

Chapter 105

Can We Remain Unchanged?

September 15th, 2001

Dear Beloved Gail,

I'm so glad that I feel you want to write again. I know I have probably been shutting you off. The demolition of the World Trade Center on Tuesday has made it hard to achieve a quiet meditative state. Please do write what you wish with these fingers.

Buck,

Take heart. I am here. You are right. Your mind has now slowed down sufficiently for me to convey to you some thoughts. You foresee the retaliation that America will take against the terrorists and you are concerned that this will just plant seeds for further conflict. And it probably will. However you are wrong in thinking that the world will not progress in spirituality in the process. You wonder how America will respond from a spiritual viewpoint and you wonder the same thing about those American attacks.

It is God's plan or law that with each experience we live through we learn something that will further us on the spiritual path. There is no exception to this. Our free will granted to us by God does allow us to learn—very little or a great deal—but learn we must. The spiritual path does not go straight up. This allows your spiritual path to be unique, as is everyone else's

Don't forget the figurative statement you used in your classes that everyone needs to learn a lesson eight times. It is only with the eighth learning that the lesson becomes clear to the intellectual and emotional minds and therefore becomes part of you. The previous seven learnings could be described as sub-rosa (in secret). Others observing you would think that you had learned nothing and were still in kindergarten.

Do you think it is possible for those 18 or 19 suicide terrorists to come over to this side and go through the life review process and remain unchanged? They will learn something. How much they learn and what they learn is a

matter of their free will. However each will have some increment of spiritual advancement. This is also true of their victims. This will also be true of you on earth who are now going through an unprecedented experience. We are all *one*.

So you do not need to be discouraged or be concerned that the world will learn nothing from all its trials. In fact, if your view were wide enough you could even see virtue in these events because people are brought face to face with some of the larger issues about life—who they are, and what they want to have as their truth. This creates a profound learning environment. This is a real step up from being mired down in the petty day to day worries that people fall prey to. This is hard to see because you let the suffering, anxiety, and fear cloud your vision.

You can have faith in your brothers and sisters that they are all learning from these events. This learning will advance the spiritual progress of your lovely world. You may not see it in the visible world. This may be because your vision is obscured or it may be because it is happening in the invisible, which includes what is going on in the minds and hearts of each of you. But it is there as sure as is the dawn.

You are very right in your thought that it is not so much a matter of what is done as it is the attitude with which it is done. It gets back to what we have talked about before. What you "do" is not as important as what you "are" [being]. Long ago we said that you can do anything including murder and it could be a virtuous act if done with the right attitude.

Marshall: I was just talking with Gordon about that. If someone is suffering greatly from terminal cancer, can not assisted death be a loving act? Yet the law calls it murder. So America's retaliation may contain virtuous elements even in the midst of the violence it delivers. Is this what you are saying?

Gail: Almost. America's military and violent response is a mixture of many things. It would be nice if that mixture contained a higher amount of spiritual concern and a lesser amount of giving back "what they deserve." You are right that both the terrorists and the vengeance seekers are using single polarity thinking which we know causes trouble. Perhaps this time there will be more people using double polarity thinking that will foster much greater advancement.

This is not a set back to the new millennium but will rather serve as a catalyst for it. It is as though you have been receiving the lessons for some time and been doing your homework diligently and now comes the time for a mid-term test. But, don't take this analogy too far and start looking and judging how things transpire in terms of whether you are passing the test or not. The results of the test will be manifest in the invisible not the visible. Further more, it isn't a test. It is more of an acceleration in learning opportunities.

Chapter 106

A View from the Other Side

September 19th, 2001

I have just received an e-mail with a reading done by psychic Al Miner about life on the other side for one of the World Trade Center terrorists. It speaks to what Gail was talking about when she said, "Do you think it is possible for those 18 or 19 suicide terrorists to come over to this side and go through the life review process and remain unchanged? They will learn something. ...This is also true of their victims..."

Here is an excerpt of that reading:

A solitary figure is seen weeping, kneeling, hands covering his face. He is approximately mid to late 20's, earth-age. He is not of the following who are called Christians. He is, in fact, one of the perpetrators of this action perpetuated earlier in your earth day [9/11].

Why is he kneeling? Why is he weeping? Because he is upon the pathway being trod by many souls; many souls whose lives have ended in the physical and have begun in spirit. And he has met, and been challenged by, many different forces.

Upon his passage through the portal called death, he continued on, believing that the impact had not yet taken place. As the illusion of the surroundings just previous to the impact faded, he found himself standing in an open place, alone. Though there were messengers of God, his guides, if you will, present, he could see them not, for his spirit was not open to see.

When he realized that he was still in existence, in the manner similar to that of the earth, when he discovered that this was not, as he was told, an act that would lead him on to paradise, he felt the anger and hatred of that which he thought to be holy, that which he thought to be a work in the name of the God that he was taught might expect same.

No songs of praise. No ceremonies of rejoicing. Only greetings by great throngs from the darkness, calling out in various ways, unimaginable, messages of the darkness, voices that choose to separate and divide, voices which perpetuate the desire for power and dominance and hatred, using the weapons of fear, and such as these, until the terror in his spirit grew to such dimension that here he is, kneeling, weeping, as he watches those souls pass by whose earth lives have ended because of his action.

The Law is perfect. And in order to pass from one realm of consciousness to that which lies beyond, to ascend, so to say, or to move into the light, as it is so often called in the earth, one must meet that which has been the journey being left behind.

Thus this man saw the lifetimes of each entity whose, as you call it, death, was a result of his action. He saw their lifetimes from birth through childhood. He saw each event of joy, of sorrow. He saw their families and knew them, and felt the love and the compassion. He felt the frustrations. He heard the lamentations of those left behind—orphaned, widowed. He felt their emotion. And finally, he saw them, as they passed by.

Here and there, he paused to look up, calling out, his hand reaching, grasping, asking, "Forgive me," pleading with the line of entities passing by, moving up individually and severally great tunnels of light, surrounded by those of the very host of God's angelic beings. Yet they heard him not.

It is not that they could not find in their spirits, many of them, the ability to answer this lad, actually young in heart and mind. It is that they saw him not. For he is veiled by the separateness of those who surround him. An eternity of such events transpired in mere earth hours.

Each soul was visited in this manner. Each Soul is now known to him. And in his spirit's heart, he knows the Law, and he feels the burden of what you call Karma. It is not that this commentary is meant to imply anything, but only to clarify. Soon those veils will part, for, ultimately, we know, he will ask of God for forgiveness, and we shall answer and embrace him, and the darkness shall fall away. And we can move him from his position within the shadows, or the darkness, as he asks it. Perhaps in time he will come to a state of understanding and he will choose as others before—perhaps even some of you who are hearing or reading these words—that he might journey in the quest of his own spirit, once again.

As we look upon this young man one final time, we can tell you that the agony, the pain, the fear, the sense of betrayal, and the sense of no reference, are beyond imagination and our capacity to express in your words. But it is not God who places these upon him, nor even the thoughts of the many-fold of the earth who direct anger and hatred toward the perpetrators. But he, himself—fueled by those in the darkness, who find some curious accomplishment by nourishing these thoughts of pain and agony.

When he looks down at his hands as the instruments of his will—that they directed the death of so many—and as he cries out "O Allah, wrest them from my body, that never again shall I commit such an action of such a nature," perhaps because his belief in this is strong, he will return to the earth without the use of his hands and arms.

We ask you to look upon this one in the moment of your sadness, your grief, your shock, your disbelief. Not he alone, but the others who were, like him, believers unto the word they were given, unto the promise they believed, with all of their being. So we would ask of you, remember them in prayer, as well.

Chapter 107

More on September 11th

September 27th, 2001

My Friend,

How are you this time? I've just come back from a trip to Utah. I was very impressed with the patriotic fervor that I saw everywhere, even Las Vegas. Please write with my fingers as you do.

Dear Buck,

You are indeed going through very interesting times. You will find it easier to get through these times if you remember what I told you earlier. Everyone, without exception, spiritually advances with every experience that they have. This seems to be counter to having free will but it is not, because of the *we are all one* principle. This will take some explaining. But first I want to repeat that even though everyone advances with every experience, the pace with which they advance is chosen by them. Thus there are many who advance at a pace that would be regarded by a snail as slow. This is how it appears at the individual separated level. As always, greater wisdom comes with expanding one's vision.

Remember also that God in his infinite abilities can take any action done by anybody no matter how horrendous and make it a cause (as in cause and effect) **for spiritual advancement. So your Hitlers, your Stalins, your Bin Ladens, in spite of themselves, spawn a whole series of stimuli for spiritual advancement.**

Marshall: I witnessed an example of that this morning at the Library Board meeting. One director works at the college and was telling us that the college is starting a lecture series aimed at our being better informed on the Middle East. His first lecturer will be trying to explain the terrorist's viewpoint. He anticipates a full house. So here we want to learn about the grievances of our fellow man. Before September 11th, we didn't want to be bothered as we were wrapped up in other things. So now we want to pay attention to the condition and ideas of people we think are unlike ourselves but are really part of the Oneship.

Gail: Yes, you can see this same thing occurring everywhere. People have gone through a major priority shift. What seemed so important two weeks ago seems less important. Much of what they took for granted they are now appreciating. To appreciate is to spiritually advance.

Also notice that there is a great surge in not being intimidated by the terrorists or their attacks. Look at that deeper. What people are saying is that they will not be afraid even though there may be more occurrences of terrorism to come. Is this not an exercise in invulnerability?

I talked earlier how we are invulnerable. That may have seemed to you kind of abstract and wishful in thinking. Now here you have many Americans deciding (free will choices) to *not* be intimidated and to not be made fearful. Instead they choose to regard themselves with greater invulnerability. There are millions of Americans who have made this choice. Now invulnerability is not so abstract. It is a practical response to a serious threat. I would say it was a spiritual lesson and spiritual response to what you regard as a horrendous event.

Do you not see that God in his infinite abilities has taken this disaster caused by the free will of individuals and made it an opportunity for your learning? Specifically in this case, people have the power to choose a higher degree of invulnerability and a lessening of fear. This is spiritual advancement by the many stimulated by what again is regarded as a disaster.

Marshall: From what you are saying I can see that the overall good to many, many people might outweigh the tragedy of the fewer. As you have said those who died are now over there. Do they see the role they played in providing the stimuli for the world's learning?

Gail: Mostly they do. It depends if they choose to see the broader perspective. Some understandably are still wrapped up in the sorrow of those they left behind. Some of those left behind are beginning to realize that there is some kind of communication with their departed ones. Others are feeling a

strange "presence" of the deceased. I use the word strange only to describe a feeling of presence they never had before. So there are some who already sense that communication with the deceased is going on.

However there are many here who are trying to contact their loved ones on earth. Unfortunately their loved ones are not open and don't know how to listen. They don't even know that communication is possible.

Perhaps you can now see the need for this book. If all those grieving ones left behind felt that it was possible to communicate with their loved one on this side they would feel uplifted. They would love to do the exercises in this book and participate in the results. We are all *one*. We are all forever. To get just a glimmer of these two truths can dissolve much grief. It also can add greatly to one's sense of invulnerability.

Chapter 108

Every Day the World Advances

September 27th, 2001

Gail,

What you are writing fascinates me. Please write what you wish with these eager fingers.

Dear Buck,

Yes this is a very stimulating time. Everyday the world advances whether or not there are disasters. This is because God has the ability to turn all events into opportunities for learning His spiritual laws. Because we are all *one*, if the Oneship advances, then all of us advance as well. This includes the terrorists and the victims.

Earlier today I wrote about how such tragic events can, with God's influence, create responses that increase our sense of oneship and invulnerability. That does not mean that the increase creates perfection or even all inclusiveness in the Oneship. However, within America there is a greater sense of inclusiveness in its citizenry than before. There is also a greater feeling of oneness in the world.

You can see the possibility that the world will advance because of the World Trade Center experience. From the broad oneship view you can get some idea of this truth. It is perhaps more difficult to see this truth from an individual viewpoint even though it is equally true. If an individual is full of hate and vengeance he or she needs to go through a learning process by which the hate and vengeance is lessened if even by a very small amount. Those who have arrived on this side are now going through a healing process that can bring about exactly that. Again, the pace at which these individuals advance is up to their free will. It has already taken them many lifetimes. How many more will be needed? This will be up to them.

But you who feel more advanced than the terrorist need to wait for your brethren (the terrorists) to join you in developing your own truth which will bring you to God. This is

hard but more effective than creating new terrorists by adopting vengeful attitudes in retaliation. The current vengeful violence can be traced back through prehistory to a long seesaw chain of perceived injustices. It is time to try something new.

Chapter 109

Thoughts are Cast Out Like Stones

September 28th, 2001

Good morning Sweetheart. What do we have today? Please write me as you wish.

Beloved Buck,

Each of us has free will. When we have a thought or take an action, it is cast out like a stone into the environment. The instant it is received by the environment it becomes subject to the laws of that environment. In the case of the stone, it becomes subject to gravity and the laws of momentum to mention just two. The nature of the stone persists but the environment and the laws of that environment determine its course.

     Put another way, each action and thought that we have is made manifest in our world. How our world reacts to that action or thought is subject to two things: the God created laws that govern our world and the free will of others. You will note I put the God created laws first. This is because His laws greatly influence (but do not determine) how the free will of others is exercised.

     This brings us to what I have said before. God, in His infinite ability takes the thoughts and actions, which we by free will have selected, and converts them into stimuli to enhance our spiritual growth. Interestingly, these stimuli act not only on the surrounding people who are effected by the thoughts and actions but also on the perpetrator of those thoughts and actions.

     I have used the World Trade Center disaster to illustrate this. It is easy to think of this event as a great step backward. It does not have to be so. With broadened perspective you can see where it can actually result in a step forward. Two reasons you regard it as a step backward is that you think in terms of the priority of maintaining the status quo and the priority of maintaining your ease in living your life. The God created laws that I have referred to above do not see these two priorities of yours as being at all vital to maintain. In

fact status quo and ease in living often stultify spiritual growth. Thus, a spiritually enhancing environment is not measured by how well the status quo is maintained nor by the ease of life.

To digest this tragic event and achieve a greater feeling of peace, understand that God is giving all of you a new and stimulating growth opportunity not only for your spirituality but for everyone's spirituality.

Take heart that everyone will grow from this event even though that growth might be so small as to be invisible to your eyes. There is a tendency to be impatient and demand visible, measurable results or you think nothing is happening. As we have said, it is like you are building a huge brick wall just one brick at a time. From a distance the addition of one more brick is invisible.

Some people will not be able to believe this because they feel that no progress is being made. There is still much hatred in the world as the events of September 11th demonstrate. There is still much suffering everywhere. However in the broader perspective there is a great deal of progress. Buck, you have lived over a period of time that would allow you to see this progress. Why don't you list some of the things that show spiritual advancement of the earth?

Marshall: I do believe you are right—much progress has been made. At the turn of the century going into World War I it was considered glorious to go to War. It was thought to bring out the best in young men. That is no longer considered true except in small enclaves of the world. The Vietnam War and to a lesser extent the Russian invasion of Afghanistan demonstrated to the government leaders that the old men in government couldn't send off the young men to fight their wars. Thus government leaders are much more cautious about getting into a war. Our current attitude toward war on a worldwide basis is much more cautious than 100 years ago.

In 1900 and well into that century our attitude toward polluting our world was also grossly ignorant and arrogant. We have very far to go but we nonetheless have a much greater love and care for our world than we did then. We are actively seeking new awareness of the polluting results of our actions.

Civil rights and human rights, which were not even on the agenda in 1900, are now worldwide concerns. Before 1900 there was no intervention into another country's sovereignty simply because they were carrying out an inhuman policy like ethnic cleansing. Before 1900 if there was intervention, it was as an excuse to annex some territory.

In my lifetime, volunteerism has blossomed greatly. There are far more organizations and groups providing help and care in many more niches than before. The principle of being your brother's brother and giving back something for what you have received is practiced by many more individuals than ever.

There are more, of course, but this illustrates that underneath the mix of good and bad events, real continuous progress can be detected in the consciousness of us all.

Gail: And that progress will not only continue it will accelerate. You live in inspiring times.

Chapter 110

Nine Comforting Thoughts

September 29th, 2001

Dear Gail,

I just took our granddaughter home. She is such a sweet child now growing nicely into adulthood. Please write to me as you wish.

Dear Buck.

In spite of everything there is much to be pleased with in your world. In the last several writings we have talked about the difficulties in coming to terms with the tragedy of September 11th. For those who have suffered a personal loss in this difficulty or any other it could bring comfort if several understandings were considered:

1. **First, any departed loved one is sharing in the afterlife.**
2. **Second, the after life is good and loving.**
3. **Third, this afterlife is not separated but is part of the Oneship. This means communication is possible with the deceased.**
4. **Fourth, there is no such thing as final. Therefore any unresolved issues are not frozen but can be addressed in the *now* and between both the earth world and the spiritual world.**
5. **Fifth, God's power includes the ability to convert any tragedy into a learning opportunity where the spiritual virtues are enhanced.**
6. **Sixth, all our brothers and sisters are evolving slowly but surely into more enlightened attitudes.**
7. **Seventh, although you may feel compelled to take actions, even violent actions, these nonetheless can be done with a greater appreciation of love, understanding, and forgiveness. Instant perfection in this direction is difficult but progress in this direction is most worthy.**
8. **Eighth, we are all *one* and each of us makes an individual and unique contribution to that Oneship. Each of us is**

granted that privilege. Each of us should have gratitude to our brothers and sisters for their unique contribution.

9. Ninth, love and union *will* prevail over hate and separation.

On earth any loss is difficult. Big losses are big difficulties. When you understand that all losses are but temporary and that all losses contain within them the seeds of enlightenment, you are closer to finding peace.

Even when you have lost a loved one, or several loved ones, you still have God's three great gifts. We are all *one*. We live forever. We have been given free choice. So too do the loved ones from whom you feel separated. Remember, the mind is the builder. This means the mind is the enabler. The attitudes and understandings you have in your mind will enable you to find or rather build peace. You will be able to communicate with all the Oneship, including your loved ones.

Do not assume that these are beyond your powers. They are not. What God gives you cannot be taken away. Even when you choose to shut down these powers by disbelief in yourself, they remain for your command. You are blessed.

Chapter 111

A Silver Lining

October 17th, 2001

Beloved Gail,

A very foggy day. Fall is really here and it is cold. I have a blanket around me as I write and it feels so good. Please use my fingers to write as you wish.

My Dear Buck,

You are concerned about the terrorists. This time it is the anthrax. You feel that the terrorists can take apart your civilization. The very systems with which you function and carry on your life is threatened. The airlines are attacked and now the mail system. What system is next—the power grid? You think it is unprecedented that the very fabric of your life can be so drastically rent. What you are thinking is contrary to what you already know. You have drawn a boundary around this current crisis which is always a great way to make things seem worse. You need to broaden your perspective not narrow it. In your lifetime you have witnessed a number of events that could all be described as threatening the very fabric of your way of life in an unprecedented way. It would do you good just to list them now so that you become aware that the current terrorist threat is in fact not the first attack on the core of your way of life.

Marshall: Okay. My first memory of such an event is of the beginning of World War II when Hitler's blitzkrieg method of war seemed totally unprecedented and devastatingly effective. His super capable war machine tore through France in just weeks even though France had a larger army and had spent millions on the Maginot line to protect itself. It seemed like there was just nothing to stop Hitler. We would all have to live under the fascist way of world order. As you say Gail, it was an unprecedented threat to civilization as we knew it.

Secondly, the threat of World War III seemed very real and we envisioned that war as being much worse than any previous war. Weapons of all types were much more powerful that in World War II. The head to head confrontation of United States with Russia was truly scary. World War III could have come about because of a number of events. There was the Korean War, the Cuban Missile crisis, and the Vietnam War. Each of those brought us to the brink of World War III and the subsequent disruption of our world.

Thirdly, there was the threat of a nuclear holocaust. It is strongly related to the threat of World War III but had the additional dimension of a surprise attack. This would have brought about mutually assured destruction. Again civilization as we knew it would have disappeared in an unprecedented way.

I think what you are trying to get me to see is that, as scary as the terrorist threat is, it is still just number four in a list of unprecedented threats to our way of life in the past sixty-five years. This doesn't diminish the threats but it does make me feel that we also have a precedent of overcoming threats to our society. That does make it seem less scary and more like something that we can handle with due diligence.

Gail: Yes that is what I mean. We could go one step further and say from a practical viewpoint this threat is starting out favorably. A nuclear surprise attack would have simply devastated the world in a very brief time and left no recourse. The current attacks take on the characteristics of warnings allowing you to generate counter measures. Here you have recourse.

You have another view about the current crisis that I would like you to think about. You are tending to see all of this from a material point of view. You are appraising your chances on a material scorecard. You count up the number of physical deaths, the number of anthrax cases, the immense cost of creating a more secure society, etc. These are all very difficult things.

However, as is always the case, the true scorecard is the one involving the hearts and minds of the people. It is how their hearts and minds change that is the true result of what you are going through. The revelation to you of the amount of hate that is out there—particularly the hate that is directed toward the United States overpowers your mind. In truth, that hate has been building up for some time. You have only been

mildly aware of it. It has now grabbed your attention, not because it has suddenly become greater but just because your awareness has become greater.

In truth, on a worldwide basis hate has diminished since September 11th. It is true that a small minority has delighted in seeing the United States, as a representative of Western civilization, suffer. But the terrorists went too far and have made vast numbers of fence sitters appalled at what the terrorist have done. They now are repulsed by this terrible manifestation of what hate is willing and able to do. The righteousness and justification of hate has been tarnished in the minds of many. This result is unseen and uncounted but of vast importance.

What I am trying to reassure you is that you need not be so appalled as if you have never been so threatened. And further there are many good things going on because of this that are not now so apparent. There is no need to be discouraged. There is no need to think the very worst is going to happen. It is in our hearts that success will come.

Chapter 112

It's the Attitude

November 15th, 2001

Dear Gail,

Please write with these fingers what you wish.

Dear Buck,

You don't feel at peace this morning. It will pass. Being at peace is a wonderful thing. While you are on earth it is difficult to be at peace all the time. You can, however, return to it. Think about acceptance in a meditative way, for example, and you will find serenity returning.

Feeling at peace is to feel close to God. This awareness of the presence of God is very enabling in dealing with the world, with learning, and with feeling part of the One. I have talked often of the importance of *being*, in contrast to *doing*. Being aware of God's presence is a central part of spiritual *being*. In this sense of *being*, what you should *do* will, without effort, come forth from you. Those on earth spend a great deal of time trying to figure out what they should do. Many, many are very sincere and wish mightily to do the proper spiritual thing but are very puzzled as to what it should be.

Recent events provide an example of this. Spiritual people wonder if this is a time to set aside spirituality and deal directly with terrorism in a realistic way. They feel if they don't retaliate in some way the terrorists are going to continue to blow them up by various means. But they feel uneasy with retaliation. How can they decide what to do?

The answer lies not in first deciding what to do, but in first deciding what to *be*. We would all like to be like Jesus or another revered spiritual master. But we are not. We are, however, on the path to becoming so. While it is unlikely that we can become Christ-like in the next twenty-four hours, we have traveled far to be where we are now. We also know we have a long way to go to become who we ultimately want to be. So we need to be patient with ourselves, to accept ourselves for what we are. We also need to have the desire to continue our journey to God.

This brings us to what we choose to be. We can choose to elevate our being in ways that will take us spiritually closer to who we want to *be*. From this, what we *do* will flow. Will such *doing* be as Jesus would do? Probably not. However that doesn't mean that it may not be a very appropriate and upward action for us to do from our place on the spiritual path.

As I have said before, what we do is not as important as what our thoughts are when we are doing it. In other words, we can do quite a variety of things and it won't matter as much as the attitude with which we do them. Murder is a serious thing. Yet when a terminal patient wants to die is it murder to help him or her? Or is it compassion and love?

Here is America fighting a war against terrorism. Some wish only to pay back the terrorists for the World Trade Center destruction. Others are not thinking so much of retaliation but of correction, sustenance and reconstruction. Therefore food is also being dropped and funds raised to help the children and refugees. This thinking reflects the presence in their being of spiritual principles.

Even though the latter also take part in violence, their attitude will help bring about a healing while the former will simply continue the seesaw of revenge and counter revenge.

I hope this illustrates the importance of who you *are* in juxtaposition to what you *do*. It is beyond most of us to be perfect but it is well within our powers to choose to promote healing in the world.

Chapter 113

Free Will and Synchronicity

October 29th, 2001

Dear Gail,

Here we are again this lovely anniversary day. Please use my fingers again to write as you wish.

Dear Sweet Buck,

I have already answered all your questions about September 11th in generalizations but I know you like specificity. So we will take the general principles and apply them directly.

There is no such thing as coincidence. All events are synchronistic. It is what you call the supreme pattern wherein everything is related to everything else. This universal inter-relatedness is the supreme pattern as you used to teach. It is very difficult to understand how this synchronicity can exist at the same time that we have complete free will. Your limited perspective and understanding says that free will exercised by so many entities is bound to throw a monkey wrench into the synchronicity. It doesn't. That is the genius and the mystery of God. If you are not already in awe of God's capabilities this realization should make you so. Not only does the synchronicity exist in spite of all that free will going around; the synchronicity is actually enhanced by free will. In fact free will is necessary for synchronicity to function. Now I know this is contrary to all your rational thinking but it is nevertheless completely true. As I have said more than once the world usually has it backwards.

This being the case, then the World Trade Center event is not outside the synchronicity but an integral part of it. The disaster, as you see it, is triggering all kinds of things both visible and invisible through this synchronicity. With your upside down thinking you see the visible war, suffering, and the remaking of your society as the most powerful result. It is not. It is what is going on in the minds and hearts of people that will create again, through synchronicity, a new and better world. Doomsayers and those who see threats at every gate have always been welcomed into the thinking of the less evolved. They are popular even in good times. How much more popular are they in times of stress.

You are fully capable of handling this situation. Do you think that we on this side would somehow *not* be fully capable of handling on our side such an event? You wonder how we can process masses of deaths that occur in a short time frame. First, this side has had plenty of practice. Secondly, as I have told you before, we on this side are not limited to doing only one thing at a time. (Although there are those on this side who still think they can handle only one thing at a time and so create this limitation for themselves.) The basic reason we can do more than one thing at a time is that here we have not separated the past, present and the future and therefore operate in all three at once. You do not understand how this can be. You assume it would be like watching three videos at once, very confusing. Earth limitations of time and space do not exist here.

When the terrorist and their victims come to this side they all go through the same process. They are not treated differently even though each comes with their own past life activities that they themselves must review. Remember those who you call terrorists are not the devil but your brothers. Remember also that being a victim does not automatically make you a saint. The terrorist in the life review process will know how it feels to be one of their victims. This is a strong stimulus to change one's thinking.

It is also true that the life review process for the victims will reveal the inward feelings of frustration and hate of the terrorist. This also is a powerful stimulus. It will make one wonder about one's indifference to the plight of one's brothers and sisters.

Although there is variation you would be surprised at the sympathy that some terrorists and some victims feel for the other.

Have you observed how the American Government and other governments are now trying belatedly to think of others? They are trying hard to show acceptance of the Muslim faith. They are thinking of the Afghan children. They are dropping food in Afghanistan.

Do you see a synchronistic pattern here involving the terrorists, the victims of terrorism, and the citizens of the world? Each of you has your part to play. The part you play is *more* than what you think and do consciously. Your thoughts are both attracting from and sending to others. For this reason, it is so very important that your thoughts be elevated.

We on this side, the recently deceased as well as older souls, are also part of this synchronicity and therefore play a role as well. Some of this is done through dreams. Some of your energies are brought forth and engaged in doing holy work. Often you are not aware of this. But again it is important that your thoughts be elevated as you enter into this.

The mass outpouring of grief and prayer after the attack had a great effect on you. You had a new assessment of what was important and what was not. Many non-Americans felt a very strong bond with America. It was a wonderful show of brotherhood. It will need to be realized that this sense of brotherhood can be achieved without the stimulus of a perceived outside common threat. The WTC event can be a tool to teach this very lesson.

The difference between what most on earth see and what the advanced on this side see is that we see the potential rose in the thorny bush and have faith that this rose will achieve its nature as given to it by God. You on earth as participants see work, suffering, and difficulties ahead of you. You feel threatened and not at all sure how it will all turn out. Can you not see that this is very necessary to give you the motivation to carry on? You *must* feel these problems as real problems so you will search for real solutions and achieve real growth in your being.

It is difficult but it would be well to consider September 11th as an opportunity to recreate your world, to recreate yourself. Somehow indifference to your brother has to be replaced with love. This seems so impossible with all the trouble spots in the world with intractable problems. When you see what needs to be done it is overwhelming. As I have said many times the solution lies more in your *being* than in your *doing*. When you discover what it is you want to *be* in fulfilling your nature given to you by God, then what to *do* becomes a much easier task. Right now you are approaching the problem backwards.

You have no need to be discouraged or even downhearted. Your world has simply been placed at a big fork in the road. You have every reason to feel that it will choose to raise its consciousness. You are anxiously awaiting the result. But I have told you before there is no final exam. There will be no final here on this side either. The only time you will become aware that you have more or less answered this problem is when you are confronted with another problem that now seems even bigger. Then you will be aware that the terrorist problem has been reduced to more livable levels.

At this time and in this place is where you will find your life in the lovely process of being fulfilled. Take joy in that. This seems incongruent but is actually congruent. I will leave you to puzzle that one out. I will meet you in the woods.

Part Six

More Wisdom to Share

Dear Reader,

As we finished up this book, a few additional questions came to us that we wanted to address. Please read on to gain yet more wisdom from Gail.

Chapter 114

Why Pain?

January 25th, 2002

My Wife,

When our dear friend Susan read the first pages of this book, she stated that she still did not understand why we have to experience pain. Please write to me on this topic.

Beloved Buck,

Pain is a puzzle. Yet it like everything else in God's universe, it has a purpose for which it is well suited. Let us begin with a couple of general statements.

One, pain is God's way of getting your attention. Attention to what? Attention to the fact that you are doing or being unsuccessful in an approach, an attitude, a habit or a perception. Further, now (the time of your pain) is the time for you to move on to a higher realization of how things work. Pain gives you the opportunity and the stimulus to focus on the lesson which has now become appropriate for you to learn.

Two, most of the lessons you need to learn hover about the lack of gratitude you feel for your life, for the tools God has given you to use in that life, and for the joys with which he surrounds you. There is specificity to what you should learn but it hovers about gratitude. To feel gratitude seems to be impossible for all the millions of people who are in dire straits. How they can do this is difficult to understand, but don't try to come to a new realization by starting out with the toughest circumstances. Don't start third grade by asking twelfth grade questions.

I died and that put you, Buck, in pain. It was the worst pain of your life. You would have been happy to trade my death for the biggest physical pain you could imagine. But, because of our talks about the death of one of us you were able to start out going in the right direction. You deliberately put your attention to thoughts of gratitude, which on the surface seemed totally contrary.

Generally, people have difficulty connecting their pain with the unsuccessful attitude they are using that prompts the pain. Although, sometimes it is direct enough that other people can see it. For instance, in the case of an alcoholic, he creates his own problems, is generally unappreciative of what he has and then risks losing it. Like so many of us, it is in losing something that brings about our true appreciation of it.

In seeking to discover what you are doing unsuccessfully and what has brought pain into your life do not wear blinders and confine your search to one small area. Again, the key is to be open. Consider things that you wouldn't normally relate to your specific pain. And remember, God is merciful. He does not necessarily require that you stay in pain until such time as you learn the lesson that caused the pain in the first place. You may need respites and He will grant them. To help you in this there are remedies—whether in the form of conventional or alternative medical treatments, stress-reduction techniques, psychological therapies or just being in nature that God makes available to you. Don't be afraid to use these.

You can seek these curatives concurrently with trying to figure out what the basic lesson is. Above all, do not think you have to just endure the pain until you figure out the spiritual lesson as a martyr would or as a bad child receiving punishment does. God has created it so there are many ways to learn your lesson. One of the above listed healing paths may lead you to a vista point from where you will be able to see the fundamental cause of your pain.

I would say that if you have pain think about these points:

1. God is trying to get your attention.
2. He wants you to pay attention to something or some attitude that is interfering with your peace.
3. The subject often hovers around your lack of gratitude.
4. Avail yourself of direct and indirect healing modes.
5. Be open. Do not be afraid to look where you have not looked before.
6. The mind is the builder of both pain and healing.
7. God loves you and is merciful.

Chapter 115

Your Searchlight

February 12th, 2002

My Dearly Beloved,

What a gorgeous day. High sixties in February. Please write to me using my fingers.

Hello Buck. God's universe is gorgeous. Ask your question.

Buck: I've been thinking what you wrote about pain and it puzzles me. You said that pain was a means for God to get our attention. I don't understand how this works. When you have pain your perspective narrows quickly to mostly just the pain itself. That's all you can think about. You've repeated often and I believe it, that it is by broadening our perspective that we find solutions. If we are doing or being something unsuccessful it would seem to me that we should broaden our perspective to find a solution—not narrow it or have it narrowed by the advent of pain. Do you see the inconsistency that I see?

Gail: It's a good question. Our readers no doubt are asking the same thing. You are forgetting the indirect feminine side of God. You seek a direct straight cause and effect with a single cause and a single effect that is clearly visible. As you yourself have stated in the past, every cause has multiple effects and every effect has multiple causes. Let us look at some of the multiple effects that come about from the cause of pain.

If you are engaging in some action or a response that is unsuccessful and inappropriate, the first thing you need to do is to stop doing it. While you are in the midst of doing it you will feel fully justified in what you are doing because of, for instance, "what they did to you." Only by stopping can you step back far enough to get a better look at it. Pain, particularly that associated with disease, will stop you if for no other reason than you need to retreat from activity. By stopping the activity you have a chance to recoup and refresh your outlook on what you are doing. Although, it is true that

with free will you might not choose to take advantage of this opportunity. There is another effect that I hope you can guess.

Buck: I don't like to disappoint you but I haven't a clue.

Gail: It is what we spent our life doing, that is seeking. We will use the verb searching, however, as it will be more clear. When you have pain you do a great deal more searching than you did before the pain. You search for relief. You search for a cure. You search for a comfortable way to position yourself to alleviate the pain. You search for something to distract your mind away from the pain. You search for the means to get out of your predicament. The result is that you have a mind that is searching. This is what you should be doing. You may feel your search is strictly limited to finding the means to eliminate the pain. It is like a searchlight (aptly named isn't it?) that may be seeking something specifically but nonetheless shines its light on many other things in the process. And so it is if you are in pain. Now, whether you are open to the other things that your searchlight shines upon is again up to your free will.

So if you find yourself in pain and start searching, open your mind to entertaining other thoughts and ideas that do not directly address the pain. If you are open in this manner, there are those who will help you by putting into your mind a new menu of choices for you to mull over. This process will, in turn, bring you new insights. When the pain ebbs and you reenter that same unsuccessful set of circumstances, you will be seeing it from a new perspective and be ready to try a new approach. If the enlightenment is sufficient, you may recognize this new perspective while the pain is still with you. Do you remember Roger when he died of cancer? A week before he left his body he found peace profound, accepting pain and his coming death with amazing equanimity. He had found his answer.

There are other effects too, such as a heightened appreciation for good health when you no longer have it. The point is, however, that you are given opportunities in many forms. These are opportunities to broaden your understanding even though they may seemingly start out by narrowing your view. Godspeed.

Chapter 116

Life on the Other Side

Dear Reader,

On many occasions, Gail has written to me about life on the other side. This is a topic that is of great interest to many. Here we have put together portions of several "inspired writings" to give you an idea of what "life" is like for our loved ones who have passed over.

My Dear Buck,

Let us talk about coming home. As we have discussed before, your home is really here in the spirit world and when you are on earth or some other venue it is like going off to boarding school and leaving your home and family behind. You are there to learn, but unlike boarding school, you get to go with other family members (your soul group).

When you pass over, it is really fun to meet your soul group here and interact with them. It is also fun to be of help to others when you can see how your help is affecting them and to be in attunement with the minds of very evolved beings. On earth you get used to thinking that work is one thing and fun is something separate. It is true there are many on earth who both work and have fun at the same time but most do not.

Part of the *one* principle is that over here work and fun are *one*, or more accurately, can be *one* if you create it so. The mind is always the builder—if a soul chooses to carry over his experience of separating fun from his work then his mind will so make it. Here we do many things which are enjoyable in the doing as well as in the sense of service.

To fully describe life on this side, then, we need a new word. It should be a combination of play, work, service, and accomplishment. This combination is what we do. It is play because we get a great deal of enjoyment from it. However play can be regarded as frivolous and not having much meaning beyond the play itself. This is not true of what we do. We do work as well but the word work carries with it a sense of obligation, a price you pay to get paid. In other words, work can be a drudge. Here work is not a drudge nor is it an obligation. The same sort of thing can be said about service.

Being of service on earth can be rewarding but also burdensome. Here service is elevating. Lastly, on earth there is a feeling of satisfaction in your accomplishments which is usually reserved for the end of some project or activity. Accomplishment is not associated with the process, but rather the result. On this side, the rewarding sense of accomplishment is a part of the process that you feel all along. If you would take the positive aspects of each of these words and leave off the limiting or negative aspects, you would have a description of what we feel in our activities here.

So what are our activities? Almost anything that is done on earth has a complementary action being done by those on this side. You have the idea that earth and its activities are totally separate from the spiritual world and its activities. This is not an unreasonable perception. After all, you don't see any effect of our spiritual world on your material plane. However, this is not an accurate perception. Everything in your world is involved with us—even though you don't see it.

Your view of the spirit world and the material world as separate is just that, a separating view. Since we are all *one* this separation can exist only in the minds of those who choose it. We of the spiritual plane, however, know of the Oneship and the lack of separation. We not only see more clearly that each world affects the other but we partake in creating this effect. When you partake in something, you know it is real. Edgar Cayce said that you are co-creators with God. That is true. We on this side are too. We join you in co-creating with God.

We need an analogy here. There are very few people in who can look at the world and say, "Oh, I see how the "fine-structure constant"* affects this world we are in." Not many say, "Isn't it fascinating to see how well it works to have the gravitational constant at 6.67?" If it were 9.67 we would not have any flying birds nor airplanes—to say nothing of the moon crashing into earth just before we fall into the sun. Yet

---

* According to Physlink.com, the "fine-structure constant" is a unitless numerical constant—whose value is approximately equal to: 1/137. In fact the exact value of the fine-structure constant is: 0.007297351 +/- 0.000000006. The inherent strength of the electromagnetic force is characterized by the fine structure constant The accepted symbol is the Greek alpha.

these two constants along with a few others have a very profound effect on your world. In fact, it would not exist if these constants were not operating or were changed slightly.

Similarly, on earth there are very few who realize the profound effect that we of the spiritual world have upon your world. That so few see it does not diminish in anyway the strength of our involvement with you or its effects. What are those effects? I told you quite some time ago that all your thoughts are dual, consisting of the thinker, you, and the contributor whom you attract. In this way, ideas are put in your mind that you have the free will to accept or discard. Thus you are influenced without being dictated to. On this side, we are not concerned with who gets credit for what. In fact we like you to think this is all your own idea, a lesson I learned repeatedly as a mother. In this way you will learn more quickly and incorporate the lesson into your being.

There are other ways in which the spiritual world influences your world but the basic pattern is the same—that you are presented with ideas and alternatives without violating your free will. Some of these influences you may regard as downright evil. Suppose you, in the twelfth grade, regarded those who cannot read as being lowly and evil. Further suppose that you wanted to correct this evil. How would you go about it? Would you give them a twelfth grade book to read and punish them when they can't read it? No, you would give them a very "lowly" lesson at their level to start them on the road of learning to read. This is what some of us do on this side. We work with the lowly by giving them lowly ideas with the intention of being helpful. Can you see this?

Again I must return to my statement that there is great diversity here. Therefore, I have only described our activities in association with your world. There are other activities here in connection with other worlds and much is done with single souls in need. There are some who are still so absorbed in themselves that they are not at all active in rendering service to others. And then there are very enlightened entities who are in a higher realm with a world of activities even more diverse!

From time to time we switch around from one kind of activity to another. We sometimes even go into an *in*activity mode. You may remember I did that a while back. It was very inspiring and I look forward to doing so again. You sort of become a blank that allows you to be only the "whole" temporarily. It is as if your individuality is turned down so that your sense of oneness can be turned up. When you are sensing this oneness you need take no action or be involved in any activity. It is, on a higher scale, similar to *being* versus *doing*.

Another thing we do is interact with other forms of life. It would be analogous to being a ranger on earth in a wilderness setting. You and I so loved to watch the wildlife. You always have this dream of the peaceable kingdom where animals would not be frightened of you and you could talk with them. We do that here. We become *one* with other life forms such as animals and renew our links with them from time to time. Some souls stay longer than others with the animals. Then, when they reincarnate on earth they have a special bond with them. Remember when our Rick was young he just seemed to know what was making an animal sick and knew what to do to make it well? The peaceable kingdom has for generations appealed to many. It is in fact a memory echo of this experience here on this side.

We also go through periods of creative activities, sometimes alone and sometimes with others in a group. It is much easier to work as a group here than on earth. The ego is not getting in the way so much. Our groups are usually made up of similar souls. This allows a much higher level of cooperation. It is fun yet with a high sense of productivity.

You can ask, "Do you sleep over there?" Sleep is necessary on earth. Here it is not but some of us do anyway. Do we drive in cars? Do we grow food? Yes some of us do one or both. All of those types of questions you could ask and the answer would be the same, "Yes some of us do." However this would do very little to give you an idea of what it is like here.

The mind is the builder. There are some here who like to sleep and their minds build a sleep situation. There are some who love cars and so their minds build them these marvelous cars that they can drive around. Those who love growing things let their minds build lovely gardens.

Now on earth, as here, the mind is also the builder. However on earth the building is partnered with the material plane which has its own set of characteristics. This modifies what your mind can build and how long it takes to build it. Another time we will go into the purpose of this joint building.

This process of co-building obscures to those with narrow perception how potent the mind is in creating. So much that they don't even understand that the mind is the builder.

On this side the material plane does not interfere with this building nor is time the same. The result is that mind building is more instantaneous. This is not completely true but the closest I can come to describing it.

This brings us to the discussion of time—here and on earth. On earth, in order to define something, you need to specify its four dimensions. Let us take the laptop computer that is under your fingers and identify it. First you need the three dimensions of height, width, and depth. You also need the fourth dimension, time. Right now the object you are trying to identify for me is under your fingers but in two hours it will be in a different place. So the time dimension you specify with be 8:22 a.m. this day. This will complete its identification.

Now we need to jump to an analogy. Let us say that you are a creature who is confined to a two-dimensional existence. You can move freely around on a tabletop but you cannot jump up and fly off in the third dimension. In fact the third dimension is invisible to you. Now let us say one day you discover a grasshopper on your flat tabletop. This gets the scientists all excited and they rush off to investigate this strange phenomenon. They photograph and measure it in great detail. In the process they inadvertently tickle it's feet. Off it jumps into the invisible. The scientists do have a very accurate record of the physicality of the grasshopper but as to the essence and functioning of the grasshopper they have no idea. It would be very difficult to explain to them.

This is the difficulty I have in trying to explain to you that time over here consists concurrently of the past, the present, and the future. You don't see how this can be. Yet we have in this "timelessness" a sequentiality somewhat analogous to what you have on earth where one thing leads to another. This sequentiality is manipulated by our minds or, in effect, with our direction. This also is not completely true but helpful to your understanding.

Actually your view of time is not two-dimensional but one-dimensional. You see it linearly. But it is not even one-dimensional as you can traverse time only in one direction—from past, to present, to future. You cannot one-dimensionally go in the opposite direction—from the present into the past. Your time concept is therefore one half of one dimension. Expressing it this way lets you see how limiting your time is. It also lets you get a glimmer of what wondrous potential there is in time that is not limited to one half of one dimension. And that is what we have here on this side.

This expanded time potential influences everything we do. It frees us to *multi-tasking* to use your phrase, and it frees us to roam in both time and space. It lets us be with you but not of you. You would rightly call it magical.

In addition to this great difference in the way we are effected by time is the quality of communication with which we can relate to each other. You know well the difficulties as well as the rewards in communicating on earth so I won't go into it. Here communication is much more open and accessible. Here we know who is entering our thoughts. We also know their true intentions, which on earth is most difficult. This makes communications here an altogether different process. What do we communicate about? It varies a great deal. Remember, there is an infinite amount to learn and understand. This means that there are all these levels of understanding to achieve. This is not the least discouraging. Quite the contrary, each level is fulfilling and exciting.

Do you remember *Todos Los Santos Day* in Cuzco, Peru, when the brass bands came through the big central cathedral doors? When the music was played outside it was wonderful but when they got inside and that brass sound could then bounce around within the cathedral sound box it became magical in resonance. And resonance is just what you feel when you come to this side and sense how much deeper the wisdom you garnered on earth is in this grander arena.

You with your dyslexia are able to fly your consciousness through a building that you are designing in your mind to see how it would all fit together. When you come to this side your consciousness also flies about but in more dimensions than just three. It is glorious, just as was the brass music was in the cathedral. The difference is that, instead of being the listener to that music, you are the music itself. Can you imagine the ecstasy this becomes? God's gifts are beyond description.

To avoid misunderstanding I must say again there is great diversity here and not everyone experiences what I just described. But it is here and it is available. In your thoughts you can hardly wait until you too can feel this. Be patient and cherish every moment on earth. The truth is that your current life experiences and the learning they allow you increases your ability to partake more fully in what I have just described when you come to this side. So right now you are in effect building the skills to participate in this and other wonders. This is true even though you have no real concept of how this is coming about. Have faith that I am telling you the truth.

Marshall: Gail, I thank you. I do remember those brass bands. It made the hair stand up on the back of our necks it was so overwhelming.

Life on this side has diversity far beyond that of the earth. This diversity includes the fact that you can find somebody over here who is doing something very similar to what is being done on earth. There are many others who are doing things that have no resemblance to earthly activities. This diversity also means that there is a huge variation in the stage of development of individuals here. There are the kindergartners, graduate students, those in between, those beyond and those below. What each is capable of doing is commensurate with their particular level of advancement.

I hope this makes clear that when you pass over you do not come as a raindrop falling into the ocean and becoming an indistinguishable part of that ocean. As hard as it is to understand, holy union is based upon you maintaining your own individuality. The raindrop falling into the ocean has a lovely poetic quality about it, but in truth, it scares people. People like their individuality even if they would like to change it drastically.

So, my dear husband, you have much to look forward to. But don't try to rush it. What you are doing now is preparing you very well for your transition. When you pass over you will slide easily into where you want to be. Good night.

Chapter 117

A Final Message from Gail

Dear Reader,

You have come and shared a journey with us. We have tried to be helpful particularly to those who have just lost a loved one, as that is what we have just gone through. I would like to leave you for now with some summary thoughts.

1. You may feel alone but you are not. Let me enumerate some of the invisible energies that keep you from being alone:

   ♦ This earth is surrounded by a healing energy. Each of you on earth is immersed in this sea of healing. If you open yourselves to it you will feel its effects and you can do so by choosing in your hearts to be open to it. One very good way to receive this healing is to *give* healing. You do not need to give the healing to any one individual, although you can. To give healing, repeat, "From God, through me to all of thee. Let the healing flow endlessly." Say this several times with a desire to *feel* it. Your expression of this healing gift will be reinforced by the healing energy field and will become stronger.

   ♦ And there is, of course, God's constant love. Often you feel that God is far away when you feel despair, fear and loneliness. This is impossible. God is always near, always everywhere. In fact, if God's love did not permeate your being and all beings, everything would disappear in an instant. It is God's love and energy that powers the atoms and your body. Without it you could not exist. Become aware of this basic fact of existence and let it be a part of your life. In the morning say, "God, I welcome you into my awareness this day."

   ♦ Your higher self is your constant companion and through it you are in contact with many, many others.

> Your higher self is trying to help you. Your construct of being lonely, which you build, cuts you off from your higher self.

How do you contact your higher self? First you must allow your mind (the builder) to realize that you have a higher self and it is there to help you. Then there are a number of techniques for making contact:

- ◆ Meditation is a very good technique.
- ◆ As you fall asleep you may ask that your higher self be in communication with you.
- ◆ When you awake remember and review your dreams. It is best to write them down.
- ◆ Or, quietly look at a beautiful flower for several minutes and try to feel its essence. Your higher self will join you in this appreciation. You will then feel your loneliness diminish.

2. Your mind is the builder. You heart tells your mind what to build. Your heart is where you live. Your heart is where you choose. If your heart is full of despair, fear and loneliness know that you can choose otherwise. Ask your mind to build otherwise. What you think is what you attract to you.

3. Furthermore, understand that your thoughts are dual, consisting of your thoughts and the thoughts of others attuned to you (the contributors). If you think despair, your mind will receive reinforcement of this despair from other minds that despair. This obviously makes it worse. It also gives you the feeling that you cannot control your mind's feeling. You have invited other despairing minds to join you in despair. You are joining with others when you do this but it is not the best way to avoid loneliness. Choose otherwise with your mind. Choose to feel gratitude for example. Instruct your mind to build an appreciation for the sun that rises in joy each day and then sets in beauty. This will attract other minds feeling gratitude to join you in this appreciation. This is a better way to dissipate

loneliness. Repeat, "My higher self is my constant companion and my best friend."

Understanding and utilizing what we offer you here will help you arrive at where you want to be. Change is inevitable. You have the power to direct it to where you want it to go. Do not look for this change outside of yourself, though it may manifest there, but rather feel it inside where it counts and where you live.

Communicating with you has been a wonderful experience for me. As my husband will tell you, I have always felt that communication was central to life's fulfillment. I have been impressed time and again with how the lack of communication leads to great difficulties. So it has been with great joy that I have entered into this communication with you and Buck. I feel a sense of peace, which in gratitude I radiate out to you. Can you feel it? It is there for you to feel.

God bless and Godspeed.

Gail Kent

"From God, through me to all of thee.
Let the healing flow endlessly."
"My higher self is my constant companion and best friend."
"God, I welcome you into my awareness this day."

Buck, six years after Gail's death.

Afterword

My Dear Reader,

I thought when I started this book that I knew what it was going to be about and that I would be the author. At the finish I am totally surprised and most pleased that Gail is my co-author. At the beginning I wouldn't have believed it. You may have a hard time believing it as well. She has introduced subjects about which I had no idea. It was a surprise that she would relate to me her parallel experience of her death to my experience of losing her. You have now read what she was feeling as well as what I was feeling as we went through her death and its aftermath.

My original intent with the book was to tell of an alternative way to deal with the death of a loved one. I struggled with the writing and made slow progress. I realized I needed help and approached Sidney Kirkpatrick and Nancy Thurlbeck to help me. I knew their work on *Edgar Cayce, An American Prophet* made them particularly appropriate for the type of work I was doing. Nancy came up with the title, *In Death We Do Not Part*. Their enthusiasm and expertise got me going on the right track.

Although I felt I had made contact with Gail through hypnosis and psychic readings, this was always through someone else and was a single episode at a time. I really yearned for direct contact with Gail on my own and with some regularity. This happened, in fact it blossomed, when I started working with Nancy and Sid. Perhaps Gail felt this was for real and started communicating regularly with me through what I call "inspired writings".

This is different from what I understand automatic writing to be. I do not take dictation word for word. I do write down what comes to me phrase by phrase, and idea by idea. When I start I do not know what the subject will be. I just start writing and the subject comes forth. I also do not know where Gail is headed with a subject or how the subject is going to be treated. Often I start a sentence and do not know how it will end.

I sit down with a deliberate attempt to avoid having any agenda myself as to what will be written. I want my mind blank on this. Yet at the appropriate time a subject comes forth and is presented in an organized manner all without any knowledge or manipulation on my part. As I said, I have been a good manager and organizer all my life and I know that organization does not

Afterword

occur by chance. A mind needs to address itself to the task of organization for it to occur. I knew that here the mind that was doing the organization was not mine.

As the writings continued it became very apparent to me that this was indeed my Gail writing to me from the other side. She had a goal in mind, a task that she wanted to be fulfilled. She wanted my help in fulfilling this task and the book was going to be the vehicle. Thus the book became not only an alternate way to respond to loss but a clear cut declaration that one can communicate with the deceased and here is how you do it.

Please do not feel that you have to accept it all as truth. Do look at it with skepticism because this is the way you develop your own truth. Test it and take what you can as your truth. One thing that we feel we would like to ask of you is to be open to the possibility that the things that are in this book are genuine. If you feel they are not proven to your satisfaction, that is fine, but do not assume that they therefore are proven false. What we don't know about our world and our existence is infinite. What we do know about it is finite and therefore subject to further surprising knowledge. Shakespeare, Huxley, and a myriad of others have all stated this idea in one way or another.

As close as I know Gail and I are (were) I know that her writings are not for me alone. Therefore with admitted trepidation I have invaded my own privacy to reveal my experiences and myself to you. I am basically an introvert and recoil at writing publicly about my inner self and feelings. However, I am so overpowered by the wisdom in these writings that I would be even more embarrassed to keep them only for myself.

In my introduction I said we would begin with what seemed like an ending. Now that the book is ending I would like to complete it with what seems like a beginning.

I continue to get communications from Gail. In fact, I just finished typing one a few moments ago. At the time that I write this afterword, I have some 230 "inspired writings." I have no doubt that by the time you have finished reading this book, I will have many more.

These writings contain a body of wisdom that I find utterly fascinating. They describe the qualities of our existence, and our relationship with our earth, the spiritual realm, each other, and with God. They describe the attributes of the Oneship.

Afterword

I have always had an unending curiosity about our existence and its meaning so I feel blessed beyond measure to receive such illumination from my dearly beloved and departed wife. While she was here we both shared this wonder. Now, here she is giving answers to questions that puzzled us both. Knowing her, she is as thrilled to be giving me these insights as I am to receive them. I also know she is not giving this wisdom just to me.

One of her basic messages is that the earth in its evolution has a reached a stage where it is now appropriate for the human-created separation of the living from the dead to diminish. How lucky we are to live at this time. How lucky I am to receive these communications in demonstration of it.

As this first book comes to an end I already see the beginning of a second book. Of the body of inspired writings that Gail has given me, less than one-tenth are found in this first book. This book focuses on the problems of death, dying, bereavement and grieving. In responding to these difficulties much can be gained by employing spiritual truths such as "living in the *now*" and understanding that separation is a construct we create with our mind as its builder. To bring into this first book all of the other wisdom in these writings would have been too cumbersome and would have lengthened the book considerably. So a second book is underway. I hope you will be as excited with the contents as I am.

Gail and I hope this first book has been an aid to you. We would particularly like to hear from you if this book helped you partake in an experience that held significant meaning for you. Gail certainly convinced me of the value in sharing. I hope you will share with us. If you do correspond with us I do not know if I will be able to reply, even though I would like to, so please accept my apologies in advance. I confess that I also feel a need to work on the second book. I am, after all, seventy-five years old and any twenty-four hour period could see me leave as Gail did.

If you would like a list of all the exercises from this book put together in a single list, we will e-mail them to you free.

E-mail your request to mkent@info11.com

You can contact me in a variety of ways:
Alleusha Publishing
P.O. Box 5212
Richmond, California 94805-5212

Afterword

You can also visit us at our Websites to order more books or to print out the exercise list from there:

Alleusha-Publishing.com
In-Death-We-Do-Not-Part.com or
Marshall-Kent.com

I thank you so very much for joining us. It has been a vast enlightenment which I have tried to share with you. It has also been an exciting adventure of the very best sort. I hope it has been so for you too. I wish you well and please, please do not limit yourself by thinking these things can't be done or that *you* cannot do them. Open your mind and find out for yourself.

We look forward to hearing from you!

Like Gail, I wish you Godspeed.

Marshall (Buck) Kent

Acknowledgements

I have learned what a tremendous undertaking the writing and publishing process can be. I could not have accomplished this task without the help and assistance of many trusted friends, family members, and colleagues. So many of my experiences with them have gone into this book. It is therefore most appropriate to say that among those deserving of special mention are my two dear parents each of whom have made their own special contribution to who I am.

I have also had many wonderful informal and formal teachers throughout my life including my Grandmother Stocking— a physician, artist, musician and friend and Robert Stirling—my teacher of piano and much else. Mrs. Heath opened my eyes to the patterns of the world through mathematics. J. D. Dawson and Beno Seghetti had faith and believed in me, Will Hewitt championed me and Walter Fogarty trusted me with his bank's money. Henry Daniels taught me to operate bulldozers and backhoes, Henry Maschal opened my imagination, Arjan Singh taught me to feel an animal's mind, Rex Kaske challenged me to retire early and Father Calvo has inspired me spiritually. My teachers also include my many students who over the years have offered cross-pollination of ideas and concepts. And there have been so many, many others.

Additionally, I have been inspired by the work of a number of organizations. They include Antioch College where I gained a broad and wonderful education, the American Friends Field Service with which I worked immediately after the war in St. Nazaire, France, the Rosicrucians whose teachings inspire me, and the Association for Research and Enlightenment (A.R.E.), the organization created by the great psychic, Edgar Cayce.

Of course, the book itself could not have been done without the experience, hard work and efforts of Nancy Webster-Thurlbeck and Sidney Kirkpatrick. We clicked right from the start.

Now, at age 75, I know that I have lived a most wonderful life and I give my gratitude to each one who has blessed me with their presence. To learn more about some of the above named, please visit their Websites:

Rosicrucians: http://**www.amorc.org**   Tel.:408-947-3600
The A.R.E: http://**edgarcayce.org** Toll Free Tel.: 1-800-333-4499
Sidney Kirkpatrick, Nancy W. Thurlbeck: **edgarcaycebooks.com**

Acknowledgements

I would also like to thank the following:

Paula Shaw,
Beyond Loss Counseling
South Pasadena, California
Telephone: 626-403-6864
E-mail:pshawlight@aol.com

Paula was very generous with her time and expertise in reading *In Death We Do Not Part* and offering us her professional feedback.

Al Miner,
Psychic
Website: **www.lamasing.net**
E-mail: susan@bellsouth.net

Al and his wife, Susan, generously gave us permission to publish the very compelling reading he did on the terrorist after September 11th.

Robert Smith
Editor of A.R.E's Venture Inward and Author of *Misdiagnosed,* a book about his wife's struggle with cancer and the conflicts between conventional and alternative medicine.
www.paraview.com/arsmith/index.htm
abob@infi.net

Bob kindly gave us permission to publish the conversation between Gail and me about his and Jane's painful experience.

I also want to express my true appreciation for those who agreed to read early manuscripts of *In Death We Do Not Part* and gave us their valuable feedback and suggestions. They include Gail's sister, Violet Feinauer, Beth Anderson, Naomi Burney, Nancy Christenson, Ross Gottstein, Betty Heyman, Betty Middlemiss, Grethe Tedrick, Richard Zoll and my son, Gordon Kent. Thank you all for your time, interest, goodwill and important feedback!

INDEX

INDEX

INDEX

INDEX

INDEX

INDEX

INDEX

INDEX

Quick Order Form

 Alleusha Publishing , P.O. Box 5212, Richmond, CA 94805

Phone Orders: 1-877-542-4792 (toll free) or 1-603-357-0236
Fax Orders: **1-877-542-4793 (toll free) or 1-603-357-2073**.
Fill out and fax this form.
By Mail: Please fill out this form and mail with a cheque to:

Pathway Book Service
4 White Brook Road
Gilsum, New Hampshire 03448

E-mail about <u>orders only</u>: pathways@alleusha-publishing.com
E-mail for <u>all other information</u>: info@alleusha-publishing.com
On-line: Visit http://alleusha-publishing.com

Visit us on-line to receive a **FREE** *list of exercises from this book, to sign up for "Gail's letter," and to learn about new publications we offer.*

Please send me _____ copies of *In Death We Do Not Part* at
U.S. $17.95/Cdn$26.00 each.

Name:_____
Address:_____
_____
Telephone:_____
Fax: _____
E-mail:_____
This contact information is for our purposes only. Please check here (__)
if you would like to receive an occasional e-mail letter from Gail.

<u>Shipping Costs:</u>
USA: $4 for the first book and $2 per additional book.
International: $9 for 1st book and $5 for ea. additional (estimate).
<u>Sales Tax:</u>
California Residents: Please add 8 % ($1.44/book) Sales Tax.

Payment: *Cheque__ Visa ___ MasterCard___
*(Please make cheques payable to Pathway Book Service.)
Card Number:_____
Name on Card:_____
Expiration Date:_____ E-Mail Address:_____

Thank you for your order. There is no such thing as a coincidence!